TOWARD A PENTECOSTAL ECCLESIOLOGY
THE CHURCH AND THE FIVEFOLD GOSPEL

Toward A Pentecostal Ecclesiology

The Church and the Fivefold Gospel

EDITED BY

John Christopher Thomas

CPT Press
Cleveland, Tennessee

Toward A Pentecostal Ecclesiology
The Church and the Fivefold Gospel

Published by CPT Press
900 Walker ST NE
Cleveland, TN 37311
USA
email: cptpress@pentecostaltheology.org
website: www.cptpress.com

Library of Congress Control Number: 2010935818

ISBN-10: 1935931008
ISBN-13: 9781935931003

CONTENTS

PART ONE

INTRODUCTION

INTRODUCTION

JOHN CHRISTOPHER THOMAS[*]

Just over a decade ago it was my privilege to deliver the 1998 Society for Pentecostal Studies Presidential Address entitled, 'Pentecostal Theology in the Twenty-First Century'.[1] As the title of this address suggests, on that occasion I sought to explore the nature and shape of Pentecostal theology as it would emerge into the twenty-first century. Among other things, I described what I deemed to be the characteristics of such theological exploration and to offer a couple of trial balloons in an attempt to illustrate the kinds of work that I envisioned and that I sought to play a small role in generating. First, I suggested that the best of Pentecostal theology would come not from those who were simply conversant with the faith but those who were part of a vibrant, worshiping Pentecostal community, those formed in and by the community to which and for which they speak. Second, I called for theological reflection a) characterized by the integration of the theologian's heart and head, b) informed by those outside the tradition through the offering of our testimony to them and in turn discerning the testimonies they offer, and c) pursued in an interdisciplinary fashion. Third, I called for Pentecostal theological reflection that would be more accountable to the broader Pentecostal academy, seeking to inform and be informed by other scholars working within the tradition, viewing such work as being held in trust for our spiritual and theological children. Fourth, I called for theological reflection that is contextual in origin

---

[*] John Christopher Thomas (PhD, University of Sheffield) is Clarence J. Abbott Professor of Biblical Studies at the Pentecostal Theological Seminary in Cleveland, TN, USA and the Associate Director of the Centre for Pentecostal and Charismatic Studies at Bangor University, Wales.

[1] J.C. Thomas, 'Pentecostal Theology in the Twenty-First Century', *Pneuma* 20.1 (1998), pp. 3-19.

and articulation, drawing upon the strength of a movement that is global in constituency and has gifts to offer to the entire tradition. Fifth, I called for a Pentecostal theology that is confessional in nature, a scholarship that allows our confessional context to help define the contours of our research with regard to both subject and approach, rather than being confined to the theological agenda set by a guild often controlled by the presuppositions of modernity.

In order to illustrate the kinds of work I envisioned I proposed two examples, one dealing with how to approach a first year graduate level course in New Testament, called 'Pentecostal Explorations of the New Testament', and a second in which I called for an exploration of Pentecostal ecclesiology informed by the five fold gospel (Jesus is Savior, Sanctifier, Holy Spirit Baptizer, Healer, and Soon Coming King) where the Church is seen as Redeemed Community, Holy Community, Empowered Community, Healing Community, and Eschatological Community, with the accompanying sacramental signs of Water Baptism, Footwashing, Glossolalia, Anointing with Oil, and Lord's Supper, respectively. Since that time, a variety of people have worked on various topics that have furthered this broad proposal, but little did I realize that one day I would be in a position to push this idea forward in order to see how it played out as a constructive approach to Pentecostal theology. However, my appointment to Bangor University as Associate Director of the Centre for Pentecostal and Charismatic Studies brought with it the opportunity, provided by Robert Pope, Head of the School of Theology and Religious Studies at Bangor, to host an international conference on a topic relevant to the work of the Centre, which was then under the direction of William K. Kay, now Professor of Theology at Glyndŵr University in Wrexham. I jumped at the chance to organize the conference, knowing immediately its potential significance and possible impact. With the conference theme agreed, I set out to assemble a group of scholars with the training, desire, and inclination to engage in constructive Pentecostal theology. Though I must admit that I did not intentionally use the characteristics highlighted in my Presidential Address to guide the choice of the conference presenters, in retrospect I am amazed at how well these characteristics do, in point of fact, fit each one of them. Diverse in terms of gender, race, nationality, denominational affiliation, and academic discipline each of these scholars embodies in their lives and work the kinds of qualities necessary to pursue this kind of constructive work. While my proposal at SPS offers the broad structure for the work of the conference, it was not something the contributors were asked to follow in a slavish manner, nor were the contributors even asked to buy into this model as the defining paradigm for a Pentecostal ecclesiology. They were simply invited to reflect on and explore—from their particular disciplines—a specific component of the five fold Gospel in ecclesiological perspective and to give some attention to one or more of the sacraments in the course of the discussion as sign of that community.

Without offering too much by way of assessment in advance—three scholars do, in fact, offer formal assessments of the conference papers, two from inside the tradition one from outside the tradition—I conclude this short introduction with the following observations. First, I was struck by the way in which this conference might serve as a model for future strategic theological discussions, for surely it is evident by now that the mammoth task of producing a global Pentecostal theology cannot be done by any one person, despite the extent of his or her individual giftedness. In point of fact, a truly global Pentecostal theology can only come from and by means of global collaboration, where each person is a full participant at the theological roundtable. Second, while the disciplinary diversity of the contributors presents some challenges in terms of uniformity of presentation, such disciplinary diversity ensures that the constructive theological task does not become the domain of only one of the theological disciplines. Rather, in keeping with the Pauline metaphor of the body of Christ, such diversity calls upon those of us in the tradition interested in theological reflection to discernment as an indispensable part of the theological task, where the contribution of each member is tested and discerned corporately by the body communally. Third, one of the many issues which the work of this conference lifts up as worthy of future reflection is the issue of leadership. For despite the reams and reams of paper and chunks of cyber space devoted to the issue of leadership, a theological model of Pentecostal leadership has yet to be discerned and articulated. The functional models of leadership that do exist within the tradition often simply build upon models inherited from other religious traditions, follow corporate leadership trends in the marketplace, evolve around a certain aspect of the tradition such as some kind of theocratic or prophetic model, or settle for a ready made proof text for leadership—the so-called five fold ministry model from Ephesians. What seems to be called for at this point is a self-consciously Pentecostal model(s) of leadership that is/are informed by the theological heart of the tradition—the five fold Gospel.

The conference upon which this book is based generated vigorous dialogue and debate, with some disagreement expressed over specific points, but the success of the conference can be judged in part by its near universal affirmation expressed in the written evaluations from the delegates themselves and a variety of conversations begun at both formal and informal levels growing out of the conference. So it is with great pleasure that I welcome the reader to this theological feast and commend the presentations, both individually and collectively, as a significant step in the articulation of a Pentecostal ecclesiology worthy of this incredible tradition.

1

THE FIVEFOLD GOSPEL AND THE MISSION OF THE CHURCH: ECCLESIASTICAL IMPLICATIONS AND OPPORTUNITIES[*]

KENNETH J. ARCHER[**]

The whole of theology is inherently developed from a soteriological point of view, salvation is not one of the main topics, along with the doctrine of God, Christ, church, sacraments, eschatology and the like, it is rather the perspective from which all these subjects are interpreted ... Carl E. Braaten[1]

The Full Gospel: A Personal Testimony[2]

After a wayward teenage lifestyle, I surrendered my life to Jesus Christ. Although I was baptized as an infant, attended weekly catechism from first through eighth grade, received first communion,

---

[*] I dedicate this essay to my first cousin Dan Archer, his wife Lisa, and Dan's mother Frances. Dan and Lisa brought me to Jesus Christ and have remained faithful Pentecostal followers of Jesus. Aunt Frances' financial generosity made it possible for me to attend my first semester at Central Bible College. Thank you for your faithfulness.

[**] Kenneth J. Archer (PhD, University of Saint Andrews) is Associate Professor of Theology at the Pentecostal Theological Seminary, Cleveland, TN, USA.

[1] Carl E. Braaten, *Principles of Lutheran Theology* (Philadelphia: Fortress Press, 1983), p. 63, as cited in Veli-Matti Kärkkäinen, *One with God: Salvation as Deification and Justification* (Collegeville, Minnesota: Liturgical Press, 2004), p. 5.

[2] In this essay, I will capitalize Full gospel and Fivefold and Fourfold. When I use Full gospel I am including both the Fivefold and Fourfold Pentecostal groups. When quoting others I will follow their spelling and construction of the terms.

went to confession, took communion regularly, and was confirmed as a Roman Catholic, I had stopped attending Mass after confirmation. I did not return to the Roman Catholic Church. Instead, I attended a Pentecostal church to which I was invited by my cousin, Dan Archer, who was concerned about my life. The community where I began my new salvific journey was an average sized Assembly of God congregation.[3] I was 'saved' at 19 years of age in a service at New Life Assembly of God, Wellington Ohio in June of 1983.

After some years of reflection, I would consider it a real conversion in the sense of an adult surrender to follow Jesus by turning away from my rebellious lifestyle.[4] I appreciated my Roman Catholic upbringing. No doubt it provided me with a Christian worldview and provided opportunities for prevenient grace to work in my life; however, it was the Pentecostal 'Full gospel' message that brought real hope to my desperate situation and a radical change to my life. My adult conversion experience brought an ontological change in my very being. As I surrendered I experienced the grace of deliverance and the hospitable embrace of the community. I became part of the family of God. Praise be to the Lord God Almighty!

I began to sense a call of God to 'full time' pastoral ministry. Various individuals in the community confirmed the call of God on my life. The pastor said I needed to go to a Bible College to prepare for ministry. In August of 1984, I set off to Central Bible College in Springfield, MO. The Central Bible College faculty grounded me in the Bible, Arminian-Pentecostal theology, pastoral leadership, and AG doctrine and polity. The four cardinal doctrines of the AG—Salvation, Healing, Spirit Baptism, and the imminent return of Jesus Christ—were especially emphasized. These experiences were understood to be promises available to Christians because they were

---

[3] The average weekly Sunday morning attendance was around 100.

[4] All grace is redemptive, especially from an eschatological perspective, but not necessarily regenerative. My understanding is more Wesleyan, moving from prevenient, to converting, to sanctifying, and on into perfecting grace. Also, this view of adult conversion would be in keeping with a more Anabaptist-pietistic perspective involving a conscious commitment which is bound up in a concerted effort of commitment to a local community and discipleship. I do not deny that as a child I had a personal relationship with Jesus and my new commitment may be more in keeping with the parable of the prodigal son. I had been really lost but now I was found!

wrought in the atoning work of Jesus Christ. The themes were explicitly addressed in certain doctrinal courses. Yet, the emphasis overall was more implicit. These themes were articulated throughout the various chapels and ministry experiences creating an 'embedded theology' focused on the experiential dimensions and practices associated with the Full gospel.[5]

Interestingly, my introduction to the history of Pentecostalism left out some of the more critical details of the movement. During my time at CBC, the argument was that Pentecostals were Evangelicals who added on the doctrine of the Baptism in the Holy Spirit with the initial evidence of speaking in unlearned tongues. Concerning the 'distinctive' doctrine of Spirit Baptism, it was understood to be a biblical doctrine that had been recovered by Charles Fox Parham at his Bible institute in Topeka, Kansas. Parham was the originator of the doctrine.[6]

The critical history and early theology would come into focus as a result of taking a course at Ashland Theological Seminary. The course was titled 'The History of Methodism and the Roots of Pentecostalism'. The textbooks for the early history and theology of Pentecostalism were Vinson Synan's *The Holiness-Pentecostal Movement in the United States*[7] and Donald Dayton's *The Theological Roots of Pentecostalism*.[8] The course gave me and my wife, Melissa, an opportunity to reflect critically upon the prehistory and early theology of Pentecostalism.[9] I did a research paper on the Azusa Street

---

[5] For a helpful discussion of embedded and deliberative theology see Howard W. Stone and James O. Duke, *How To Think Theologically* (Minneapolis, MN: Fortress Press, 1996), pp. 13-21. I adapted their definition of embedded theology. They define it as an implicit theological understanding of Christian faith disseminated by the Christian community's various ministry practices and assimilated by its members.

[6] As best as I can remember, the Azusa Street revival was not the focus and the controversial details of Parham's life, maintaining Jim Crow laws, and other interesting theological doctrines he held were not addressed. It was his contribution to the development of the doctrine of Spirit baptism with speaking in other tongues that was highlighted.

[7] Donald W. Dayton, *The Theological Roots of Pentecostalism* (Peabody, MA: Hendrickson Publishers, 1987).

[8] Vinson Synan, *The Holiness-Pentecostal Movement in the United States* (Grand Rapids, MI: Eerdmans, 1971).

[9] Melissa and I were in our second pastorate and she began to attend ATS. We graduated the same year.

Revival. The attempt at racial reconciliation, the volume of miraculous healings, and the transformation power experienced by individuals who had received Spirit Baptism were of particular interest to me. William Seymour, an African American male, became my new hero. The early literature I read reinforced Dayton's theological analyses. The theological DNA that produced the Pentecostal movement was a fusion of particular Nineteenth century themes into a new gestalt identified as the 'full gospel' of Jesus Christ.

When I read Dayton's monograph, I had already been a senior pastor for over four years. The proclamation of the Full gospel of Jesus Christ as the Savior, Healer, Spirit Baptizer and Soon Coming King was the focus of most if not all my ministry. We included in our weekly Sunday worship services a time to lay hands on the sick and anoint them with oil as we believed God for their healing. I practiced the 'shot gun' approach to altar calls. You began with a call to salvation, and then you include calls for consecration and recommitments (sanctification), then opportunities for those to experience healing and deliverance whether that special need be an emotional, spiritual, and or physical concern. Everyone knew that Jesus was coming, the signs were everywhere. Therefore it was important to be baptized in the Holy Spirit. Hence, calls for being Baptized in the Holy Spirit were also included in the invitation. These may not have been the normative ministry practices of most Pentecostal preachers at that time; however, I venture to suggest that themes of the Full gospel were heard regularly through sermons and testimonies in many Pentecostal churches. As a result, the Full gospel was embedded into the ministry practices of many Pentecostal communities. The Full gospel served as the very heart of my Pentecostal spirituality—a dynamic, pietistic, christocentric soteriology. As I read Dayton's book, I said, here is an outsider that understands us better than most insiders—the book impacted me because it brought into critical focus my embedded spirituality. In fact, after class one day as we were in the car on the way home I had Melissa write down in the front of my copy of Dayton's book a possible doctoral dissertation topic ... a Pentecostal systematic theology based upon the Full gospel.[10]

---

[10] My doctoral research focused on Pentecostal hermeneutics. The Pentecostal community, as a distinct narrative tradition, is an essential and necessary com-

Today, Donald Dayton's work is still appreciated for retrieving the theological prehistory and early theological core of Pentecostalism. His work in historiography and historical theology has helped liberate certain understandings about the Wesleyan Holiness and Pentecostal traditions in North America. These traditions should not be considered as a subtype of North American Reformed-fundamentalist evangelicalism. His works have shown that Pentecostalism is deeply rooted in the more radical wing of the Wesleyan holiness movement of the late Nineteenth century.[11]

In his monograph, *The Theological Roots of Pentecostalism,* Dayton demonstrates that in North America certain theological themes coalesce into a four-fold pattern creating a distinct tradition called Pentecostalism. He acknowledges that historically a fivefold pattern was part of the earliest phase of Pentecostalism.[12] The fivefold pattern retains Jesus the Sanctifier as an essential part of the full gospel. Dayton does affirm that an emphasis on holiness and sanctification can be heard in most, if not all, Pentecostal traditions. However, he argues that the 'four-fold pattern expresses more clearly and cleanly

---

ponent of a Pentecostal hermeneutic. I argued that the Full gospel was the very heart of the 'central narrative convictions' of the Pentecostal story which shaped its community's identity. See the published version of my PhD thesis, Kenneth J. Archer, *A Pentecostal Hermeneutic for the Twenty-First Century: Spirit, Scripture and Community* (JPTSup 28; New York: T&T Clark, 2004), chapter 4. Paperback edition: *A Pentecostal Hermeneutic: Spirit, Scripture and Community* (Cleveland, TN: CPT Press, 2009). I moved away from the 'systematic' and embraced narrative. I am still in the process of writing a fully developed Pentecostal narrative theology grounded in the Fivefold gospel. For a provisional attempt see my *The Gospel Revisited: Towards a Pentecostal Theology of Worship and Witness* (Eugene, OR: Pickwick Publications, forthcoming).

[11] Donald W. Dayton, 'The Limits of Evangelicalism: The Pentecostal Tradition', in D.W. Dayton and R.K. Johnston (eds.), *The Variety of American Evangelicalism* (Downers Grove, IL: InterVarsity, 1991), pp. 36–56 (49). See also Archer, *A Pentecostal Hermeneutic: Spirit, Scripture and Community,* pp. 18-22.

[12] See Donald Dayton, 'Introduction' in Yung Chul Han (ed.), *Transforming Power: Dimensions of the Gospel* (Cleveland, TN: Pathway Press, 2001), pp. 11-18. Dayton writes, 'for a decade or so all of Pentecostalism was sharply Wesleyan/Holiness until this theme was suppressed by some under the influence of W.H. Durham' (p. 13). *Transforming Power* was the first attempt by a group of scholars to address themes of the Fivefold gospel.

the logic of Pentecostal Theology'.[13] The fusion of these themes serves as the very heart of the tradition.[14]

Dayton's analysis is appreciated by most as a helpful backdrop to the theological emergence of Pentecostalism. The current question being raised is can the full gospel continue to serve as the narrative core to produce a fully orbed contemporary Pentecostal Theology? That is, can the early Pentecostal Full gospel be retrieved in such a way that it moves from the place of background to foreground?

The Fivefold Gospel: Soteriology and Ecclesiology

Steven J. Land on Soteriology and Mission

Steven J. Land's ground-breaking *Pentecostal Spirituality: A Passion for the Kingdom* affirms the significance of Dayton's analysis of early Pentecostalism's theological uniqueness shaped by and articulated through the Full gospel as essential to *contemporary* identity, spirituality, and theology of Pentecostalism.[15] Land argues that a distinct Pentecostal approach to theology is attained by identifying and further developing its spirituality. 'Theology is concerned with the relationship between God and creation.'[16] This relationship moves from God, in God, and to God. The community is caught up into the missionary history of the triune God. Pentecostal spirituality is formed through and in such a relationship. The very heart of Pentecostal spirituality is love for God and others manifested in a passion for the full realization of the Kingdom of God.

---

[13] Dayton, *Theological Roots of Pentecostalism*, p. 21.

[14] Dayton, *Theological Roots of Pentecostalism*, pp. 17-23. For one important contribution as to why the theological theme of Jesus the Sanctifier understood from a Wesleyan perspective should be retained for the doctrine of healing, see Kimberly Ervin Alexander *Pentecostal Healing: Models in Theology and Practice* (JPTSup 29; Blandford Forum, UK: Deo Publishing, 2006). See also Simon Chan, *Pentecostal Theology and the Christian Spiritual Tradition* (JPTSup 21; Sheffield: Sheffield Academic Press, 2000), pp. 69-70, who is concerned to ground Spirit baptism into the experience of sanctification.

[15] Steven J. Land, *Pentecostal Spirituality: A Passion for the Kingdom* (JPTSup 1; Sheffield: Sheffield Academic Press, 1993). Land's monograph was a revision of his Emory PhD dissertation. It is now available as *Pentecostal Spirituality: A Passion for the Kingdom* (Cleveland, TN: CPT Press, 2010).

[16] Land, *Pentecostal Spirituality*, p. 196.

For Land, 'Salvation is a partaking of and a participation in the divine life.'[17] The believer is brought into a real union with the triune God and participates in God through Jesus Christ via the Holy Spirit. This is a mystical journey of transformation into the image and likeness of Christ.[18] A journey caught up in the missionary fellowship with God. Therefore the focus of Land's work is identifying early Pentecostal spirituality-theology (chapters one and two), and revisioning it into a contemporary Pentecostal theology-spirituality (chapters three and four). The Fivefold gospel provides the contextual atmosphere and thematic structure for his articulation of Pentecostal spirituality-theology.[19]

Steve Land was one of the first to take the Fivefold gospel as the essential fabric of early spirituality of Pentecostalism. He followed Walter J. Hollenweger's argument that the first 10 years of Pentecostalism was its spiritual maturity and not its infancy.[20] Drawing upon the first 10 years of the literature, Land affirms the significance of the Fivefold gospel in shaping the spirituality of the movement. Land writes, 'It is generally recognized that the early Pentecostal revival built on this Wesleyan-Holiness foundation in embracing the 'fivefold' or 'full gospel' of justification, sanctification, Sprit baptism, divine healing, and the premillennial return of Jesus; all of these were to be definite experiences flowing from the atonement.'[21] The earliest Pentecostals, coming from the Wesleyan holiness tradition, understood salvation 'in the terms of the fivefold gospel and three blessings.'[22]

Steve Land identifies Donald Dayton and William Faupel as the most influential works shaping the monograph. 'Dayton', Land points out, 'was one of the first to assert that Pentecostalism is a distinct theological development and not merely an experiential epi-

---

[17] Land, *Pentecostal Spirituality*, p. 128.

[18] Land, *Pentecostal Spirituality*, pp. 76 and 23.

[19] Land, *Pentecostal Spirituality*, see summary of chapters 1 and 2 on pp. 123-24. Land retrieves early Pentecostal soteriology and re-appropriates it in a Wesleyan-Eastern fashion. This is why sanctification must be retained as essential to the Full gospel.

[20] Land, *Pentecostal Spirituality*, p. 47. See Walter J. Hollenweger, *The Pentecostals* (Peabody, MA: Hendrickson Publishers, 1988), p. 551.

[21] Land, *Pentecostal Spirituality*, p. 48.

[22] Land, *Pentecostal Spirituality*, p. 210, see also pp. 18 and 82-93.

sode in twentieth-century Christianity.' Faupel's work, according to Land, offers the most 'clear, complete, meticulously documented work on North American Pentecostalism available anywhere' and is deeply in touch with the Pentecostal ethos.[23] Precisely for Land, it is Faupel's argument that eschatology provides the impetus for early Pentecostals' concern for Spirit baptism. Faupel's argument is taken up into his work on Pentecostal Spirituality with the goal of advancing the case for understanding Pentecostalism as primarily a trinitarian eschatological missionary fellowship.[24]

Dayton's works on the Full gospel is affirmed but with a clear concern to retain sanctification from a Wesleyan understanding. Sanctification is necessary in order to integrate properly the power of Spirit baptism into love and purity of God via the blessing of initial and entire of sanctification.[25] The Christian affections are grounded in its source which is God and oriented towards others in love and truth. The Fivefold gospel is necessary in order not to lose an ontological, transformative, experiential understanding of sanctification.[26] If sanctification is dismissed as the second blessing subsequent to justification, then purity will be separated from power. The tragic result would be the loss of Pentecostal spirituality as perfecting love. Furthermore, Land is clear that Spirit baptism is necessary and tongues may serve as the initial sign, but the essential sign

---

[23] Land, *Pentecostal Spirituality*, p. 28. Land writes, 'Initial sanctification, associated with real change accompanying new birth reaches its goal in entire sanctification. The fullness of freedom associated with new birth moves forward the fullness of love in entire sanctification as one walks in the light of scripture' (p. 147). Land rejects any notion of a static understanding of entire sanctification (p. 149). Sanctification is moral integration and growth associated with the lifelong process of discipleship (p. 211).

[24] Land, *Pentecostal Spirituality*, pp. 29, 34, and 206.

[25] Land, *Pentecostal Spirituality*, pp. 54, 176, and 126.

[26] Kimberly Ervin Alexander demonstrates the importance of fully retrieving a Wesleyan soteriology as it relates primarily to healing, thus Jesus as Sanctifier must also be included in the Full gospel. Sanctification is understood as an ontological crisis-process of human spiritual development. According to Alexander, Wesleyan Pentecostalism offers a particular theological trajectory which impacts their understanding of the practice and process of reception of healing which is different than the Baptistic or Finished Work stream of Pentecostalism. '"How Wide Thy Healing Streams Are Spread": Constructing a Wesleyan Pentecostal Model of Healing for the Twenty First Century', *Asbury Theological Journal* 59.1, 2 (Spring and Fall, 2004), pp. 63-76 and Alexander, *Pentecostal Healing: Models in Theology and Practice*.

of such an experience is love manifested in missionary zeal for God's Kingdom.[27]

Land is not writing a historiography or even identifying the theological views of early Pentecostals but instead moving forward in presenting a contemporary Pentecostal Spirituality based upon the early Pentecostal beliefs and ethos associated with an understanding of the gospel. Land's thesis is to 'explicate a Pentecostal spirituality which is apocalyptic, corporate, missional and essentially affective.'[28] He desires to ingrate the beliefs (know) and practices (do) into the affections (be). The affections are the integrating center of spirituality and thus the heart of Pentecostal theology.[29] The Fivefold gospel is the means to participation in the very life of God with sanctification as its very heart. Sanctification forms and transforms the affections and thus serves as an essential link between the blessings of justification and Spirit baptism. Regeneration, sanctification, and Spirit baptism trigger an ontological change in the believer as she/he is caught up into the life of God and God's community. They build on each other and flow into one another, thus one grows into the image of Christ through the presence of the Holy Spirit. However, this threefold blessing soteriology was forged from a particular apocalyptic vision. The contextual atmosphere for a particular Pentecostal spirituality was and should be eschatological. The impetus for the pouring out of the Holy Spirit is fueled by a passion for the full realization of the Kingdom of God. Jesus the King is soon coming! The outpouring of the Holy Spirit constitutes the Church as a missionary fellowship which is caught up into the trinitarian mission of God.

In sum, Steve Land's monograph envisions the Fivefold gospel as the means to participation in the very life of the triune God. Sanctification is the very heart because sanctification forms and transforms the affections. The Fivefold Gospel with its threefold blessing provides the thematic structure and apocalyptic atmosphere for the development of his Pentecostal spirituality. He offers Pentecostals a theology whose 'spirituality correlates more closely

---

[27] Land, *Pentecostal Spirituality*, pp. 201-202.

[28] Land, *Pentecostal Spirituality*, p. 31.

[29] Land, *Pentecostal Spirituality*, pp. 56, 44, and 132-36.

with the fivefold gospel's emphasis on Jesus' and 'the three-dimensional understanding of soteriology'.[30]

Steve Land's *Pentecostal Spirituality* reveals a number of significant insights. Early Pentecostal soteriology was logically connected by three distinctive blessings—regeneration, sanctification (both initial and entire), and Spirit baptism. Land understands this soteriology as union with and participation in the life of God with the goal being transformed into the image of Christ. Although a threefold *ordo salutis* is maintained, he emphasizes the motif of mystical journey through out the monograph. The Pentecostal *via salutis* is as important, if not more so, than the Pentecostal *ordo salutis*. Pentecostal spirituality demands both, because its soteriology is thoroughly synergistic and participatory. What may be missed is that this echoes the Eastern orthodox tradition of *theosis* or divinization. What is obvious is that this emphasis upon sanctification, as a distinct crisis-process experience(s) in which the affections are transformed and developed, is in keeping with Wesleyan soteriology.[31] For Land, Pentecostal soteriology involves real ontological change in the believer and Christian community as they journey with and in the trinitarian life of God. Sanctification is the heart for it provides for the means for integration of spirituality which in turn develops a real hunger or passion for the Kingdom of God. Apocalyptic eschatology becomes the primary context for the development of the affections and motivation for right practices. This particular vision of the soon coming King creates a contextual atmosphere which draws the Christian into a Spirit baptismal experience. The experience further develops both the fruit of the Spirit and empowers the believer into faithful missional witness. This reinforces his concern of developing a Pentecostal spirituality as eschatological trinitarian missionary fellowship.[32]

One can argue that sanctification plays a more significant role than either justification or Spirit baptism because sanctification is the integrative center of the Christian affections. Pentecostal affec-

---

[30] Land, *Pentecostal Spirituality*, p. 211.

[31] John Wesley's soteriology is centered on a life of sanctification with the goal of moral transformation of the human affections into the image of God which manifests itself in perfecting love for God, people, and God's creation.

[32] The historic trinitarian mission of God is developed in dialogue with Jürgen Moltmann's work.

tions generate the community's passion for the Kingdom. However, Land does not dismiss justification or Spirit baptism. A Christian must experience justification-regeneration in order to 'qualify them for heaven' and sanctification is necessary in order to be 'fit for heaven'. Spirit baptism, as a distinct experience, is necessary to produce a sense of courageous urgency to get 'everyone ready for heaven' by overcoming the devil and the world.[33] These three logically ordered soteriological blessings produce a passion for God who is moving history towards the coming Kingdom, the consummation of salvation for all creation.

Before moving on to other Pentecostals' exposition on soteriology and ecclesiology as it relates to the Fivefold gospel, I will raise two concerns. First, Land affirms the significance of the Fivefold gospel, but the heart of his soteriology is sanctification flanked by justification and Spirit Baptism. Justification prepares you for sanctification and Spirit Baptism throws you back to sanctification while simultaneously propelling you forward into the Kingdom of God. Empowered witness for the Kingdom both ethically and vocationally is the goal of Spirit Baptism. Soteriology is explicitly connected to a present spirituality of three blessings which correlate with Jesus as Savior, Sanctifier, and Spirit Baptizer. Jesus the King who is com-

---

[33] Land correlates the three blessings with three affections. Justification-regeneration produces gratitude because one has been made and continues to be made righteous in relationship with God. 'Righteousness is imputed in order to be imparted' (p. 140). The testimony of such an experience is ' I have been saved' and corresponds to the statement that Jesus is the Savior. Gratitude is the foundational structure of Pentecostal affections. Sanctification begins in regeneration and is actualized more fully in a subsequent dynamic yet definitive act of entire sanctifying experience. Sanctification produces compassion because it is grounded in God's holiness which is characterized by love. Compassion is an affection associated with love and peace. The testimony of such experience (s) is 'I have been sanctified' and corresponds to the statement that Jesus is the Sanctifier. The affection correlated with Spirit baptism is courage. One has power over the Devil and courage to follow the Lord in faithful mission because one has authorized power from God to be a courageous witness in word and deed. Joy and hope are characteristic fruit of the affection of courage. This affection of courage corresponds to the testimony that 'I have been Spirit baptized' and is articulated by the Fivefold gospel as Jesus is the Spirit baptizer. Land consistently argues that these affections are connected, interrelated and in dynamic development as one journeys with God. The threefold blessings of the Fivefold gospel are all necessary experiences for the development of distinct Pentecostal affections. Furthermore these experiences are a penultimate realization of the coming Kingdom (p. 82). See his helpful charts on pages pp. 125 and 139.

ing soon is no longer an explicit soteriological concern but more of an eschatological passion which fuels missionary zeal. It creates an apocalyptic vision which alters the affections in a distinctive qualitative gestalt. The Pentecostal affections produce urgency for the missionary task. Divine healing, which is another important aspect of the Fivefold gospel, serves simply as a sign of the Kingdom breaking into the present. Land does not integrate healing into his presentation on Pentecostal Spirituality beyond the affirmation of testimony to the present in breaking of the Kingdom which has not yet fully come. The point here is that Land's spirituality based upon the Fivefold gospel contributes to a Pentecostal spirituality but does not, as yet, move beyond soteriology. In fact, the Fivefold gospel is not completely integrated into soteriology beyond the three blessings, Land does not assign an affection to either divine healing (Jesus the Healer) or the Second Coming (Jesus the soon coming King).[34]

I wholeheartedly agree with Land that soteriology is essential to any theology and is directly connected to communion with God (theology proper), participation in Christian community (ecclesiology), and the coming of God's reign (eschatology). From my perspective, the Fivefold gospel needs to be further developed in order to produce a fully orbed Pentecostal theology that does not loss its grounding in its present relational experiences of its mystical spirituality.[35] Land, even though he affirms the centrality of the Fivefold gospel, does not move it into an integrating paradigm for an overarching contemporary theology. Of course the focus of his monograph is Pentecostal *spirituality*. As he has demonstrated, the spirituality generated by the Fivefold still remains essential to soteriology. Land's monograph only *implicitly* contributes to the community as a missionary fellowship. I believe it would be beneficial to develop further and integrate *explicitly* the Fivefold gospel into ecclesiology

---

[34] Building on the work of Land, J.C. Thomas has recently proposed that the experience of Jesus as Healer and soon coming King might be accompanied by the affections of joy and hope, respectively. Cf. J.C. Thomas, 'What the Spirit Is Saying to the Church: The Perspective of a Pentecostal Working in New Testament Studies', in K. Spawn and A. Wright (eds.), *Spirit & Scripture: A Symposium on Renewal Hermeneutics* (London: Continuum, forthcoming).

[35] Steve Land, following his presidential address to the Society of Pentecostal Studies, stated to the society that in his future work he would like to focus upon a Pentecostal soteriology based upon the Fivefold gospel.

in order to strengthen theologically a Pentecostal understanding of the mission of God.[36]

Land's emphasis upon the Pentecostal affections shaped by the Fivefold gospel as distinctive for Pentecostal theology has caused concern for some Pentecostal theologians. Frank Macchia is the most recent in raising this concern. In his *Baptized in the Spirit: A Global Pentecostal Theology*[37] Macchia states that for Land Spirit baptism is not *the* distinctive contribution of Pentecostal theology. While Macchia may be correct as far as he goes, it is an exaggerated overstatement to suggest Land's monograph, *Pentecostal Spirituality*, 'represents a significant shift in the axis of Pentecostal distinctives'.[38] Macchia argues that Pentecostalism's distinctive is the doctrine of Spirit baptism and that Land's monograph represents a shift away from the doctrine.[39] For Land, the Pentecostal distinctive is its soteriology articulated through the Fivefold gospel which generates a particular spiritual formation of the individual's affections. The Fivefold gospel's declaration of Jesus as Sanctifier and King coming soon are the key to the formation of Pentecostal affections. Spirit baptism is *essential* but not *distinctive*—the Fivefold gospel which includes Spirit baptism is distinctive.[40] Land writes, 'Both the

---

[36] See D. Lyle Dabney, 'Saul's Armor: The Problem and Promise of Pentecostal Theology Today', *Pneuma* 23 (2001), pp. 115-46. I agree with Dabney that early Pentecostal spirituality has an 'implicit theological impulse' that needs to be explicitly developed (p. 144). I believe the implicit theology should be developed around the Fivefold gospel with an intentional move towards pneumatology. He argues that it needs to be done from a pneumatological perspective, or the third article of the Creed. Amos Yong has followed this trajectory for the development of Pentecostal theology.

[37] Frank D. Macchia, *Baptized in the Spirit* (Grand Rapids, MI: Zondervan, 2006).

[38] Macchia, *Baptized in the Spirit*, p. 24. He also engages Land's work more positively on pp. 42-46.

[39] Frank Macchia's thesis in *Baptized in the Spirit* is that Spirit baptism is the distinctive feature of Pentecostal theology and should be the integrative principle for a Pentecostal theology (p. 56). Spirit baptism must be defined more broadly than the traditional classical Pentecostal views yet still remain true to Pentecostal experience and distinct theological accents (p. 26). His monograph is an attempt to articulate a descriptive Pentecostal theology integrated by Spirit baptism. He, like Land, is concerned with the relationship between sanctification, eschatology, and Spirit baptism.

[40] Macchia states that it would be helpful if Land would further develop his understanding of Spirit baptism for Pentecostal theology. Macchia believes this is

character and vocation of a Pentecostal were bound up in the doctrines of sanctification and Spirit baptism, respectively.[41] For Land, the necessity of the early Pentecostal articulation of the Fivefold gospel as the essential distinctive of Pentecostal theology is necessary in order to retain a proper ontological development in the believer between the experiences of sanctification and Spirit baptism. If Spirit baptism is divorced from sanctification it becomes destructive, if it is removed from the category of soteriology it becomes misdirected. Without the soteriological blessing of Spirit baptism, there would be no *Pentecostal* fusion of the Christian affections, thus no distinct Pentecostal spirituality.

Secondly, Land is passionate about the Kingdom of God. But how does the Fivefold gospel contribute to his proposal that the Pentecostal community (ecclesiology) is a missionary fellowship longing for the Kingdom of God? Simply put the community of the Spirit is the Church on the way to the Kingdom.[42] In this sense the eschatological missionary community is a church who worships God rightly and witnesses to the world rightly. How the Fivefold gospel relates to ecclesiology is not specifically stated. The practices of prayer, praying for the sick and caring for the suffering, working towards racial integration, gender equality, and testifying to the lost are all affirmed as essential practices of the missionary community. Yet, we are left wondering if there might be a way to integrate further the Fivefold gospel into an organic ecclesiology that further strengthens a dynamic christocentric-pneumatic Pentecostal eschatological missionary fellowship without losing the personal-communal dimensions of soteriology. Pentecostal theology needs to find a way explicitly to connect and integrate ecclesiology with and into soteriology without losing its eschatological orientation or pneumatological accent.

My two concerns, that the Fivefold gospel has not been fully integrated into soteriology and only has contributed implicitly to ec-

---

important in light of Land's concern to address the fractured existence of purity and power, see Baptized *in the Spirit*, p. 45. Land would most likely respond that sanctification properly understood and experienced would remedy the problem. For Land's reflections on Spirit Baptism cf. his 'The Nature and Evidence of Spirit Fullness', in R. White (ed.), *Endued with Power: The Holy Spirit in the Church* (Nashville, TN: Nelson, 1995), pp. 55-82.

[41] Land, *Pentecostal Spirituality*, p. 124.

[42] Land, *Pentecostal Spirituality*, p. 178.

clesiology, will be picked up later. Let me conclude this segment on Steve Land's monograph with words of affirmation and appreciation. His monograph served as a liberating moment with a lasting impact upon Pentecostal theology. It moved the endeavor from evangelical-fundamentalist theological categories and thinking into the larger dialogue of Christian traditions. The monograph reads differently than typical theological works because it expresses theology through the genre of spirituality. As a result of the Fivefold gospel, he was able to argue that Pentecostal spirituality is distinct. Thus, its theology must also offer a particular vision of Christianity. His work has served as a theological voice, resource, and inspirational motivational force for the developing network of scholars who share similar concerns.[43] The monograph was ambitious, fluid, and brief which left many a reader wondering as to the exactness of meaning of his theological concepts. However, Land was and still is convinced that his monograph demonstrates that Pentecostal spirituality is Christocentric (the fivefold gospel) because of its pneumatic starting point. 'In the Spirit Christ saves, sanctifies, heals, baptizes in the Holy Spirit and is coming soon as king.' And 'given the nature and history of Pentecostalism, the theological task is best understood as a discerning reflection by the eschatological missionary community upon the living reality of God with us.'[44] Land is correct that the heart of Pentecostal Spirituality is Jesus. Maybe this is why he begins chapter 1 with the words 'Jesus Christ' and ends the monograph with the words 'Jesus Christ' which serves as a fitting *inclusio* for his argument of the necessity of the Fivefold gospel for Pentecostal spirituality.[45]

Veli-Matti Kärkkäinen on Pentecostal Soteriology

Ecumenical and Pentecostal theologian, Veli-Matti Kärkkäinen, has brought Pentecostal theology into dialogue with other traditions

---

[43] His monograph was the first to be published in the Journal of Pentecostal Theology Supplemental Series. The theological conversations were still being developed but one in particular was hermeneutics as it relates to interpretation and community formation, see, pp. 22, 40, and 75. The cited dialogue partners are Cheryl Bridges Johns and Rickie Moore: Bridges Johns in formation and Moore in hermeneutics.

[44] Land, *Pentecostal Spirituality*, p. 183

[45] Land, *Pentecostal Spirituality*, pp. 13 and 223. J.C. Thomas brought this to my attention.

through his numerous writings on ecumenism, theology, and mission. His publications make a significant contribution to the growing awareness of developing Pentecostal theology(s), especially in broader Christian circles. Kärkkäinen's theological monographs are written with an eye towards the global and ecumenical perspective. In his more ecumenical works he generally includes a section on Pentecostal contribution(s) to the subject matter. Pentecostalism, then, is brought into the theological dialogue with other traditions. Pentecostalism is presented as an active contributor which elevates its status from mere interesting religious phenomena to an actual theological dialogue partner. By highlighting certain contributions that Pentecostals bring to the theological topic being addressed, Kärkkäinen exposes Pentecostals' theological perspectives on divine reality.[46]

In his *One with God: Salvation as Deification and Justification*[47] Kärkkäinen argues that soteriology could 'be a catalyst for a more serious concern for unity' among divided Christian communities.[48] He writes, 'The ecumenical work on the doctrine of salvation is a good textbook example of the challenges and fruits of a real ecumenical theologizing.'[49] The purpose of this work is not to develop a homogenous uniformed doctrinal position on soteriology, but to work towards a 'common perspective on salvation'. The symphonic testimony of salvation will have various movements, complex rhythms, and at times be a cacophony of voices, yet Kärkkäinen believes it is essential to the witness of the ecclesiastical traditions to come to some basic consensus.[50] Soteriology may serve as common ground for what now appears to be a hopelessly divided Church. The common soteriological consensus he proposes is union with God.[51]

---

[46] I will limit my focus to two of Veli-Matti Kärkkäinen monographs that address the topics of soteriology and ecclesiology. The goal is not to summarize his view on the subject but to highlight his understanding of Pentecostal contributions to these theological topics as it relates to the Fivefold Gospel and mission.

[47] Veli-Matti Kärkkäinen, *One with God: Salvation as Deification and Justification* (Collegeville, Minnesota: Liturgical Press, 2004).

[48] Kärkkäinen, *One with God*, p. 5.

[49] Kärkkäinen, *One with God*, p. 7.

[50] Kärkkäinen, *One with God*, p. 5. The metaphor of symphony is his; I elaborated on it.

[51] Kärkkäinen, *One with God*, see chapter seven, 'One with God: In Search of a Consensual View of Salvation'.

In his analysis, Kärkkäinen includes Pentecostalism's understanding of spirituality and soteriology. He places Pentecostal soteriological understanding in the trajectory of Wesleyanism.[52] He teases out Pentecostal soteriology in dialogue with Eastern Orthodoxy.[53] He writes, 'Pentecostal spirituality is shaped by Christ-centeredness. Jesus Christ is depicted as the Justifier, Sanctifier, Healer of the Body, Baptizer with the Holy Spirit, and Soon Coming King. This is the classical 'fivefold' gospel, or as it is sometimes known by Pentecostals, the 'Full Gospel.'"[54] The Full Gospel functions as a means of Pentecostal theological identification and as a way of entering into soteriology. Pentecostals are christocentric not pneumatocentric. Yet, because of the Full gospel, the Holy Spirit is essential to their understanding of soteriology, in particular sanctification.[55] What he lifts up is the important role the Holy Spirit plays in drawing the believer into the divine life and transforming her/him into the image of Christ Jesus. Spirit Baptism is understood as empowerment for witness and service. But more importantly for his exposition on soteriology, the Spirit is the essential key to sanctification and a victorious life over sin.[56] Because of this, Eastern Orthodoxy and Pentecostalism share a very mystical and experiential understanding of soteriology.[57] 'Both emphasize that to

---

[52] Kärkkäinen, *One with God*, see section titled 'Deification and Sanctification in Methodism', pp. 72-81.

[53] Kärkkäinen, *One with God*, see section titled 'Beyond Salvation: Christian Transformation in Orthodox-Pentecostal Perspective', pp. 108-17. For this segment, Kärkkäinen relies primarily upon the doctorial thesis of Edmund J. Rybarczyk cf., *Beyond Salvation: An Analysis of the Doctrine of Christian Transformation Comparing Orthodoxy with Classical Pentecostalism,* PhD dissertation, Fuller Theological Seminary, 1999. The dissertation was revised and published as *Beyond Salvation: Eastern Orthodoxy and Classical Pentecostalism On Becoming Like Christ* (Paternoster Theological Monographs; Eugene, OR: Wipf and Stock Publishers, 2004).

[54] Kärkkäinen, *One with God*, p. 112.

[55] Kärkkäinen writes (*One with God*, p. 112), 'Whereas Christ is the basis for the believers' justification and sanctification, the Holy Spirit is the person of the Trinity who draws the believer to—and makes the believer become like—Christ in the process of progressive sanctification'. I suggest his understanding reflects more of a Fourfold or Baptistic view than the traditional Wesleyan-Eastern Fivefold view. It appears that Spirit Baptism serves a vocational function, not an ethical formational role in the life of the Pentecostal believer. I would like him to clarify this a bit more.

[56] Kärkkäinen, *One with God*, p. 112.

[57] Kärkkäinen, *One with God*, pp. 109-10.

be a Christian is to experience Christ and the Holy Spirit, not only in conversion, but throughout one's life, "in the deepest recesses of one's being'".[58]

Pentecostalism, like the Orthodox and Wesleyan tradition, is also deeply concerned about the transformative nature of salvation. What happens *in* the Christian is the focus, not just what happens *to* the Christian. The agency of the Hoy Spirit in cooperation with human will (synergism) creates an active relational participation in the life of God. This results in an authentic transformation of the Christian into the image and likeness of Christ. For Pentecostals and Wesleyans this process would be communicated doctrinally through sanctification. The Orthodox tradition explains this mystical transformative union through the doctrine of *theosis*. The Spirit's active role in salvation and the synergistic understanding of soteriology generates a mystical experiential spirituality which both holds in common.[59] 'The focus' then 'of Pentecostal spirituality is experiencing God mystically as supernatural.'[60]

Kärkkäinen's analysis of Pentecostal soteriology underscores the importance of Steve Land's articulation of Pentecostal soteriology as participation in God and union with God. If one reads Steve Land's monograph and then reads Kärkkäinen's segment on 'Deification and Sanctification in Methodism' one cannot miss the significant role that Wesleyanism sanctification plays in Land's understanding of Pentecostal soteriology. Land's work has both a historic

---

[58] Kärkkäinen, *One with God*, p. 110. His citation is from Rybarczyk—see n. 48 above.

[59] Kärkkäinen concludes the discussion of Orthodoxy and Pentecostalism by highlighting two common ties. The two ties that connect Orthodoxy and Pentecostalism are the emphasis upon the working of the Holy Spirit in salvation—a mystical experiential union, and the synergistic view of salvation. Furthermore he points out that the Orthodox tradition does emphasize the sovereignty of the Holy Spirit to work independently of Scripture, Liturgy and Church structures (pp. 111-15).

[60] Veli-Matti Kärkkäinen, *Pneumatology: The Holy Spirit in Ecumenical, International and contextual Perspective* (Grand Rapids, Michigan: Baker Academic, 2002), p. 91. In this volume on *Pneumatology*, Kärkkäinen's presentation of Pentecostalism (pp. 87-98) is a similar version of his presentation of Pentecostalism in his volume, *An Introduction to Ecclesiology: Ecumenical, Historical & Global Perspectives* (Downers Grove, IL: InterVarsity Press, 2002), pp. 68-78. The difference is the specific focus. Concerning pneumatology, he writes, 'The single most important aspect of Pentecostal pneumatology is the doctrine of Spirit baptism' (p. 95) which is an essential aspect of the Full Gospel.

theological connection with Wesleyanism and presents a mystical orientation that is consistent with Eastern Orthodox soteriological view.[61] For Land, it is the Fivefold gospel which generates certain affections that would both affirm salvation as union with God yet still be distinct from Orthodoxy and Wesleyanism.

Land, like Kärkkäinen, clearly affirms Spirit baptism as important for vocational witness. However, Land also affirms Spirit baptism as important contribution for moral development. The apocalyptic outlook that fuels the passion for Spirit baptism is also the furnace where the affections are formed. Land affirms the threefold blessing in a qualified sense; hence Spirit baptism is a soteriological or redemptive experience. By qualified, I mean that Land emphatically highlights sanctification (holiness) as both prerequisite to Spirit baptism and continuing contribution to it. Empowerment (power) must be infused with divine love (purity) which is manifested in missionary zeal (passion) for God's Kingdom.[62]

Veli-Matti Kärkkäinen and Frank Macchia on Pentecostal Ecclesiology

Veli-Matti Kärkkäinen in *An Introduction to Ecclesiology* points out that Pentecostals have not written much on ecclesiology. Pentecostals stress spirituality as a lived reality, and so ecclesiology is important. The importance of ecclesiology is generally expressed with such language as community or fellowship of believers (*koinonia*) and is associated with mission.[63] Frank Macchia states that 'Pentecostals have tended to highlight a charismatic/missionary ecclesiology'.[64]

---

[61] The notion of the mystical nature of Pentecostal soteriology was first 'overtly' championed by Simon Chan as an important means of retrieval and revision of both Spirit baptism and sanctification within the matrix of a synergistic soteriology articulated through a sacramental theology. Here sacraments and church become significant in the traditioning of Pentecostal spirituality. He calls for a retrieval and revision of the Fivefold gospel because it includes a clear affirmation of the necessity of sanctification as an ontological experience and important prerequisite for the Spirit baptismal experience. See his, *Pentecostal Theology and the Christian Spiritual Tradition*.

[62] This is also a concern of Frank Macchia, *Baptized in the Spirit,* see pp. 30, 56, 59, and 257-62.

[63] Kärkkäinen, *An Introduction to Ecclesiology*, p. 75.

[64] Macchia, *Baptized in the Spirit*, p. 208.

As for the governmental structure of the Church, Pentecostals point out that the NT does not endorse one structure but allows for various structures.[65] A distinct Pentecostal ecclesiology has not yet been articulated.[66]

Kärkkäinen makes an important observation. He writes,

> The identity of a Pentecostal theology that informs and shapes its ecclesiology can be characterized with the help of their preferred label, the 'full gospel.' This full gospel comprises five theological motifs: 1. Justification by faith in Christ. 2. Sanctification as a second definite work of grace. 3. Healing of the body as provided for in the atonement. 4. The premillennial return of Christ. 5. The baptism in the Holy Spirit evidenced by speaking in tongues. This last motif came to be the most distinctive feature of classical Pentecostalism.[67]

Interestingly, even though he affirms the Fivefold gospel as important for informing and shaping ecclesiology, he never explains how it does so. It seems that the classical Pentecostal Fivefold gospel illustrates that 'the central point to note is the accent on lived Charismatic spirituality rather than on discursive theology.'[68] From this he moves to affirm that the distinct contribution would be a view of the Church as a pneumatologically constituted community of charismatic fellowship.[69]

---

[65] Kärkkäinen, *An Introduction to Ecclesiology*, pp. 73-74.

[66] Steve Land in *Pentecostal Spirituality* agrees that Pentecostals do not have a stalwartly developed ecclesiology. According to Land this is a result of living in the eschatological tension of the Kingdom of God already but not yet. This tension is both a strength and also a weakness for a Pentecostal ecclesiology (p. 178). According to Land, the church is a movement on the way to the Kingdom whose bishop is the Holy Spirit (pp. 157-58). This aspect is important because it offers some resistance to the institutionalism of the church. It is a weakness because Pentecostals often do not have 'sufficient biblical and theological controls and directives worked out for the church's life outside the worship and witness settings' (p. 178).

[67] Kärkkäinen, *An Introduction to Ecclesiology*, pp. 71-72. He suggests prophethood of the believer as a possible sixth motif.

[68] Kärkkäinen, *An Introduction to Ecclesiology*, p. 72.

[69] Kärkkäinen, *An Introduction to Ecclesiology*, p. 75. Kärkkäinen draws upon the important work of Peter Kuzmic and Miroslav Volf, 'Communio Sanctorum; Toward a Theology of Church as a Fellowship of Persons', an unpublished posi-

Kärkkäinen often refers to the Fivefold or Full gospel when discussing Pentecostalism. This is especially true when he gives a historic overview of the movement.[70] In his earlier works, the importance of the Full gospel functions as a segue way into his reflections upon the Pentecostal contributions on a given theological theme. However, the importance of the Full gospel is secondary to the Pentecostal distinctive—Spirit baptism. Jesus the Spirit baptizer is the most distinctive feature of classical Pentecostalism.[71] In Kärkkäinen's comments on Pentecostalism Spirit Baptism is the *distinctive* of the *distinctives*. For example, he writes 'The single most important aspect of Pentecostal pneumatology is the doctrine of the Spirit baptism.'[72]

In a later publication he gives further reflection to the importance of encounter and charismatic Spirituality of Pentecostalism. In '"Encountering Christ in the Full Gospel Way": An Incarnational Pentecostal Spirituality'[73] Kärkkäinen states that 'The center of Pentecostal theology is the idea of the 'Full Gospel' which speaks of Christ in various roles as Saviour, Sanctifier, Healer, Baptizer with the Spirit, and Soon-coming-King.'[74] 'Pentecostal spirituality is based on a passionate desire to "meet" with Jesus Christ as he is being perceived of as the Bearer of the Full Gospel.' Therefore, Pentecostalism is primarily a 'Christocentric Sprit movement' not a free spirited pneumatological movement focusing upon the charismatic gifts of the Holy Spirit. At the very core of Pentecostal spirituality is a desire to encounter Jesus through the Holy Spirit in worship, in healing, in charism, etc.[75] As Kärkkäinen correctly observes, 'Like Christians of the primitive Church, Pentecostal evangelists and missionaries who went out to cities and villages in their own

---

tion paper read at the International Roman Catholic-Pentecostal Dialogue, Riano, Italy, May 21-26, 1985. See further pp. 77-78 where he delineates seven 'salient features of Pentecostal/Charismatic ecclesiologies'.

[70] Kärkkäinen, *Pneumatology*, p. 96. He identifies and briefly explains the two versions of the 'classical' Pentecostal *ordo salutis*.

[71] Kärkkäinen, *Pneumatology*, p. 93.

[72] Kärkkäinen, *Pneumatology*, p. 95.

[73] Veli-Matti Kärkkäinen, '"Encountering Christ in the Full Gospel Way": An Incarnational Pentecostal Spirituality', *Journal of the European Pentecostal Theological Association* 26.2 (2007), pp. 9-23.

[74] Kärkkäinen, 'Encountering Christ in the Full Gospel Way', see pp. 9-12, 9.

[75] Kärkkäinen, 'Encountering Christ in the Full Gospel Way', p. 9.

countries and abroad to preach the *Full gospel* (they) did not go out to preach the Good News of the Spirit.'[76] Yet, Spirit baptism evidenced with other tongues 'came to be the most distinctive feature of classical Pentecostalism'.[77]

I wonder how this more emphatic emphasis upon the Full gospel as the center of Pentecostal theology will influence Kärkkäinen's future work on Pentecostalism, especially his use of the language of most *distinctive*. Spirit baptism evidenced in speaking in other tongues is certainly a *new* doctrine, but without the other confessions associated with the Fivefold gospel, it *most* certainly is not the distinctive of Pentecostalism.

Frank Macchia's longest chapter in his book *Baptized in the Spirit* is on ecclesiology.[78] He makes an insightful suggestion concerning the Fivefold gospel and ecclesiology. He writes, 'Their (Pentecostals) fivefold gospel of regeneration, sanctification, Spirit baptism, healing, and eschatological expectation isolated by Donald Dayton as *distinctive* (my italics) to Pentecostal theology can be seen as the ecclesiological "marks."'[79] According to Macchia, the Fivefold gospel's emphasis is 'on the charismatic and missionary church, faithful to Jesus' charismatic ministry'.[80] Later on in the chapter he reiterates the importance of the marks of Christ articulated by the Fivefold gospel as 'the Pentecostal take on the marks of the Church'. The Fivefold gospel 'places a special focus on the need for a sanctified and missionary church to proclaim healing to all the nations in the power of the Spirit.'[81]

The problem for me is that Macchia never identifies or explains the fivefold marks of the Church beyond reasserting the Fivefold gospel. How does the Fivefold gospel shape ecclesiology beyond offering a Pentecostal commentary upon the marks of the Church mentioned by the Nicene-Constantinopolitan Creed? The Fivefold provided the marks because the 'organizing principle' of Macchia's

---

[76] Kärkkäinen, 'Encountering Christ in the Full Gospel Way', p. 11. My italics and parenthetical.

[77] Kärkkäinen, 'Encountering Christ in the Full Gospel Way', pp. 14-15.

[78] Macchia's chapter on ecclesiology is 101 pages in length and makes up almost a third of the book.

[79] Macchia, *Baptized in the Spirit,* p. 208.

[80] Macchia, *Baptized in the Spirit,* p. 208.

[81] Macchia, *Baptized in the Spirit,* p. 241.

theology is the outpouring of the Spirit or Spirit baptism.[82] The reader is left wondering why Macchia so positively affirms the importance of the Fivefold gospel since it really does not make any substantial contribution to his ecclesiology. Maybe if it served as an organizing paradigm, which you might be led to believe it should because the Fivefold gospel articulates Pentecostal marks of Christ and Christ's Church, then maybe this lengthy section would have offered the reader a more explicit Pentecostal ecclesiology.[83] Instead, as helpful as this might be, it reads as an exploration into the possibility of a Pentecostal ecclesiology through a dialogical engagement of ecclesiological insights and concerns of other traditions.[84]

---

[82] Macchia, *Baptized in the Spirit,* p. 256

[83] In an earlier essay, 'Theology, Pentecostal', in Stanley M. Burgess (ed.), *New International Dictionary of Pentecostal and Charismatic Movements* (Grand Rapids: Zondervan, 2002), pp. 1120-141, Macchia rejects the Full gospel as a framework. Frank Macchia has argued that the Full gospel 'is important for understanding the origins and enduring accents of emerging pentecostal theologies' (p. 1124). But as a framework for Pentecostal theology, it is unable to address the full spectrum of theological *loci*. Macchia writes 'such a framework is potentially Christomonistic (in which devotion to Christ defines every area of theological concern) and dominated by a concern with the way of salvation.' Thus, 'pentecostal theology cannot be confined to this paradigm if it is to speak to a broader configuration of *loci*' (p. 1124). Interestingly in the same essay, in section two titled 'Theological Issues', he addresses theological issues that are directly connected and specifically related to the Fivefold gospel. The following is a list of *all* the topics addressed in this section: A. The Godhead and the Christ of the Full Gospel; B. Regeneration, Sanctification and Spirit Baptism; C. Water Baptism and Spirit Baptism; D. Speaking in Tongues; E. Divine Healing; F. The Gifted Congregation and G. Revisioning Eschatology. It would appear that the Fivefold gospel served as a productive framework for his presentation on Pentecostal theology.

[84] I realize that Macchia is working towards the development of a Pentecostal ecclesiology. See also Amos Yong, *The Spirit Poured Out on All Flesh: Pentecostalism and the Possibilities of a Global Theology* (Grand Rapids, MI: Baker Academic, 2005). In the section titled 'Sketching a Pneumatological Soteriology' Yong writes, 'The fivefold gospel is expanded here in light of the foregoing Lukan Spirit soteriology by discussing the seven dimensions of salvation' (p. 91). He does not expound on nor specifically connect any aspect of the Fivefold to the seven dimensions. Yet he also recognizes the significance of the Fivefold because at the end of the chapter on soteriology he states, 'In this way, we can give preliminary systematic articulation to the pentecostal intuition of the fivefold gospel' (p. 120). Just the fact that Yong mentions the Fivefold gospel in a contemporary articulation of soteriology testifies to the depth of the formational power upon the spirituality of Pentecostal scholars.

For many Pentecostal theologians, Spirit baptism serves as *the distinctive* of the distinctives. Yet almost always, Pentecostal theologians and historians of Pentecostalism come back to the Fivefold gospel or Full gospel as significant for early 'classical' Pentecostal identity and theology. For example, Allan Anderson, in *An Introduction to Pentecostalism: Global Charismatic Christianity*, devotes 15 pages to defining Pentecostalism.[85] He is correct to recognize differences between 'classical' and 'neo' Pentecostalism, as well as charismatic manifestations of Christianity. He argues that '"Pentecostal" is appropriate for describing globally all churches and movements that emphasize the working of the gifts of the Holy Spirit, both on phenomenological and theological grounds—although not without qualification'.[86] Furthermore, Anderson will use the term Pentecostalism in a broad sense so as 'to include all the different forms of "spiritual gifts" movements'.[87] Anderson, in his essay titled 'Pentecostalism' states, 'The various expressions of Pentecostalism have one common experience and distinctive theme: a personal encounter with the Spirit enabling and empowering people for service, and experience often called the 'baptism in (or with) the Spirit".[88] Yet, in his works he addresses aspects directly related to a Pentecostal understanding of the Full gospel because the Full gospel is essential to Pentecostal ministry practices.

I would agree with those that affirm the significance of Spirit baptism closely associated with tongues (signs and wonders), and expressive-experiential worship as a necessary and key indicator of Pentecostalism.[89] I agree with Keith Warrington's important point that 'central to their (Pentecostals) faith and practice are the concepts of "encounter" and "experience"'.[90] However, 'to know God

---

[85] Allan Anderson, *An Introduction to Pentecostalism* (Cambridge, UK: Cambridge University Press, 2004, reprinted 2006), pp. 1-15.

[86] Anderson, *An Introduction to Pentecostalism*, pp. 13-14.

[87] Anderson, *An Introduction to Pentecostalism*, p. 14.

[88] Alan Anderson, 'Pentecostalism', in William A. Dyrness and Veli-Matti Kärkkäinen (eds.), *Global Dictionary of Theology: A Resource for the Worldwide Church* (Downers Grove, IL: InterVarsity Press, 2008), pp. 641-48 (642).

[89] For an extensive articulation of my theological method see 'A Pentecostal Way of Doing Theology: Method and Manner', *International Journal of Systematic Theology* 9.3 (July 2007), pp. 301-314.

[90] Keith Warrington's *Pentecostal Theology: A Theology of Encounter* (London, England and New York, New York: T&T Clark, 2008). Warrington argues that

experientially' one needs a narrative to make sense of their experience with God. The Biblical story provides the narrative. The Five-fold gospel provides the central narrative convictions which both motivate and testify to such transformative encounters.[91] Furthermore, I and most likely all Pentecostal theologians would agree with Allan Anderson that Spirit baptism is necessary and essential for a Pentecostal theology. But by itself, it is not the single identifying marker of Pentecostalism. It functions as the linchpin which holds the Pentecostal Full gospel together as the distinctive of Pentecostalism. This of course would not be true of other spirit-movements or even charismatic movements. Kärkkäinen's argument presented in his "'Encountering Christ in the Full Gospel Way'" further collaborates with my earlier work. The storied articulation of the Full gospel is necessary for making sense of the encounter.[92] The Five-fold gospel establishes the 'Pentecostal' parameters and expectations of such transformative encounters.

The Fivefold Gospel: Toward a Pentecostal Soteriological Ecclesiology

The historical importance of the Fivefold gospel and its ongoing significance in shaping Pentecostal spirituality is undeniable.[93] The

'Pentecostal theology may be best identified as a theology of encounter—encounter of God, the Bible and the community' (p. 21). Mark J. Cartledge in his *Encountering the Spirit: The Charismatic Tradition* (MaryKnoll, New York: Orbis Books, 2006) makes a similar argument. He writes, 'The central motif of the charismatic tradition is "encounter with the Spirit" both corporately within the worshipping life of the Church and individually through personal devotion and ongoing work and witness in the world' (p. 16). Interestingly, he discusses all the confessions associated with the Fivefold gospel.

[91] Warrington is on the right track when he quotes MacDonald who identifies Pentecostal spirituality as "'fully experienced gospel" or "Christ-centred, experience-certified theology"'. *Pentecostal Theology*, pp. 21-22.

[92] See Kenneth J. Archer, 'Pentecostal Story: The Hermeneutical Filter for the Making of Meaning', *Pneuma* 26.1 (Fall 2004), pp. 36-59.

[93] For an important essay that challenges some historiography which down plays or simply dismisses the influence Wesleyan sanctification and Fivefold gospel in the early British Pentecostalism see Mark J. Cartledge, 'The Early Pentecostal Theology of *Confidence* Magazine (1908-1926): A Version of the Five-Fold Gospel?, *Journal of the European Pentecostal Theological Association* 28.2 (2008), pp. 117-30. He writes, 'I wish to test the hypothesis, namely that the theology of *Confidence* and by implication Alexander Boddy was based upon a five-fold Pentecos-

question remains, how should a fully orbed contemporary Pentecostal theology be written which reflects the centrality of the Fivefold gospel? The response has been that it cannot because it does not address all the theological loci. Or that the Fivefold gospel can no longer function in the same way as it did in the early classical period of Pentecostalism. Furthermore, some argue that we must speak of Pentecostalisms not Pentecostalism and such a work would be too narrow and only be representative of a narrow USA version of Pentecostalism. First, such a Pentecostal theology would not pretend to offer *the* definitive Pentecostal theology, nor attempt to be a *global* Pentecostal theology. It would be an attempt at producing a *local* Pentecostal theology. However, it should be conversant with other traditions, enriched by other Pentecostal regional accents and emphases, and it will most likely resonate and intersect with other contextualized forms of Pentecostalism incarnated in different parts of the world. Secondly, a fully orbed Pentecostal theology would have to be written differently, then say the typical systematic theologies. This is especially true if Pentecostalism is a distinct Christian tradition and not Evangelicalism with a speech impediment. Thirdly, given the social locations and global perspectives of the contributors to this conference, one could argue that a diverse and collective group of Pentecostals could contribute to global perspectives on Pentecostal theology focused upon the Fivefold gospel.

John Christopher Thomas: The Fivefold Gospel as Integrative Centerpiece

John Christopher Thomas, Pentecostal New Testament scholar, was the first to call specifically for an integrative Pentecostal theology constructed around the Fivefold gospel. In his 1998 Presidential address to the Society for Pentecostal Studies, he stated, 'By means of the work of Don Dayton and Steve Land, among others, I have come to be convinced that standing at the theological heart of Pen-

---

tal understanding of the gospel' (p. 117). After his analysis he states, 'I have not found the language of the "five-fold gospel" anywhere in the magazine. However, I would argue that the key ideas are clearly present' (p. 128) and further states 'I would suggest that the hypothesis that *Confidence* was a vehicle of a version of the five-fold gospel in all but name has substantial corroboration, at least from 1908-1917' (p. 130). His analysis demonstrates that British Pentecostalism has more Wesleyan influence than was previously recognized (p. 128).

tecostalism is the fivefold gospel.'[94] He argued that a contemporary
Pentecostal theology should be structured around the Fivefold gospel. He stated that 'It is my belief that when a Pentecostal theology
is written from the ground up, it will be structured around these
tenets of Pentecostal faith and preaching.'[95]

I suggest that what Thomas found in Dayton and Land's work
resonated deeply with his own spirituality. He was formed in a
Church of God Pentecostal community and continues to serve as
an official minister in the Church of God community. The Fivefold
gospel is the historical distinctive of early Pentecostalism and still
functions as spiritually formative in Pentecostal traditions and
churches. For Thomas, the tenets of the Fivefold gospel are the
spiritual and theological heart of Pentecostalism. He recognized the
significance of the Fivefold gospel's formational spirituality both
past and present. Therefore he argues that it should be a paradigm
for developing a distinct contemporary Pentecostal theology. He
writes, 'In fact, I have to admit a great deal of surprise at my col-
leagues in theology proper that this approach has not been taken up
formally, for it seems like such a natural place to begin and appears
to have so much promise for the articulation of a theology that is
distinctly Pentecostal.'[96]

Thomas offered a proposal to the Society to demonstrate the viability of such a project. He selected ecclesiology as a test case in
order to illustrate that the fivefold could *explicitly* serve as the integrative center. He pointed out that most discussions of ecclesiology
appear 'near the end, often in a somewhat detached fashion.'[97] If
the Fivefold was adopted as the paradigm, then 'reflection about the
nature, mission and identity of the Church' would be included in
each discussion of one of the tenants of the Fivefold gospel. 'Each
of the five major divisions would conclude with a section devoted

---

[94] John Christopher Thomas, 'Pentecostal Theology in the Twenty-First Century', *Pnuema* 20.1 (Spring 1998), pp. 3-19 (17). Thomas refers specifically to Dayton's *Theological Roots of Pentecostalism* and Land's *Pentecostal Spirituality*.

[95] Thomas, 'Pentecostal Theology in the Twenty-First Century', p. 17.

[96] Thomas, 'Pentecostal Theology in the Twenty-First Century', p. 17. He
writes, 'One of the very helpful things about this paradigm is that it immediately
reveals the ways in which Pentecostalism as a movement is both similar to and
dissimilar from others within Christendom.' He identifies the Holiness tradition
as similar and evangelicalism as dissimilar.

[97] Thomas, 'Pentecostal Theology in the Twenty-First Century', p. 18.

to the Church.'[98]   In this way the theological work would not follow typical evangelical theology where you discuss soteriology and then move to the next theological loci, ecclesiology. Instead, the Fivefold gospel as the distinctive, would serve as the organizing paradigm of the work.

Thomas creatively joined each tenant of the Fivefold gospel with a particular understanding of the nature of the community. Furthermore, he associated a biblical and sacramental sign to that particular understanding of the Church. The following is an outline of his proposal:

> Jesus is Savior. The Church as the Redeemed Community and the ecclesiastical sign is Water Baptism.
>
> Jesus is Sanctifier. The Church as a Holy Community and Footwashing is the ecclesiastical sign.
>
> Jesus is Spirit Baptizer. The Church as an Empowered Missionary Community and the ecclesiastical sign is Glossolalia.
>
> Jesus is Healer. The Church as a Healing Community with the ecclesiastical sign of praying for the sick with the laying on of hands and anointing with oil.
>
> Jesus is Coming King. The Church as an Eschatological Community with the Lord's Supper serving as the ecclesiastical sign.[99]

As we can discern, this is not a forced association. The confessional testimonies articulated by the Fivefold gospel and community practices associated with it are not unfamiliar to Pentecostals. Instead, it is an organic development of the relationship between soteriology and ecclesiology as understood by Pentecostal spirituality. Thomas has extended the discussion of the Fivefold from a soteriological emphasis into the broader theological framework. He does so by *explicitly* interconnecting Christocentric spirituality with soteriology and ecclesiology. In this manner, the Fivefold gospel contributes to ecclesiology in unambiguous and explicit ways. Thomas' proposal demonstrates both the possibility and the viability of the

---

[98] Thomas, 'Pentecostal Theology in the Twenty-First Century', p. 18.

[99] Thomas, 'Pentecostal Theology in the Twenty-First Century', pp. 18-19.

Fivefold gospel serving as the integrative centerpiece of a Pentecostal theology.[100]

Kenneth J. Archer: A Soteriological Ecclesiology centered in the Fivefold Gospel

Stories are essential to shaping, forming and communicating personal and societal identity. All human communities have stories which explain who they are as a people, why they exist, and what activities they are to perform. Stories shape worldviews which in turn enable the community to make sense of reality. The Pentecostal story is a particular twist to the basic Christian story. The Pentecostal story explains why the Pentecostal community exists, who they are and what responsibilities they are to perform as a community. Pentecostals will engage Scripture, do theology, and reflect upon reality from their own contextualized communities and narrative tradition.[101] The Pentecostal community is a distinct coherent narrative tradition within Christianity. Pentecostal communities are bound together by their charismatic experiential worship and their common story. The heart of our common story is the Full gospel.

Developing the insights of others, I have argued that the Fivefold gospel served as the central narrative convictions of the earliest North American Pentecostal communities. The central narrative convictions function as a cohesive narrative web. Jesus is the center of the web, the Fivefold serves as stabilizing theological strands. Woven into this narrative web are personal testimonies, biblical stories, experiences, and scriptural passages which further strengthen the whole web.[102] Or we could illustrate the importance of the centrality of the gospel in terms of a hub. Ted Peters, in his systematic theology entitled *God—the World's Future*, writes: 'If we were to think of Christian systematic theology as a wheel, the gospel of Jesus Christ would be located at the center. It is the hub around

---

[100] William K. Kay, *Pentecostalism* (London, UK: SCM Press, 2009), in an insightful section titled 'Pentecostal systematics', identifies five starting points for developing a Pentecostal theology, pp 259-63. He reviews J.C. Thomas' proposal and affirms its potentiality for the development of a constructive and imaginative Pentecostal theology. He writes, 'A fully fledged, multi-volume systematic theology could take the elements of the fivefold gospel (or fourfold if sanctification is removed as a separate item) and start to weave a coherent discourse covering the whole of Christian theology' (p. 263).

[101] See my, *A Pentecostal Hermeneutic for the Twenty-First Century*, pp. 94-126.

[102] Archer, *A Pentecostal Hermeneutic for the Twenty-First Century*, p. 117.

which everything else revolves … the gospel is that which establishes one's identity as Christian.'[103]

The Fivefold gospel is a formative doxological confession which is testimonial in nature and relational in character.[104] The Full gospel can still be heard with some important modifications throughout Pentecostalism globally.[105] Jesus is the Savior, Sanctifier, Healer, Spirit baptizer, and coming King. The doxological testimonies generate anticipated encounters concerning the redemptive work of God. Through these central narrative convictions Pentecostals identify themselves as participants in the redemptive mission of the Social Trinity living in the last days. Worship and witness provide the important relational and missional concerns of Pentecostal theology grounded in the Fivefold gospel.[106] In the words of Steve Land, 'The Spirit of the end groans, sighs and is pressed within in order to drive out toward the world in witness and toward God in worship.'[107]

As a result of my spiritual formation and hermeneutical studies, I was convinced that the Fivefold gospel *could* and *should* function as the heart of a Pentecostal narrative theology. J.C. Thomas' proposal enabled me to connect the dots, if you will. That is, his creative proposal made sense. In the words of Veli-Matti Kärkkäinen, 'I am drawn to the Pentecostal—Spirit-led, I am sure—focus on Jesus

---

[103] Ted Peters, *God—the World's Future* (Minneapolis, MN: Fortress Press, 1992), pp. 43–44.

[104] For a helpful discussion of the role and hermeneutical function of testimony see Jean-Daniel Plüss, 'Religious Experience in Worship: A Pentecostal Perspective', *PentecoStudies* 2.1 (2003).

[105] Veli-Matti Kärkkäinen, 'Encountering Christ in the Full Gospel Way'. I agree with Kärkkäinen's observation that 'Pentecostalism employs the categories of the Five-fold Gospel in a creative and not always in a constant way' (p. 15).

[106] This summary is based upon my article, 'A Pentecostal Way of Doing Theology: Manner and Method'. See also Mark J. Cartledge, 'Pentecostal Theological Method and Intercultural Theology', *Transformation* 25.2 & 3 (April and July 2008), pp. 92-102. Cartledge compares and contrasts the Church of God School of Theology's Pentecostal hermeneutic (Thomas and Archer) and theological method (Archer) with that of Walter J. Hollenweger. Also see Terry L. Johns, 'Dancing with The Spirit: Story, Theology and Ethics', in S.J. Land, R.D. Moore and J.C. Thomas (eds.), *Passover, Pentecostal and Parousia: Studies in Celebration of the Life and Ministry of R. Hollis Gause* (JPTSup, 35; Blandford Forum, UK: Deo Publishing, 2010), pp. 191-208, where the Fivefold gospel and pentecostal hermeneutical method shapes a storied pentecostal ethic.

[107] Land, *Pentecostal Spirituality: A Passion for the Kingdom*, p. 192.

Christ as the center of the (five or fourfold) Gospel ... it is a precious methodological gateway to a balanced theology.'[108] I picked up the mantel and started further developing his proposal in my theology courses on Pentecostal theology. This led to my published theological essay titled 'Nourishment for our Journey: The Pentecostal *Via Salutis* and Sacramental Ordinances.'[109]

In that essay I offered narrative expansion and further development concerning the sacramental nature of the signs associated with the Fivefold gospel and the mystical nature of Pentecostal soteriology. Sacramental ordinances are community acts of commitment ordained by Christ as means of grace with particular symbolic significance for our Pentecostal identity (story) and Christian journey (*via salutis*).[110] By locating the sacramental ordinances in the Pentecostal story, the sacramental ordinances take on a spiritual-metaphorical-narrative nature. The metaphorical and narrative nature of the sacraments gives the Holy Spirit opportunity to work redemptively in our lives by strengthening and reshaping the community in her journey (*via salutis*) with the Social Trinity. The sacramental ordinances are metaphorical-narrative signs that re-enact the redemptive story of Jesus for the community. The participants experience the redemptive presence of God through these proleptic worship experiences. The community anticipates and participates in the ecclesiastical rites which convey grace. Furthermore, through the metaphorical-symbolic act we encounter the Holy Spirit and continue to proclaim and participate in the mission of the Social

---

[108] Veli-Matti Kärkkäinen, 'David's Sling: The Promise and Problem of Pentecostal Theology Today: A Response to D. Lyle Dabney', *Pneuma* 23 (2001), pp. 147-152 (152).

[109] Kenneth J. Archer, 'Nourishment for our Journey: The Pentecostal *Via Salutis* and Sacramental Ordinances', *Journal of Pentecostal Theology* 13.1 (October 2004), pp. 79-96.

[110] I connected sacramental to ordinance (suggesting the term 'sacramental ordinance') as a way of affirming that these five ecclesiastical worship activities (water baptism—salvation, footwashing—sanctification, glossolalic speech—Spirit baptism, praying for and anointing the sick with oil—healing, and the Lord's Supper—Coming King) are commanded by Jesus Christ (ordinances) and opportunities to experience redemptive encounters with God (sacramental). In this way the 'sacramental ordinances' are directly connected to the commands of Jesus and enable us to continue our salvific journey with God through the Spirit. In doing so I clearly reject the Zwinglian understanding of these rites.

Trinity.[111] I believe that by connecting a sacramental ordinance to each of the doxological confessions (originally identified by Thomas) that Pentecostal theology could move from soteriology into ecclesiology in an organic pneumatic way.[112] Furthermore, this approach to ecclesiology actually gave me opportunity to integrate more fully the Fivefold gospel into a dynamic synergistic soteriology. Hopefully, this shows that a narrative approach to Pentecostal theology may be able to address the various theological loci in such a manner that it allows for them to be informed and developed by each other around the theological center—the Gospel.[113]

Keith Warrington notes, 'Pentecostals do not own a distinctively Pentecostal theology of the church.'[114] Pentecostals will move from a discussion of soteriology to ecclesiology.[115] As Amos Yong correctly noted 'the what of the church is by definition related to the question of what it means to be saved.' Therefore 'pentecostal ecclesiology is intimately connected with its (Pentecostalism) doctrine of salvation.'[116] In this final section, I will offer a brief proposal to strengthen a soteriological-ecclesiology structured around the Fivefold gospel.[117]

In order to strengthen a Pentecostal ecclesiology without decentralizing the gospel, I suggest that we integrate the fivefold ministry

⤷ Are you attempting to push your agenda? (Proceed with caution)

---

[111] See also Wesley Scott Biddy, 'Re-envisioning the Pentecostal Understanding of Eucharist: An Ecumenical Proposal', *Pneuma* 28.2 (Fall 2006), pp. 228-51.

[112] I realize that the essay did not fully develop a Pentecostal ecclesiology.

[113] For another exploration see Chapter 3 of my forthcoming monograph, *The Gospel Revisited: Toward a Pentecostal Theology of Worship and Witness,* titled 'Jesus the Spirit Baptizer: Signifier of a Pentecostal Narrative Theology.' I attempt to integrate the more prominent themes of a Pentecostal theology into three interrelated theological categories (Social Trinity, Synergistic Soteriology, and Ecclesiology).

[114] Warrington, *Pentecostal Theology: A Theology of Encounter*, p. 131.

[115] See also Kenneth J. Archer and Andrew S. Hamilton, 'Anabaptism-Pietism and Pentecostalism: Scandalous Partners in Protest', *Scottish Journal of Theology* 63.2 (2010), pp. 185-202, where I argue for a Pentecostal synergistic soteriological approach to ecclesiology.

[116] Yong, *The Spirit Poured Out on All Flesh*, p. 127.

[117] Hopefully, this might contribute the ongoing development of a distinctly Pentecostal ecclesiology.

gifts of Christ into the Fivefold paradigm proposed by Thomas. The fivefold ministry gifts are listed in Eph. 4.11-13.[118]

> It was he who gave some to be **apostles**, some to be **prophets**, some to be **evangelists**, and some to be **pastors** and **teachers**, to prepare God's people for works of service, so that the body of Christ may be built up until we all reach unity in the faith and in the knowledge of the Son of God and become mature, attaining to the whole measure of the fullness of Christ (NIV).

Generally Pentecostals have distinguished these five gifts from the rest of the gifts mentioned in Scripture. All gifts come from God for the benefit of the community and the individual-in-community (Jas 1.17). In Eph. 4.11 these five gifts (apostles, prophets, evangelists, pastors and teachers) are given to the Church by Jesus Christ.[119] The rest of the gifts mentioned in the NT are distributed to the community by the Holy Spirit. The Church lives under the Lordship of Christ through the indwelling and empowering personal presence of the Holy Spirit.[120] These gifts are distributed by Jesus Christ for the purpose of building up and the maturation of the community. The gifts enable the community to worship God and witness to the world. The local church is to carry on the mission of Christ through the powerful presence of the Spirit.

The functional ministry of the Church then is never reduced to an instrumental purpose of evangelistic mission. Witness is the responsibility of the community in ministry to the world which flows out of the worship of God. Witness is not so much a pragmatic activity but rather an ontological existence in the world. Pentecostal worship is not a means to an end but an end in itself. Worship and witness are doxological activates. They are reciprocal and inseparable relational privileges of the Pentecostal community.

---

[118] See Andrew T. Lincoln, *Ephesians* (Word Biblical Commentary, 42; Waco, TX: Word, 1990, republished by Nelson Reference and Electronic), pp. 249-69, for the difficulty of this passage.

[119] See Warrington, *Pentecostal Theology*, pp. 138-43. I commend him for including this section on the ministry gifts of Christ in his monograph.

[120] See Peter Hocken, 'Church, Theology of', in Stanley M. Burgess and Gary B. McGee (eds.), *Dictionary of Pentecostal and Charismatic Movements* (Grand Rapids, MI: Zondervan, 1988), pp. 211-18. Concerning Pentecostal polities, the retrieval of the fivefold ministry gifts could be seen as a distinctive, see p. 213.

The following is a delineation of the fivefold ministries gifts that builds on Thomas' proposal.[121]

> Jesus is the Savior. The Church as the Redeemed Community and the ecclesiastical sacramental ordinance is Water Baptism. To this I would add apostles and the *apostolic* function of the community.

> Jesus is the Sanctifier. The Church as a Holy Community and Footwashing is the ecclesiastical sign. To this I would add teachers and the *teaching* function of the community.

> Jesus is Spirit Baptizer. The Church as a Charismatic Community and the ecclesiastical sign is Glossolalia. To this I would add the prophets and the *charismatic* function of the community.

> Jesus is the Healer. The Church as a Healing Community with the ecclesiastical sign of praying for the sick with the laying on of hands and anointing with oil. To this I would add pastors and the *pastoral* function.

> Jesus is Coming King. The Church as a Missionary Community with the Lord's Supper serving as the ecclesiastical sign. To this I would add the evangelists and the *evangelistic* function of the community.

I would argue that these gifts refer primarily to the ministry function of the Church. I would emphasize function of the collective community without denying the reality and possibility of such offices existing. Pentecostals are not cessationists when it comes to gifts and are restorationists when it comes to recovering and restoring NT practices, polities, and beliefs to the Church.[122]

The local church is apostolic in function. Her authority is derived from Christ. Thus it has authority to proclaim the gospel and call the inhabitants of the world into the way of salvation. The redeemed community is a contrast society sent by the commissioning of Christ and in the power of the Spirit to carry forth the mission

---

[121] This working proposal, of course, needs further development and reflection.

[122] I am not opposed to the importance of these gifts having reference to actual 'persons', in fact all those so gifted are identified at various points in Scripture.

and message of God. She desires to retain apostolic authority, purity, and power. Her apostolic authority is further demonstrated through the restoration of apostolic signs such as healing, miracles, prophecy, speaking in tongues.[123] The Church is the Body of Christ—the redeeming presence of God in the world.

The local church is to function as a teaching community. As such it will tutor and disciple the believers into mature followers of Jesus Christ. The community is to be sanctified. Teachers instruct the community as how they are to live rightly in perfecting love with a loving and holy God and one another. We are to be holy because God is holy. The Church then is a community of priests.

The local church is prophetic in function. It testifies to the world by the ongoing inspiration of the Spirit. The proclamation of the Scripture through the prophetic anointing of the Spirit enables the activity to transmit grace and initiate a revelatory encounter with God. Furthermore, the community is to speak forth the word of God for today. Thus she must not lose her prophetic function to live and testify to social-political issues. The local churches must allow for the prophetic gifts to express the justice of the Lord to both the Church and to the nations. She lives as a protesting society to the demonic powers and unjust structures in the world. The Church is an empowered missionary community because it is charismatic—the temple of the Holy Spirit. And as such, it is anointed, like Christ, to perform signs and wonders for the coming Kingdom of God. The local church is a community of prophets.

The local church is to function pastorally. As a healing community the Church nurtures the broken hearted. She embraces those on the margins, the sick, lonely, rejected, and victimized. She gathers up the little children and mothers them into maturity. She provides hospitable opportunities for transformative growth. She casts out demons setting the captives free. She is the proleptic foretaste of the healing that is still to come in fullness. The Church is to have many mothers and fathers, yet if the Church is not your mother, then God is not your Father. The Church is the family of God.

The local church is evangelistic in function. As a redeemed and charismatic community it moves out into the ends of the earth sharing the Full and whole gospel. As an eschatological community

---

[123] Kärkkäinen, *An Introduction to Ecclesiology*, p. 77.

it offers a proleptic foretaste of the salvific benefits that find their ultimate reality in the Kingdom that is coming. The proclamation and demonstration of the Fivefold gospel embraces all aspects of human life not just the so-called spiritual interior live. The local community and its members go forth as the Spirit leads in apostolic authority with prophetic anointing. Everyone is an evangelist because they have been empowered by the Spirit to witness in words and deeds of the transforming Gospel.

In sum, Pentecostals are sent out with apostolic authority and prophetic empowerment to proclaim the gospel to the ends of the earth. The good news of salvation includes living as an alternative society within the world. The community exists as a contrast society *in* the world and *for* the world without being *of* the world. The community is not a product of worldly systems or existence—it is a redeemed community. The community pastorally nurtures and hospitably protects one another in its journey—it is a healing community. The Church as a community of teachers instructs one another so that it remains faithfully to the teachings of Christ, living honorably with one another, and able to discern the leading of the Spirit. The Church is to embody before the world a distinct sociopolitical alternative because it is sanctified unto the Lord—a holy community. As such, the local church is a sacramental presence of Jesus Christ in and to the world. The Church as the dwelling place of the Holy Spirit is a prophetic witness of life to a dying world and a charismatic sacred space within the world—a charismatic community. The Church as a contrast and charismatic community is embodied by the presence of the Holy Spirit and empowered by the Holy Spirit in order to carry on the redemptive evangelistic mission of our Lord Jesus Christ—a missionary community. The very nature and character of the Church equipped with the fivefold ministry gifts and sustained by the transformative grace of the sacramental ordinances enable a community to participate faithfully in the mission of the Social Trinity.

The Fivefold gospel marks the very character of the Church, shapes its relational identity and directs its salvific path. The fivefold ministry gifts provide nurture and discernment as the community is led by and empowered by the Spirit so that it can faithfully continue the ministry of Jesus Christ for the sake of the world. The marks of the Church are organically connected to the marks of the Fivefold gospel which serve as the ministry marks of Jesus Christ. The fivefold ministry gifts of Jesus Christ, as listed in Eph. 4.11, further fortify the missional function of the Church.

The local communities are presently to model the 'glorious human fellowship—a recreation of shalom' that is to come fully at the consummation of the second coming of Christ Jesus. The body of Christ will not be dissolved at the second coming of Jesus, but instead, it will be fully glorified. The Church will be unified through its diversity and remain localized in the space-time continuum in creation. Therefore, the Fivefold gospel coupled with the fivefold ministry gifts of Jesus Christ should enable the further integration of a distinct narrative Pentecostal ecclesiology.

PART TWO

THE PENTECOSTAL CHURCH AS REDEEMED COMMUNITY

2

THE CHURCH AS A REDEEMED, UN-REDEEMED, AND REDEEMING COMMUNITY

WYNAND J. DE KOCK*

Introduction

As a boy, I grew up in a wonderful 'spirit-filled' church in a small city outside of Johannesburg in South Africa. Pentecostalism wasn't part of mainstream Christianity then; we were often ridiculed for our faith. I remember conversations—or maybe they were more like debates—with school friends about doctrines like charismatic gifts, believers' baptism and freedom of choice, election and predestination. From a young age I was passionate about what I believed, but I often found that my passion did not keep up with my ability to explain my faith. Many times I found myself retreating into the stance: you may take away everything, but you can't take away my experience.

Imprinted on my memory is the image of our pastor's hand on someone's head, with the veins bulging in his neck as he called on God to bring deliverance. That head was often mine; I needed prayer more often than most. There was always olive oil and tissues available to invoke the Spirit's presence and to deal with the nasal consequences of the Spirit's work, respectively. I was baptized soon after my eighth birthday and experienced 'baptism in the Spirit' in that same year. These baptisms shaped my faith and spirituality as a

* Wynand J. de Kock (DTh, University of South Africa) is Principal of Tabor College Victoria, Australia and Professor of Theology in Residence at Eastern University in Philadelphia, PA, USA.

child. I agree with Steve Land when he describes water baptism as '… the acceptance to become a holy witness in the power of the Holy Spirit. It was a death and resurrection ritual of remembrances and hope'.[1] At age eighteen, I found myself ready to respond to what I believed was God's call on my life to become a pastor. Giving up my dreams to be an engineer, I set off for the local university to study theology.

My understanding of God's redemption plan was simple: God loves the world; the world is sinful; Jesus died on the cross for our sins generally and mine specifically. I need to accept his offer of atonement, so that God's anger can be mollified: If I don't, I will remain damned and will go to hell or remain behind when the rapture occurs. The presence of the gifts, especially speaking in tongues, was evidence that one was living a holy life, since the Holy Spirit can only indwell those who are sanctified. This was the full gospel for me; that after all, was the name of our church.

It was clear to me that Jesus was the embodiment of the 'full gospel'. Week after week, Jesus was presented as the Saviour, Sanctifier, Baptizer with the Spirit, Healer of the body, and the Soon-Coming King.[2] Kenneth Archer's discussion of the place of the 'full Gospel' rings true. He writes:

> Pentecostals embrace the Full Gospel, which places Jesus and the Spirit at the center of God's dramatic redemptive story. Pentecostals, as the end-time people, are participating in the 'Latter Rain' of this redemptive story. The proclamation of the Full Gospel is the declaration of the redemptive activity of God in Christ Jesus and the Holy Spirit to the community.[3]

While these sermons shaped my personal piety, they did little if anything to expose and deal with the deep-seated racism I nurtured as a young South African male. I did not experience the in-breaking of God's Kingdom to bring healing, transformation, and reconciling power over all of God's creation. While the Kingdom of God

---

[1]   Steven J. Land, *Pentecostal Spirituality: A Passion for the Kingdom* (JPTSup 1; Sheffield: Sheffield Academic Press, 1993), p. 115.

[2]   See Donald W. Dayton, *Theological Roots of Pentecostalism* (Grand Rapids: Zondervan, 1987).

[3]   Kenneth J. Archer, 'A Pentecostal Way of Doing Theology: Method and Manner', *International Journal of Systematic Theology* 9.3 (July, 2007), p. 312.

may be the 'key theological motif for Pentecostal spirituality in its search of a holistic vision',[4] it was not my experience.

I agree with Kärkkäinen[5] that the 'interesting mixture of Anabaptist, Wesleyan-Holiness, and Catholic heritages, focuses on the inner transformation', but I did not experience it as the 'the key to social transformation'. While I did experience Pentecostalism's emphasis on the 'rebirth of a person by the Spirit', I did not experience that rebirth as 'anticipation of the transformation of the cosmos'.

Today I can agree with Kärkkäinen, that Pentecostalism taken to its logical conclusion could expect that: 'The person filled by the Spirit of God is impelled by that same Spirit to cooperate with God in the work of evangelism and social action in the anticipation of the new creation.'[6] But that expectation was foreign to the Pentecostalism of my youth.

The church that nurtured my faith was deeply racist in its attitudes. While there will be some who will dispute this, the history of the Full Gospel Church of God in South Africa tells the sad tale of racial segregation and discrimination. In fact, most Pentecostal churches were in cahoots with the Nationalist Government of the day. When an official of the Full Gospel Church had declared the Church's position on Apartheid, it could state with glee that it 'was already practicing it'.[7]

White Pentecostals participated in the suppression and even torture of those considered 'enemies of the state'. The story of Frank Chikane[8] is a painful reminder of this. He grew up and was ordained in one of the largest Pentecostal churches in South Africa.

---

[4] Veli-Matti Kärkkäinen, 'Spirit, Reconciliation and Healing in the Community: Missiological Insights from Pentecostals', *International Review of Missions* 94.372 (2005), p. 44.

[5] Kärkkäinen, 'Spirit, Reconciliation and Healing in the Community', p. 44.

[6] Kärkkäinen, 'Spirit, Reconciliation and Healing in the Community', p. 45.

[7] Wynand J. de Kock, 'Geloof, Geloofsinhoud en Geloofsontwikkeling: 'n Fowleriaanse Interpretasie van 'n Kerk in Krisis', DTh Thesis (University of South Africa, 1990), p. 187

[8] Lyn S. Graybill, *Truth & Reconciliation in South Africa: Miracle or Model?* (Boulder: Lynne Rienner Publishers Inc., 2002), p. 138. For Frank Chikane's account of this incident see Ron Sider, 'Interview with Rev. Frank Chikane', *Transformation* 5 (April/June, 1988), pp. 9-12 and his autobiography, Frank Chikane, *No Life of My Own* (Maryknoll, NY: Orbis Books, 1989).

As a young minister, he became aware of the injustices of the South African society. In response to his deeply held theological convictions, he joined the South African Student Organisation in the seventies and later became its leader. The political credentials of this organisation are beyond any doubt, since Steve Biko was its inaugural president in the sixties. It did not take long before Chikane's political activities landed him in hot water with the government, as well as with the white leadership of his Pentecostal denomination. They cold-heartedly defrocked him for his ungodly behaviour. It would already be sad if this was where the story ends, but we know that it does not finish with an unfair dismissal. Over the years of activism, this diminutive and softly spoken Pentecostal believer was detained and imprisoned on numerous occasions. On one of these occasions, he was interrogated and tortured by another Pentecostal believer. This believer was ordained and ministered in the same denomination that once ordained Chikane. One would expect that his torture would be less severe since it was under the supervision of a fellow believer and Pentecostal, but instead we read:

> Following his release, he was unable to walk because of torture. Over the next several years he was detained several times and was beaten, abused and had his hair torn out. On one occasion, his appearance in court so shocked his church that a number of youth members slipped over the border to Mozambique to join the ANC guerrilla forces.[9]

My own racism was exposed as a Graduate student at a Pentecostal Theological Seminary in Cleveland, TN. It was during a clinical placement as Chaplain at Egleston Children's Hospital that I met a little black boy who displayed the classic symptoms of acquired foetal alcohol syndrome. His face and head were severely malformed and he suffered from mental retardation. James was the Quasimodo of the ward, and I had to care for him. As much as his malformations disgusted me, matters were only made worse by the colour of his skin. Deep down in my twisted mind, I concluded that this little boy was suffering like this because black people were all the same: they needed Europeans to take care of them.

---

[9] *Dictionary of African Christian Biography*, Frank Chikane, http://www.dacb.org/stories/southafrica/chikane_frank.html, Internet; Accessed 23 March 2010.

But on a destined day James and I met in the long and wide corridor of the Egleston Children's Hospital. There was a thunder storm outside that day and James came out into the corridor frightened by the thunder. I was surprised, even shocked, by his presence. Before I could do anything, a petrified, slobbering, shaking little black boy was holding on to me. Many thoughts flashed through my mind, but to my shame the dominant thought was that I needed to get him off my clean pants. My disgust for the little boy and for all that he represented was coming to the surface. I managed to get him back onto his bed, still doing everything in my might to free myself from his boyish grip. As I peeled his last finger from my arm, he swung around, now holding on to a stuffed toy animal. His eyes were cold and I looked away.

James' action exposed me. I felt deeply ashamed, ashamed of my inhumanity. This boy, who needed a human to hold him and love him, found in me only disgust and an inability to respond. If his mother was addicted to a *teratogenic*[10] drug and it produced a little 'monster', then my motherland was also on drugs to produce that kind of behaviour in me.

I have no doubt that the churches that nurtured Chikane's torturer and the heartless chaplain were communities of the redeemed. I don't question the authenticity of my youthful encounters with God and to this day I celebrate the significance of being baptized into a 'counter-cultural community'[11] of the redeemed. But I now realize that this community was also in need of redemption. Our brand of 'counter-culturalism' did not free our motherland from her addictions. The redeemed community was, and is, in need of redemption in order to be a redeeming presence in this world. In the remainder of this paper, I wish to explore the Church as a community that is redeemed, needs redemption and has a redeeming presence in this world.

---

[10] Alcohol is a *teratogenic* drug which can cause serious birth defects in some children whose mothers ingest alcohol during pregnancy. The term *teratogenic* comes from the Greek word for monster.

[11] Kenneth J. Archer, 'A Pentecostal Way of Doing Theology', p. 314.

The Church as the Community of the Redeemed

The analogy, albeit of an indirect kind, between the being of God and the Church is a well-trodden theological path. Because God called creation and Church into existence through his word, there seems to be an *analogia entis* between God and the Church. Even if the traces of the trinity, *vestigium trinitatis*, are faint and even if analogy refers to comparisons amidst ever greater contrasts,[12] the challenge remains to appreciate the analogy between the being of God and that of the Church.

Colin Gunton says, 'The Church is what it is by virtue of being called to be a temporal echo of the eternal community that God is'.[13] As the community of the redeemed 'the church may be said to be a vestige of the Trinity, in so far as it consists in personal communion.[14] The Cappadocian fathers used the word *perichoresis*[15] to describe the communal nature of God. Thomas Torrance explains that it points to a 'dynamic three-way reciprocity' between Father, Son, and Spirit, in what he calls 'the *perichoretic* co-activity of the Holy Trinity'.[16] Miroslav Volf adds that, 'In every divine person as a subject, the other persons also indwell; all mutually permeate one another, though in so doing they do not cease to be distinct persons.'[17]

God is therefore a being who shares life, who is in his very essence a community, a God who creates out of the overflow of his being and who calls his creation to participate in this shared life. The implications for our understanding of the Church are substan-

---

[12] See Miroslav Volf, *After Our Likeness: The Church as the Image of the Trinity* (Grand Rapids: Eerdmans, 1998), p. 199.

[13] Colin Gunton, 'The Church on Earth: The Roots of Community', in Colin Gunton and Daniel Hardy (eds.), *On Being the Church* (Edinburgh: T. & T. Clark, 1989), p. 75.

[14] John Zizioulas, *Being As Communion: Studies in Personhood and the Church* (Crestwood, NY: St Vladimir's Seminary Press, 1993), p. 66.

[15] The Greek *perichoreuo* means to 'dance around'. Like so many Greek verbs, this is a compound verb—two words making up one new word. The verb *choreuo* is to dance and when it is joined by the preposition *peri*, it closely resembles *perichoreo*, which means to 'encircle' or 'encompass'.

[16] Thomas F. Torrance, *The Christian Doctrine of God: One Being Three Persons* (Edinburgh: T. & T. Clark, 1996), p. 198.

[17] Miroslav Volf, *After Our Likeness: The Church as the Image of the Trinity* (Grand Rapids: William B. Eerdmans, 1998), p. 209.

tial. The Church is the community that has been 'swept into a divine world of mutual love and begun to experience the very goal of our nature as spiritual and social beings'.[18] Volf applies *perichoresis* to the life and ministry of the church when he writes:

> Each person gives of himself or herself to others, and each person in a unique way takes up others into himself or herself. This is the process of the mutual internalization of personal characteristics occurring in the church through the Holy Spirit indwelling Christians. The Spirit opens them to one another and allows them to become *catholic persons* in their uniqueness. It is here that they, in a creaturely way, correspond to the catholicity of the divine persons.[19]

The Cappadocian[20] fathers also described the Holy Spirit as the personification of the love between the Father and the Son. Stanley Grenz picks up on this view of the Spirit when he writes:

> The bond between the Father and the Son is the mutual love they share. Throughout all eternity, the Father loves the Son, and the Son reciprocates that love. Out of love, the Father generates the Son, and the Son in turn reciprocates the love of the One who generates him.[21]

Grenz helps us to appreciate that love describes God's inner life. Millard Erickson agrees:

> They are bound to one another in love, *agape* love, which therefore unites them in the closest and most intimate of relationships. This unselfish love makes each more concerned for the other than for himself. There is therefore a mutual submission

---

[18] Clark Pinnock, *Flame of Love* (Downer's Grove: IVP, 1996), p. 38.

[19] Volf, *After Our Likeness*, pp. 211-12.

[20] Two brothers, Basil the Great (330-379 CE) and Gregory of Nyssa (330-395 CE) and a close friend Gregory of Nazianzus (329-389 CE), became defenders of Nicene orthodoxy and carried forward the work of Origen, Tertullian, and Athanasius in formulating the doctrine of the Trinity.

[21] Stanley Grenz, *A Theology for the Community of God* (Nashville: Broadman & Holdman Publisher, 1994), p. 74.

of each to each of the others and a mutual glorification of one another. There is complete equality of the three.[22]

Pinnock writes, 'Spirit is leading us into union—to transforming, personal, intimate relationship with the Triune God.'[23] Soteriology is then, says Steven Land, about 'participation in the divine life more than the removal of guilt.'[24] It is more than a destination, it is a spiritual journey, 'a life lived in, through, and for God'.[25] With the help of John Christopher Thomas, Kenneth Archer argues that the ordinances of Christ 'aid us in our salvific journey because they give the Holy Spirit necessary opportunities to keep the community on the right path—the way of salvation'.[26] As such they function as media that transmit the grace of God;[27] they function as sacraments.[28] Jesus, as the redeemer, instructs his followers to baptize new believers, because baptism, says Anthony Cross, is:

... closely connected to the forgiveness of sins and the reception of the Spirit (Acts 2.38), union with Christ in his death and res-

---

[22] Millard Erickson, *God in Three Persons: A Contemporary Interpretation of the Trinity* (Grand Rapids: Baker, 1995), p. 331.

[23] Pinnock, *Flame of Love*, p. 149.

[24] Land, *Pentecostal Spirituality*, p. 23.

[25] M. Robert Mulholland, Jr, *Shaped by the Word: The Power of Scripture in Spiritual Formation* (Nashville, TN; Upper Rooms Books, rev. edn, 2000), p. 26.

[26] Kenneth J Archer, 'Nourishment for our Journey: The Pentecostal Via Salutis and Sacramental Ordinances', *Journal of Pentecostal Theology* 13.1 (2004), p. 85. See also Kenneth J Archer, 'A Pentecostal Way of Doing Theology', p. 313, for a summary of John Christopher Thomas' proposal. 'John Christopher Thomas has creatively connected each doxological confession of Jesus with a particular biblical-sacramental sign. Thus, 'Jesus is our Savior' is connected with the ecclesiastical rite of 'water baptism', 'Jesus is our Sanctifier' with 'footwashing', Spirit Baptizer with glossolalia speech, Healer with praying for and anointing the sick with oil and Jesus as Coming King with the Lord's Supper. Thomas has set forth a proposal that is more integrative theologically by interconnecting ecclesiology and soteriology with Christology.'

[27] Pinnock, *Flame of Love*, p. 122.

[28] Kenneth J Archer, 'Nourishment for our Journey', p. 89, agrees with John Christopher Thomas that: 'The sacraments are directly connected to proclamation of the gospel and specifically connected to commands and promises of Jesus Christ. In this light, Pentecostals who embrace the fivefold gospel might consider expanding the number of sacraments from three to five'. See also, J.E. Colwell, *Promise and Presence: An Exploration of Sacramental Theology* (Milton Keynes: Paternoster, 2005), pp. 113-14.

urrection (Rom. 6.3-9), incorporation into the body of Christ, the church (1 Cor. 12.13), and regeneration (Tit. 3.5).[29]

But the redeemed community is also a sacrament, since the Spirit enables the Church to transmit the grace of God, in Christ, throughout the world. The Church signals to the world that there is life, in and beyond this life and that intimacy with God is possible, in and beyond our broken relationships.

The Church as a Community in Need of Redemption

While it is true that Trinitarian persons could not live apart or in segregation from one another, the same cannot be said for human beings. Genesis reveals that humans were created to be in communion with God and the rest of creation—Genesis chapters one and two tell us this with great clarity. However, in chapter three, things change. A serpent enters the story and suggests a way of living that is separate from God. It can be said that the serpent introduces the notion of separation: separation between God, others, and creation, a life that is selfish. From here on human beings have acquired the ability to live as human beings apart from others or even in enmity.

The intimacy that existed in God and creation was disturbed by the intrusion of evil. Aida Spencer describes the rest of life in the Old Testament as being *under the curse*.[30] After the fall, we read in Genesis that God said to the serpent that from now on it would be cursed among the animals. The news was not any better for the first human couple. He said that Eve would endure great pain in childbirth and Adam would toil to produce a crop because the earth was cursed. In addition, God warned they would need to leave Eden and their marriage would be marked by a power struggle. 'You'll want to please your husband,' He said to Eve, 'but he'll lord it over you.'[31]

When Gilbert Bilezikian reflects on the tragedy of Genesis 3, he introduces the reader to a helpful illustration. He writes:

---

[29] Anthony R. Cross, 'The Evangelical sacrament: *baptisma semper reformandum*', *Evangelical Quarterly* 80.3 (2008), p. 202.

[30] This is a term borrowed from Aida B. Spencer, *Beyond the Curse: Women Called to Ministry* (Nashville, TN: Thomas Nelson, 1985).

[31] The Message, Gen. 3.16

A visual representation of oneness may be created instantly by clasping one's hands together. The hands are separate entities, each distinctively independent from the other. Yet the inter-locked fingers of one's clasped hands suggest a bonding that makes them one body. After creating man and woman from one body, God declared them united into one flesh (Gen. 2.22-24). This joining together of two independent lives into oneness provides the basic model for biblical community.[32]

He goes on to say that the separation caused by *diabolos* can be illus-trated by yanking apart the clutched hands. The consequence of this separation was far reaching. Bilezikian explains, 'Unfortunately, the damage inflicted on oneness was far greater than mere separa-tion. It led to an hierarchical view of life. This tragedy may be en-acted with one hand made into a fist over the other.'[33] Power strug-gles and the battle for survival begin to dominate human existence. From here on the Bible tells the story of polygamy, slavery, murder, war, and children at risk. This is life *under the curse.*

Paul Tillich, a theologian who wrote most of his theology during and after the Second World War, also reflects on the human plight. According to Tillich, as fallen creatures humans came face-to-face with the stark reality of *non-being.* As a result of the fall, human be-ings have been separated from God, who is our Ground of Being,[34] and consequently humans have become deeply anxious about the prospect of non-being.

Non-being has become our deepest and ultimate concern, says Tillich. This concern is experienced at a universal and personal level. At a universal level we are threatened with the total extinction of being, with nothingness as our final destiny. At a personal level, we are threatened with personal mortality. Tillich would say that we suffer from the loss of being what we were created to be and be-coming what we were supposed to become.[35] The anxiety that marks human existence is the result of our separation from God.

---

[32] Gilbert G. Bilezikian, *Community 101: Reclaiming the local church as Community of Oneness* (Grand Rapids: Zondervan, 1997), p. 45.

[33] Bilezikian, *Community 101*, p. 45.

[34] Paul Tillich, *The Courage to Be* (London: Fontana Library, 1952), p. 157.

[35] See Tillich, *Courage to Be*, pp. 44-48.

Ted Peters, a student of Tillich, continues this reflection on human anxiety in *Sin: Radical evil in soul and society*.[36] Human existence is marked by anxiety, according to Peters. Faith is when we seek to overcome this separation with the means of grace that God provides. This is perhaps the 'Road Less Travelled', as M. Scott Peck reflected on life. The most common response to anxiety is one of unfaith, says Peters. Unfaith manifests in our attempts to take matters into our own hands.

According to Peters, pride is the first evidence of unfaith. Instead of trusting God, we place our trust in our own human efforts. Pride is followed by Concupiscence. This is a very old English word. Its basic meaning is 'desire' but more generally it is to want what others have. In the most basic sense, concupiscence manifests in sexual lust and greed. Peters explains it like this: 'More generally concupiscence is the desire to acquire, to own, to indulge, to take pleasure, to consume. It causes us to covet and disposes us to greed and avarice'.[37]

Self-justification follows short on the heels of concupiscence. In essence self-justification is a web of lies that we tell ourselves. We know deep down that concupiscence will not work; we know that ultimately we will die and our effort to take life from others will come to nothing. Peters explains it when he says: 'In order to maintain the illusion that concupiscence will in fact succeed, we invent lies—lies that identify us with what is good. Sometimes these lies identify some others as evil, justifying the conclusion that they should die and we should live.'[38]

When we willfully use our power over those we have turned into scapegoats, we move from self-justification to cruelty. 'The suffering of others works like a drug; the cruel person needs increasingly larger doses to attain the same high. The ultimate fix is the death of the other.'[39] It seems that Peters might even be right when he invokes the Lifton principle: 'Killing others relieves our own fear of being killed.'[40]

---

[36] Ted Peters, *Sin: Radical Evil in Soul and Society* (Grand Rapids: Eerdmans, 1994).

[37] Peters, *Sin*, p. 125.

[38] Peters, *Sin*, pp. 161-62.

[39] Peters, *Sin*, p. 194.

[40] Peters, *Sin*, p. 194.

The next step from here is blasphemy. We blaspheme if we destroy the means by which someone else can experience grace. 'Blasphemers', says Peters, 'tarnish the name of God to the point that people no longer think to call on it to ask for divine grace.'[41] Normally, we would associate blasphemy with using God's name inappropriately. While I can understand that using God's name in vain is blasphemy, it is ironic that we can be cruel and even torture people in the name of God—yes, even claiming to do this as an act of worship.

There are many expressions of how humans attempt to alleviate this deep-seated anxiety; some are obviously evil while others seem quite harmless. The Church is not immune to this. Allow me a brief excursion into two areas where the Church seems to be faltering as it deals with anxiety at the core of its being.

Excursion #1: No place to disagree. Eugene Peterson gets the gist of Paul's thinking when he writes: 'The World is unprincipled. It's dog-eat-dog out there! The world doesn't fight fair.'[42] But Paul is optimistic about how followers of Jesus treat those in and outside the Church. According to Paul, 'We don't live or fight our battles that way.' Our weapons are not carnal, he says.

Carnality points to our fallen—*under the curse*—way of existence. It is an existence where we want to achieve one-upmanship. The carnal way is to subdue and to dominate; it is to manipulate, out-manoeuvre, and cajole. Eugene Peterson says, 'The tools of our trade aren't for marketing or manipulation, but they are for demolishing that entire massively corrupt culture.' On another occasion, Paul explains how we get to this place of carnal thinking when he writes: 'We demolish arguments and every pretension that sets itself up against the knowledge of God and we take captive every thought to make it obedient to Christ.'[43]

Sometimes it feels like the redeemed community is not very different from others when it comes to the strength of our self-interest and opinions. While this is not the focus of this paper, I see this same tendency in the church of the 21st century. Christians won't speak to other Christians because they don't have the same

---

[41] Peters, *Sin*, p. 17.
[42] 2 Corinthians 10.3-5.
[43] The NIV, 2 Cor. 10.5.

view about the rapture, or church leaders won't attend conferences because the speakers are too Catholic, too Charismatic, too Fundamentalist, too Missional, or too Emergent. Christian authors publish books about each other and write web-blog entries that are tantamount to committing character assassination. Paul uses the picture of a prison to illustrate the carnal way of thinking because such thinking always leads to imprisonment.

When our answers, theories, and practices become towers of pride,[44] we become less willing to engage questions, leaving us imprisoned in thought, action, and passion. If there is no space for questions, then faith will quickly be replaced by prideful thoughts. David Dark calls the Church to repentance, when he writes:

> I believe deliverance begins with questions. It begins with people who *love* questions, people who *live with* questions and by questions, people who feel a great joy when questions are asked. ... When we're exposed to the liveliness of holding everything up to the light of good questions—what I call 'sacred questions'—we discover that redemption is creeping into the way we think, believe and see the world. The *re*-deeming (re-valuing) of what we've made our lives, a redemption that perhaps begins with the insertion of a question mark beside whatever feels final and absolute and *beyond* questioning, gives our souls a bit of elbow room, a space in which to breathe and imagine again, as if for the first time.[45]

Excursion #2: Power over others. The 48 Laws of Power was a best seller in 2002. In the pocket-size version of this book, Robert Greene confirms our insatiable hunger for power: 'The feeling of not having power over people and events is generally unbearable to us—when we feel helpless we feel miserable. No one wants less power; everyone wants more'.[46] Power seems to be the default posi-

---

[44] Though pride is the one ingredient that would weaken and even dissolve the binding power of faith-seeking-meaning (*fides quaerens*), it is not true that unreasonable certainty is always associated with pride. As we mentioned before, if all four rooms of life have potential to contain vices, then pride is most likely to be found here.

[45] David Dark, *The Sacredness of Questioning Everything* (Grand Rapids: Zondervan, 2008), p. 14.

[46] Robert Greene, *The 48 Laws of Power: Concise Edition* (London: Profile Books, 2002), p. xi.

tion we return to when we feel anxious. We counter anxiety by grabbing power to assert ourselves over others. As we already noted, Paul Tillich argues that this anxiety results from our separation from the *ground of our being*.

The western world is currently entangled in power-struggles across the globe. Greed and economic-myopia have caused financial pain right around the world—and especially in economically marginalized nations. But, it seems that money isn't the real prize, power is. Even at a personal level, we are preoccupied with our careers. Getting to the top of our professions is the priority and achieving this will, we believe, will secure our future. The survival of the fittest permeates our thinking. So, we have become obsessed with self-help, self-improvement, self-actualization and leadership.[47] After all, Harry Truman said that: 'Leadership is the ability to get men to do what they don't want to do and like it'.[48]

Leadership is a hot topic in the Church. Preachers point out that Aaron and Miriam struggled with Moses' popularity, while Moses himself grew weak under the pressure of leadership. They draw lessons from the leadership struggle between Saul, the first king of Israel, and his successor, David, who was the darling of the masses. The Church loves to reflect on David as a worthy model for leadership. He is often used as justification for centralising the leadership in one person in a local church—power by one over others. This obsession with leadership is something that even the disciples of Jesus struggled with. In an intimate moment, the mother of two brother-disciples of Jesus approached him with a burning request. 'Grant that one of these two sons of mine may sit at your right and the other at your left in your kingdom',[49] she asked. The kingdom

---

[47] A quick survey on the internet reveals how we are preoccupied with leadership. When I searched the web in 2004, Google delivered 21,500,000 articles on leadership in 0.17 seconds. In 2010, I found 125,000,000 in 0.24 seconds. I wonder what it will be by the time you read these statistics. Results achieved on ADSL in Australia. Type 'Leadership' into Google and see how many books are available today. Any respectable bookshop would reveal the general interest in leadership as well. In 2004 a librarian could stock their shelves with 85,665 books on leadership; five years later it was a bulging 372,859 volumes. I think we are obsessed. Type 'Leadership' into Amazon.com's search engine and see how many books are available today.

[48] Allan R. Cohen *et al.*, *Effective Behavior in Organizations* (Homewood, IL: Irwin, 1984), p. 310.

[49] The NIV, Mt. 20.21.

was about to be revealed, the masses were about to be ruled by a new king, and he would need lieutenants.

Jesus' response has been a pet scripture of pastors through the ages as they have preached on the topic of servant leadership. He said: 'whoever wants to become great among you must be your servant, and whoever wants to be first must be your slave—just as the Son of Man did not come to be served, but to serve, and to give his life as a ransom for many'.[50] But the motivation of this response is often ignored. Jesus said that Gentile rulers 'lord it over'[51] those that they are supposed to lead; something Jesus despised.

By the time of Constantine, the Church had a pope, a man of authority, and the emperor of the Church. The Church succumbed to the demands of civil society and, like the people of Israel, chose to place power in the hands of one man. Powerful men in positions of power and authority today are still leading most of the Church. Even in the newer expressions of Christianity, such as the Pentecostal, Charismatic, and Apostolic movements, power is often centralized in a male who can hold this office on account of his anointing and maleness.

Conservative evangelicals, like Wayne Grudem and John Piper,[52] insist that that the issue of women in leadership will be settled when we agree on the interpretation of 1 Cor. 14.34-35 and 1 Tim. 2.11-15. For Pentecostals, who have a proud history of women church-planters and leaders and who long for the fulfillment of the prophecy of Joel, the issue should be a bit easier—but it is not. In fact, it would be fair to say that the view of women in Pentecostal history is 'complex and contradictory'.[53] Cecil M. Robeck points out that the ordination of women to the pastorate has become even more controversial for Pentecostals in recent times, because of their

---

[50] The NIV, Mt. 20.26-27.

[51] The NIV, Mt. 20.25.

[52] John Piper and Wayne Grudem, 'Charity, clarity, and hope: The controversy and the cause of Christ', in J. Piper and W. Grudem (eds.), *Recovering Biblical Manhood & Womanhood: A Response to Evangelical Feminism* (Wheaton, IL: Crossway Books, 1991), pp. 403–22.

[53] R.M. Griffith, and D.G. Roebuck, 'Women, role of', in S.M. Burgess and E.M. van der Maas (eds.), *The New International Dictionary of Pentecostal and Charismatic Movements* (Grand Rapids: Zondervan, 2002), p. 1203.

increased exposure to Biblicist paradigms.[54] The monarch seems to be well and alive even in Pentecostal churches today. This seems to be a throw back to life *under the curse and a call for redemption.*

The unfolding story of scripture suggests that God's love can break into our anxiety-ridden existence. God climbs onto a cross and puts his existence at risk, not so that we escape hard realities of life, but that we learn to live faithfully in it.

The Church as Redeeming Community

Jürgen Moltmann's recollection of Elie Wiesel's[55] story has given us a vivid picture of the lengths God will go to break into our anxiety-ridden existence. It is about a young Jewish boy who was hung by the Nazis along with two other men in the camp at Buna. The boy did not die immediately; his death was prolonged by 30 minutes of suffering. The onlookers around Wiesel asked: 'Where is God now?' Somehow Wiesel heard the answer coming from within himself: 'Where is he? He is here. He is hanging there on the gallows.' Moltmann comments with great insight and tender pastoral grit:

> Any other answer would be blasphemy. There cannot be any other Christian answer to the question of this torment. To speak here of a God who could not suffer would make God a demon. To speak here of an absolute God would make God an annihilating nothingness. To speak here of an indifferent God would condemn us all to indifference.[56]

Moltmann introduced us to a God that is not cold and aloof—like a judge or distant government official. He is more like the God that Shillito described in his *Jesus of the Scars:* 'The other gods were strong, but Thou wast weak; They rode, but Thou didst stumble to

---

[54] Cecil. M. Robeck, 'National Association of Evangelicals', in *The New International Dictionary of Pentecostal and Charismatic Movements,* p. 925.

[55] Wiesel survived Auschwitz, Buna, Buchenwald, and Gleiwitz. In 1968 he was awarded the Nobel Peace Prize.

[56] Jürgen Moltmann, *The Crucified God: The Cross of Christ as the Foundation and Criticism of Christian Theology* (trans. R.A. Wilson and John Bowden; London: SCM Press, 1974).

a throne; but to our wounds only God's wounds can speak, and not a god has wounds, but Thou alone.'[57]

God was not looking for vengeance when He sent His Son to the cross. According to Moltmann, when God's Son cries out from the cross for help, the Father does not turn away from Him as if to say, 'I know it hurts now, but your pain will soon be over'. But instead, God (Father, Son, and Spirit) put his own existence on the line to achieve a new reality for humankind. We are well acquainted with Jesus' side of the suffering on the cross, but God the Father and Spirit were suffering too. The relationship between Father and Son was stretched to breaking point. As the bond of love, the Spirit was at pains to keep the Godhead from separating.

The death and resurrection that has marked Christian Theology 'is a trinitarian event in which the three Persons experience the mutuality and reciprocity characteristic of the triune God'.[58] When Jesus was here on earth there wasn't a vacancy in God's being—the Trinity was still three in one. The Trinity was still a perichoresis. So when the man Jesus died on the cross, the perichoretic union was turned into a dance of great distress—a funeral waltz. Elie Wiesel's picture of God liberates me.

This was the darkest point in human history; this was the most dangerous 'moment' in divine existence. What happened on the cross expressed the most profound ontological threat to the Trinity. Jesus' death may not have been the death of God[59] as the 'God is dead theologians' contended in the 1960s, but it was the death in God.[60] There can be no more profound description of despair— God enters the depth of the human condition of separation.

But there is good news. God overcomes despair as the Bond of love raises Jesus from the grave. The resurrection is therefore as important as the cross in our understanding of what God did at Easter. This is the moment when God in himself overcomes despair. This is when Father, Son, and Spirit overcome the 'dark night of the soul' and hope becomes available to all of humankind. It is

---

[57] Edward Shillito, 'Jesus of the Scars', *Areopagus Proclamation* 10.7 (April 2000).

[58] Pinnock, *Flame of Love*, pp. 92-93.

[59] Thomas J.J. Altizer and W. Hamilton, *Radical Theology and the Death of God* (Indianapolis: Bobbs-Merrill, 1966), p. 135.

[60] Moltmann, *Crucified God*, p. 243.

as if, at this moment, God makes a statement about the significance of humanity. In Jesus, the statement is clear—humanity can overcome despair and doubt and be a vehicle for hope. Human life does not have to be marked by separation; union is possible.

This *perichoretic* understanding of God suggests that God might be interested in more than penal justice; it suggests that there is more to God than a mere thirst for retribution. Could it be that God is more interested in overcoming alienation and enslavement than he is in being judicially satisfied? The events of Easter as earthly expressions of the divine drama—when 'death in God' was crushed, could in fact be pointing to God's intention to lift humanity out of its morbid existence.

Fatedness is James Fowler's choice term for morbidity. Fatedness suggests that sin has placed human life on a predetermined path that takes us away from the freedom that God intended for us. 'In fatedness, destinies and futures become congealed in destructive forms that are in enmity against God's future', says Fowler.[61] In a way, fatedness becomes a colonising power that drains creation of all its spiritual vitality and leaves humans with death as the inevitable conclusion of life. In Jesus, however, God enters our stagnant pools of 'subverted destiny and freedom'[62] and in the Christ act God makes Himself known as the liberator and redeemer. Through the Spirit a redemptive community is awakened. This is how Michael Welker explains the constitutive role of the Spirit.

> The direct result of the descent of God's Spirit is the gathering, the joining together of people who find themselves in distress. The support of their fellow persons is acquired; a new community, a new commitment is produced after the descent of the Spirit.[63]

The Church as the redeeming community joins God in his mission to break open the stagnant pools of 'subverted destiny and freedom'. Our vocation is to be activists of God's coming reign. David Bosch's vision of this is that Christians 'erect in the here and now,

---

[61] James W. Fowler, *Faith Development and Pastoral Care* (Philadelphia: Fortress Press, 1987), p. 43.

[62] See Fowler, *Faith Development,* p. 44.

[63] Michael Welker, *God the Spirit* (Minneapolis: Fortress, 1993), p. 57.

in the teeth of those structures, signs of God's new world'.[64] That is what Jesus did. When he returned from his ordeal in the desert, he declared his intention to agitate against the congealed pools of human existence. In his first public appearance, he read the words from the prophet Isaiah: 'God's Spirit is on me; He's chosen me to preach the message of good news to the poor, sent me to announce pardon to prisoners and recovery of sight to the blind, to set the burdened and battered free, to announce, "This is God's year to act."'[65]

This is our vocation as we respond to the call of God that takes us *beyond the curse*. Christians are commissioned to join God in his mission to decommission the colonising powers of sin and death. God provides 'Pentecostal power for a Pentecostal task'.[66] Pentecostals are well positioned to explain how the gifts of the Spirit function as a 'realization of God's presence to empower believers for service'.[67] Even 'speaking in tongues' has a special place in the redeemed communities faithful response to God's call. For Frank Macchia believes that '*Glossolalia* is not only a yearning for the liberation and redemption to come, it is an "evidence" that such has already begun and is now active'.[68]

It might be true that women were treated badly *under the curse*, but there was a shift after Easter, when women became the first witnesses to Jesus' resurrection. This was a big deal in a world where women could not be witnesses in a law court. Paul advocated for women to be educated in theology. There is even evidence that a woman instructed a man.[69] How outrageous! These shifts point to the trajectory of the storyline that curves towards freedom in Christ.[70]

---

[64] David Bosch, *Transforming Mission: Paradigm Shifts in the Theology of Mission* (Maryknoll, NY: Orbis Books, 1991), p. 176.

[65] The Message, Lk. 4.18-19.

[66] Wynand J. de Kock, 'Pentecostal Power for a Pentecostal Task: Empowerment through Engagement in South African Context', *Journal of Pentecostal Theology* 16 (2000), pp. 102-16.

[67] Frank Macchia, 'Tongues as a Sign: Towards a Sacramental Understanding of Pentecostal Experience', *Pneuma* 15.1 (Spring, 1993), p. 63.

[68] Frank Macchia, 'Sighs too Deep for Words: Toward a Theology of Glossolalia', *Journal of Pentecostal Theology* 1 (1992), p. 70.

[69] Acts 18.24-26.

[70] See Gal. 4.8-11.

The trajectory is clear: It points towards Paul's vision: 'In Christ's family there can be no division into Jew and non-Jew, slave and free, male and female. Among us you are all equal.'[71] As for our family, we would be swept along on this redemptive trajectory as we responded to the call of God to work against any form of one-upmanship in the Church and broader society.

Paulo Freire, an educator among the poor in Brazil, gives us the language to describe what happened to these early believers.[72] The poor can often not think for themselves as their thoughts have been colonised by the dominant ideas of those in power. But the poor are 'conscientised' when they develop the critical awareness that gives them the vocabulary to express their own thoughts and values; and even the courage to take action against the oppressive elements of their world. This meant that they could no longer feel the same about non-Jews or continue to stereotype women. It also meant that economic adjustments were inevitable. While their resources were insufficient, they soon discovered that when one partners with God on a mission that cannot be accomplished through human strength, it opens the door for the mighty wind of God to rush in.

These very ordinary Galileans, some of whom might even have belonged to the most despised in Palestine, experienced a conscientisation that transformed the way they viewed God, nation, and self. Moltmann explains theologically what happens when believers experience the Spirit: 'In the Holy Spirit, the eternal God participates in our transitory life, and we participate in the eternal life of God. This reciprocal community is an immense, out-flowing source of energy.'[73] They became 'holy things' through whom God's *presence* would be made known. Instead of having bread and wine with Jesus, they became the bread and wine. His body is broken for their sake and his blood is spilt to give them a new future. Their lives had been given new significance, since they had been engaged in God's redemptive mission on earth. Kärkkäinen says it much better than what I can:

---

[71] The Message, Gal. 3.28.

[72] See Cheryl Bridges Johns, 'Affective-Conscientization: Pentecostal Re-Interpretation of Paulo Freire', EdD dissertation (Southern Baptist Theological Seminary, 1987), p. 154.

[73] Jürgen Moltmann, *The Spirit of Life: A Universal Affirmation* (trans. Margaret Kohl; London: SCM, 1999), p. 196.

The Spirit makes the church a missionary movement that not only founds communities but also cultivates them. In their theology, Pentecostals appeal to the biblical idea of the transfer of the charismatic Spirit from Jesus to the disciples. The transference of the Spirit at Pentecost means the transference of Jesus' own mission to the church. The church, by virtue of its reception of the Pentecostal gift, is a prophetic community of empowerment for missionary service, healing and reconciliation. The Holy Spirit is looked upon as the One who empowers people with the charisms for witness and social service. Healing and reconciliation happen in the community, even when people are separated from each other and suffer alone.[74]

Conclusion

In 1989, the then Minister of Law and Order and life-long member of the Dutch Reformed Church Adriaan Vlok, ordered the assassination of Frank Chikane. The attempts on Chikane's life failed.

The political transformation of 1994 ended not only his political career, but a way of life. In 1995 his wife committed suicide, provoking a period of soul-searching that led him eventually to appear before the Truth and Reconciliation Commission (TRC) in 1997, one of only a few of the top leaders in the old regime to do so.[75]

In 2006, Vlok went to Chikane's home and washed his feet. Believing that he had sinned against the Lord and Chikane, he asked for forgiveness. Chikane accepted his forgiveness with these words:

I see it as a pointer to where we are now and where we may be headed, in our journey to mature reconciliation after past wrongs. It could just become a harbinger of inspiring acts that help transform our nation's psyche further and free us from the pain and horror of the past.[76]

---

[74] Kärkäinen, 'Spirit, Reconciliation and Healing', p. 46.

[75] Quoted in Katie Day, 'The Curious Conversion of Adriaan Vlok', *Journal of Religion, Conflict and Peace.* http://www.plowsharesproject.org/journal/php/article. php?issu_list_id= 12&article_list_id=38/ (accessed 23 March, 2010).

[76] Day, 'The Curious Conversion of Adriaan Vlok'.

Although Vlok, as part of the Church, was redeemed in some ways, he was also in need of redemption in others. Chikane, as part of the Church, became a redeeming influence in his life.

I have sought in this study to argue that the Church in many ways is experiencing different levels of redemptive reality. Through the Spirit's presence it is redeemed. Yet, it also finds itself in need of ongoing redemption, and is in fact trapped in certain facets of its life and practice. By overcoming this it becomes a redeeming presence within society and the world. It is at once redeemed, un-redeemed and a redeeming force.

3

THE REDEEMING COMMUNITY:
THE GOD OF LIFE AND THE COMMUNITY OF LIFE

DARÍO ANDRES LÓPEZ RODRÍGUEZ[*]

> … anyone who really says 'yes' to life says 'no' to war. Anyone
> who really loves life says 'no' to poverty. So the people who truly
> affirm and love life take up the struggle against violence and in-
> justice. They refuse to get used to it. They do not conform. They
> resist.[1]

1. Introduction

These challenging words of Jürgen Moltmann, regarding the Christian witness in the contemporary world, place several themes related
to the holistic mission of the Church on the discussion table. The
Church, as redeeming community, made up of all those who have
experienced the saving grace of Christ, and as a visible sign of the
presence of the reign of God in history, is called to be a community
of life which loves and defends the life of all human beings.

Precisely, to confess that Jesus saves, as Pentecostals have in-
sisted, and continue to insist in light of the fivefold Gospel which
they proclaim, more than affirming that the salvation which Christ
offers to all people is a 'salvation of disembodied souls', is the af-

---

[*] Darío Andres López Rodríguez (PhD, Oxford Centre for Mission Study) is
Pastor and Teacher in Lima, Peru. This chapter was translated by Richard Wal-
drop (DMiss, Fuller Theological Seminary), Missionary Teacher and Educator in
the Church of God, Cleveland, TN, USA.
[1] Jürgen Moltmann, *The Spirit of Life: A Universal Affirmation* (Minneapolis,
MN: Fortress Press, 1992), p. xii.

firmation that Jesus saves the whole human being within the historical reality in which they are found. Coming together in this historical reality are diverse social, political, economic, cultural, and religious factors which affect all human beings, whether they be believers or non-believers.

What does this signify? It means that the salvation that Christ brings about in a human being completely liberates and converts him or her into a missionary placed in the world to proclaim the reign of the God of life. Consequently, the Church as redeeming community whose members know and enjoy the fullness of life which Christ offers and imparts, is called to affirm and defend life as a gift from God. This is the mission of salvation which has been entrusted to her. This is a holistic, integral salvation which liberates human beings from all oppressions.

In order to explain in greater detail my understanding of the Church as redeeming community, whose mission horizon is the salvation of the complete human being within a concrete historical reality, it will be helpful to examine the panorama of the New Testament. In this review, so that we not be distracted by issues unrelated to our particular interest, we will concentrate on the themes which, according to our judgement, are keys in capturing the theological texture of the Church as redeeming community. Afterwards, we will dicuss the lessons that are derived from this review, focusing our reflection on certain key aspects of Pentecostal ecclesiology.

Our biblical review takes the Pentecostal affirmation, 'Jesus Saves', as a hermeneutical key. The concrete questions which we will attempt to answer will be the following: From what does Jesus save? For what purpose does Jesus save? Into what community must those who are saved be integrated? What message must be proclaimed by the community which is made up of those saved by Christ? What is her mision in the world? What dimensions of her holistic mission must be emphasized in these times in which thousands of human beings, particularly those in the Global South, suffer the damaging consequences of institutionalized injustice or structural violence?

2. The Perspective of the Gospels

According to the testimony of the Gospels, Jesus of Nazareth went about shaping a new life-carrying and life-defending community during his missionary journeys through the cities and villages of Palestine. This was a community which, by its social composition and lifestyle, emerged as an alternative society from the surrounding society. It was a community in which all those who were marginalized by the society of the first century could find a place. According to John Howard Yoder:

> ... in a society characterized by very stable, religiously under-girded family ties, Jesus is here calling into being a community of *voluntary* commitment, willing for the sake of its calling to take upon itself the hostility of a given society.[2]

In this community of voluntary committment, the poor and excluded of society were seen, treated, and valued as full and worthy human beings, and as subjects and agents of the reign of God.

Who were the poor and excluded ones with whom Jesus of Nazareth intentionally related while he went about the cities and villages preaching the good news of the reign of God? They were concrete human beings with concrete needs, such as tax collectors (Mt. 9.9-13; Lk. 19.1-10), lepers (Mt. 8.1-4; Lk. 17.11-19), women (Mt. 8.14-17; 9.18-26; Mk 12.41-44; Lk. 7.11-17), the infirm (Mt. 9.1-8; 12.9-14; 14.34-36), children (Mt. 19.13-15), and Samaritans (Lk. 17.15-19; Jn 4.1-12).

This was a missionary practice of preferential option for the proscribed of the earth which finally caused serious confrontations between Jesus and the leaders of the established religion (Mt. 9.3; 12.14; Mk 2.6-7; 2.16; 3.3; Lk. 5.30; 13.14). However, this radical missionary practice of Jesus was in tune with his messianic platform which was expounded in the synagogue of Nazareth (Lk. 4.16-30), and had a close relationship with the good news of the reign of God which he proclaimed (Mt. 9.35; Mk 1.38-39; Lk. 4.42-44; 8.1).

The reign of God was already among us. With his person and his ministry, Jesus himself was making it happen (Mk 1.14-15), and the destiny of the poor and oppressed was beginning to be re-

---

[2] John Howard Yoder, *The Politics of Jesus: Vicit Agnus Noster* (Grand Rapids, Michigan: William B. Eerdmans Publishing Company, 1972), p. 37.

versed, as had been announced by the maiden Mary in her messianic canticle (Lk. 1.52-53). A new reality had been introduced into history. It was a new reality announced by the angel sent to excluded human beings, such as the shepherds of the mountains of Judea, called *news of great joy for all the people* (Lk. 2.10). It was a new reality identified by the elderly Simeon and Anna as the advent of the time of longed-for liberation and evoked by the pious people of Israel (Lk. 2.25-32; 38).

Jesus' answer to the messengers of John the Baptist, with concrete actions of liberation for those who were oppressed and with words that gave witness of his messianic role, illustrate that, in effect, the regin of God had broken into history:

> When the men came to Jesus, they said, 'John the Baptist sent us to you to ask, "are you the one who was to come, or should we expect someone else?" ' At that very time Jesus cured many who had diseases, sicknesses and evil spirits, and gave sight to many who were blind. So he replied to the messengers, 'Go back and report to John what you have seen and heard: The blind receive sight, the lame walk, those who have leprosy are cured, the deaf hear, the dead are raised, and the good news is preached to the poor' (Lk. 7.20-22).

In his answer to John the Baptist, in addition to reiterating what he had manifested in his messianic program revealed in the synagogue of Nazareth, Jesus expressed that the reign of God was related to liberation from all oppressions that affected concrete human beings. For Jesus, the presence of the reign implied, then, a direct confrontation with the forces of evil which disfigured and distorted the purpose of God, namely that all human beings live full and dignified lives as God's creation.

In light of this quick journey through the gospels, it can then be affirmed that the community of the kingdom was well aware of the liberating mission of Jesus of Nazareth, of the impartiality and gratuitous nature of the love of God, of the leveling effect that the proclamation of the good news of salvation brought, and of the open confrontation which the public announcement of the gospel provoked *vis-à-vis* the anti-kingdom.

This community of the kingdom, or redeemed community, as the resurrected Christ commissioned his disciples, was entered into through water baptism as a public sign of repentance and of having received forgiveness of sins (Mt. 28.19; Mk 16.16; Acts 2.38). Baptism in water was then the sacramental sign of belonging to the Church as redeemed community. It was understood thusly by the primitive church (Acts 2.38; 8.12, 36-38; 9.18; 16.15, 33) and was also the practice of the Pauline communities such as the one in Corinth (1 Cor. 1.13-17).

3. The Perspective of the Acts of the Apostles

Luke, in his record of the missionary practice of the primitive church, registers that he followed the example of Jesus with regard to his concern for the poor and excluded. There was a clear personal and collective concern for the poor and fragile, such as the widows (Acts 2.44-45; 4.34-37; 6.1; 9.36, 39; 11.28-30; 20.35). And in their missionary advance, as they broke with the religious and cultural prejudices characteristic of Jewish society of the first century, such as those which the apostle Peter had (Acts 10.28), the hellenistic Jews who converted to the Christian faith proclaimed the gospel among the gentiles (Acts 8.8; 11.19-20).

This fact is valuable because, according to the Jewish religious and cultural patterns of the time, the gentiles were part of the world of those who were excluded. But these gentiles who came from the diverse social strata of the Graeco-Roman world of the first century made up the communities of disciples which became established in different points of the Roman empire (Acts 13.42-43, 48; 16.14, 27-34; 17.4, 34; 18.8; 1 Cor. 1.26-28).

In addition, continuing the missionary route opened by Jesus of Nazareth, the reign of God was also the message which the primitve church proclaimed when she began to spread across the length and breath of the Roman empire (Acts 14.22; 28.23). It was also the doctrine that was transmitted to the communities of disciples that were being formed in different places (Rom. 14.17; 1 Cor. 4.20; 6.9; 15.24; Gal. 5.21; Eph. 5.5; 2 Tim. 1.5; Heb. 12.28; Jas 2.5).

This announcement of the reign of God, whose center was the presentation of Jesus of Nazareth, a Jew crucified by the imperial power, as *Kyrios* and *Christos* (Acts 2.36; 11.17; 15.26), had five precise ingredients: Christ incarnated, crucified, resurrected, exalted, and coming King (Acts 3.13-16; 4.10-12, 33; 7.55-56; 10.36-43; 13.27-38).

4. The Perspective of the Pauline Correspondence

The Pauline correspondence also registers that the churches with which Paul had written communication had a genuine concern for the poor and defenseless (Rom. 15.25-28; 1 Cor. 16.1-4; 2 Cor. 8.1-16; Gal. 2.10; Eph. 4.28; Phil. 4.10-20; 1 Tim. 5.10; Tit. 3.14). It is additionally clear that Paul transmitted to the new disciples the gospel which he himself had received (1 Cor. 15.1-4). This was the gospel related to the announcement of the reign of God as Paul himself recognized in his farewell discourse given to the elders of the church of Ephesus (Acts 20.25), and in several of his letters to the churches (1 Cor. 6.9; Gal. 5.21; 2 Thess. 1.5).

In the same way, the Pauline letters underscore that the presentation of Jesus as *Kyrios* and as *Christos* was central in the *kerygma* that was transmitted to the churches located outside of the Jewish cultural world (Rom. 5.11; 7.25; 1 Cor. 1.10; 5.4; 2 Cor. 1.2; 8.9; Gal. 1.3; 6.14; Eph. 3.11; 5.20; Phil. 2.11; 3.20; Col. 3.24; 1 Thess. 3.11; 5.23; 2 Thess. 1.1-2, 12). From the Pauline correspondence there also emerges other very valuable themes which trace an aproximate picture of the Church as redeemed community. According to Samuel Escobar:

> ... from the era of the New Testament onward, the church appears as a new community that arises in contrast to the predominant society.... The epistles themselves and the book of Acts offer additional material which reflect the alternative practices of this community, in terms of the use of money, power, sex, attitude toward the authorities, and diverse forms of social solidarity.[3]

In effect this is so, since in the Pauline corpus it is highly clear that the Church is a new humanity in Christ Jesus (Ephesians 2) and that the practice of good works (1 Tim. 6.18; Tit. 3.8, 14) constitutes a distinctive note of following Jesus of Nazareth: *For we are God's*

---

[3] Samuel Escobar, *Tiempo de Misión: América Latina y la misión cristiana hoy* (Santafé de Bogotá-Ciudad de Guatemala: Ediciones Clara Semilla, 1999), p. 123.

workmanship, created in Christ Jesus to do good works, which God prepared in advance for us to do (Eph. 2.10).

What has been pointed out has a clear correlation in opposition to what Paul previously calls *fruitless deeds of darkness* (Eph. 5.11), because the disciples, as children of light, must denounce the works of darkness (Eph. 5.8, 11). Said in a different way, to be coherent with biblical faith, the private and public conduct of believers who live in diverse historical contexts, must be radically distinct from the practices of death imposed by the surrounding society. It must be so because:

> Love of God inevitably leads us to want what God loves, consequently, the practice of justice is not something added from outside to our friendship with God, but is an intrinsic element in our relation with God.... No one can love God and practice injustice, because the exploitation and despoilment of the poor, like the resultant rejection of God, is a choice of death.[4]

In light of the Pauline correspondence, then, that the churches as communities of redemption, as liberated and liberating communities, and as the firstfruit of a new humanity, must be a counterculture which affirms and defends life and human dignity as a gift from God. In this sense, the practice of good works oriented toward the common good and the active resistence of the practices of death of the autocratic powers (political, military, and religious), are two concrete forms of loving and defending life, especially a life of dignity for the poor and excluded of society.

5. The Perspective of Other Letters

The concern for the poor and excluded of the world, as well as the prophetic critique of those who oppress them, is also noted in the call that is given in the Epistle of James (2.1-26; 5.1-6). In addition, the references to the reign of God which appear in these letters, although with lesser frequency than in the Pauline correspondence, indicate that it was not a strange or marginal theme in the churches (Jas 2.5; 1 Pet. 1.11; Heb. 11.28). In the same way, as in the case of

---

[4] Gustavo Gutiérrez, *The God of Life* (Maryknoll, New York: Orbis Books, 1991), p. 16

the Pauline communities, the presentation of Jesus of Nazareth as *Kyrios* and *Christos*, formed part of the *kerygma* which the churches received and to whom these letters were directed (Jas 1.1; 1 Pet. 1.3; 2 Pet. 1.8, 14, 16; 2.20; 3.18; Jude 4, 21).

All of these facts, taken together, express that the New Testament churches had a common theological underpinning from which they derived their missionary practice as well as the private and public ethic of the believers. Precisely connected with the believers' private and public ethic there emerged a critical issue (persecution because of their faith) which directly affected the churches to which Peter directed his letters. This explains why the message of 1 Peter is centered in a call to persevere, practicing that which is good within a socieity which is contrary to the lifestyle of the followers of the the God of life.

What was happening to the believers and the churches in the historical moment in which Peter wrote his letter? According to Donald Señor:

> Christians were ridiculed because of the change of lifestyle that had come with their conversion…. Some Christians who lived in situations which were much more vunerable, such as slaves and wives of non-Christians, had to face more cruel sufferings since they had to walk a tightrope between their social responsibilities and and faithfulness to the gospel. In addition, Christians were small groups dispersed in a mass environment which was many times hostile….[5]

Senior's reconstruction of the historical framework in which the Petrine communities were located can explain, on the one hand, why the author of the letter insists on underlining the fact that following Jesus is a road of obedience marked by suffering. And, on the other hand, it can explain why the affirmation of Christian hope becomes a prophetic critique of the kingdoms of this world and why believers should be warned of their temporal, transitory, and finite nature.

---

[5] Donald Señor, 'Los Fundamentos de la Misión en el Nuevo Testamento', in *Biblia y Misión: Fundamentos Bíblicos de la Misión* (Estella: Verbo Divino, 1985), pp. 188-422 (403).

6. The Perspective of the Apocalypse

Juan Stam, when he deals with the historical circumstances in which this book was written, states:

> The focus of the Apocalypse corresponds ... to the situation of congregations who were being threatened. In the same way that the Lamb gave his life, the faithful must follow the Lamb unto death.... Here, the theology of the death of the Lamb is, at the same time, an ethic of radical discipleship which calls the believer to be faithful until the last consequences.... John of Patmos also shows us that he is resolutely opposed to all efforts to reduce the radical demands of the gospel ... or to soften his prophetic denounciations toward the Empire.... This makes these faithful witnesses dangerous to the system: to proclaim the victory of the Lamb is in this context an announcement of the end of the Empire....[6]

Donald Señor notes that the cosmic Christology of St. John

> ... and his concern for the redemption of the world brings him to his theology of witness: a theology which does not admit any compromise.... Christians are asked to suffer persecution and even martyrdom, before they would compromise their faithfulness to Christ and his work of redemption.... The consequences of such a position could lead to a retreat from the social and political spheres of Graeco-Roman society. This is a posture which is completely different from that of 1 Peter's letter.... The retreat from society by Christians is a prophetic act of witness before society and in favor of society. Christians should proclaim the good news of universal salvation before the world, and her pulpit become the heroic negative response to the call to compromise with a system which they see is alligned with the forces of sin and death.[7]

---

[6] Juan Stam, 'La misión en el Apocalipsis', in C. René Padilla (ed.), *Bases bíblicas de la misión: Perspectivas latinoamericanas* (Buenos Aires: Nueva Creación and Grand Rapids: Eerdmans, 1998), pp. 351-80 (356, 360-61).

[7] Senior, 'Los Fundamentos de la Misión en el Nuevo Testamento', pp. 414-15.

So, what is the message that is latent in the Apocalypse and which builds toward a better understanding of the Church as redeeming community? In the Apocalypse a call is given to the Church to be a community of active resistence against the anti-Kingdom forces intertwined with the Roman Empire, clearly distancing themselves from the practices of death which are promoted and defended by the empire and its political, military, and religious agents.

If the churches follow upon this missionary path, they should not be surprised that those who have the power of the religious and political kingdoms of this world in their hands would feel uncomfortable with their presence and message or that they would try to silence, persecute, and exterminate her; even more so, when it is discovered that the churches see themselves as communties of active resistance toward the politics of death imposed by the temporal lords and eventually implemented by their political enforcers.

7. Final Words

From this examination of the documents of the New Testament, although panoramic and inexhaustive, and from the idea of the Church as redeeming communty called to love and defend life, come five concrete characteristics that give shape to her mission in the world. These characteristics have to do with her kerygmatic, inclusive, leveling, destabilizing, and prophetic nature.

What implications for her mission as redeeming community does each one of these characteristics have? More particularly, what implications for the social and political dimensions of her mission as redeeming community come out of her kerygmatic, inclusive, leveling, destabilizing, and prophetic nature? We will breifly look at each one of them:

Her Kerygmatic Nature. The church as redeeming community has a public truth that must be proclaimed among the diverse human audiences: the reign of God. The nucleus of this truth is the presentation of Jesus of Nazareth, incarnated, crucified, resurrected, exalted, and coming King as Lord and Messiah. This is a public truth that cannot be accommodated to the lower interests of the politicians and religious leaders, nor can it be lowered as if it were merchandise subject to the supply and demand of the various contemporary religious markets.

Her Inclusive Nature. This is a reality which is visibly expressed in her social composition, particularly so, because in the church as redeeming community, persons of diverse social, political, cultural, and religious realities are found. This is a characteristic which goes against the current of the social, cultural, and religious patterns of exclusion which are commonly accepted in asymmetric societies such as those of Latin America.

Her Leveling Nature. This is one clear sign of the social reversal that the reign of God brings. In the church as redeeming community, all differences of race, sex, age, or economic position imposed by the surrounding society as 'normal' must disappear. These are differences which condemn hundreds of defenseless human beings to social ostracism.

Her Destabilizing Nature. The announcement of the reign of God, with words and concrete gestures of liberation of the poor and oppressed, constitutes a political critique of the kingdoms of this world and is an announcement that their end has come. The sole presense of the church as redeeming community, with her radically distinct values and lifestyle from those of the surrounding society, destabilizes and dismantles the messianic pretensions of those who presume to have the final word in history.

Her Prophetic Nature. The church as redeeming community does not fit into the surrounding society and becomes highly uncomfortable for those who are accustomed to exercising political and religious power in a despotic way. This converts her into a kind of alternative society which, due to her countercultural character, emerges as a community of active resistance toward the predominate political and religious system.

From this public truth which the redeeming community must proclaim among all human audiences, which is the good news of the reign of God whose center is the presentation of Jesus of Nazareth as Lord and Christ, various concrete tasks for her saving mission in the temporal frameworks in which she is found can be inferred. These tasks are connected to the christological affirmations present in the New Testament: Christ incarnated, crucified, resurrected, exalted, and coming King.

What do these christological affirmations indicate, particularly in regards to the social and political dimensions of the Church as redeeming community? They indicate the following:

• The incarnation of Christ shows that human beings and that which is human have an immense value, so that if that were not so, God himself would not have pitched his tent among us, inserting himself into a concrete temporal framework (Jn 1.14).

• If Christ died for all human beings, then the life of each human being has immense value since it cost the life of the Messiah himself. And for this reason, no one can trample upon it, violate it or mistreat it and go unpunished.

• If Christ was resurrected, triumphing over death, then life and not death, has the last word in history. Consequently, disciples are called to be ambassadors of life, and churches are called to be defenders of the dignity of all human beings as God's creations.

• The exaltation of Christ to the right hand of the Father (Mk 16.19; Acts 7.56; Rom. 8.34) indicates that he sovereignly governs above all things, and this of course includes the kingdoms of this world which are, from a biblical perspective, transitory, temporal, and finite.

• The promise of the return of Christ constitutes in itself a political critique of all human empires, since if Christ is coming again then the power and authority of all human lords are fragile, realtive, and perishable. Consequently, the church as redeemed community must not bow before any human power nor must give religious legitimation to any corrupt and repressive government.

From all this it is deduced that the proclamation of Jesus of Nazareth, incarnated, crucified, resurrected, exalted, and coming King, is linked closely to the holistic mission of the Church. This holistic mission must have the unrestricted defense of the dignity of all human beings as God's creations as one of its central axis, especially the dignity of the poor and oppressed, because:

Belief in the resurrection entails defending the life of the weakest members of society. Looking for the Lord among the living leads to commitment to those who see their right to life being constantly violated. To assert the resurrection of the Lord is to assert life in the face of death.... The message of the resurrection of Jesus and of our resurrection in union with him is clear: life, not death, has the final Word in history.[8]

To struggle actively so that the poor and oppressed may live with dignity, as human beings created in the image of God, is not constructed as a task belonging exclusively to the 'theologies of liberation' or a matter which concerns only the social activists related to human rights organizations, or a theme tied to the ideological interests of the political left. It is better understood as a legitimate dimension of Christian witness which desires to be faithful to the God of life and, for that same reason, becomes a concrete way of living in the power of the Spirit.

In light of historic Pentecostal ecclesiology which was articulated, proclaimed, and lived out by the first Pentecostals, themes such as the defense of the dignity of all human beings as God's creations, and the direct struggle against the forces of evil which oppress human beings, should be a natural part of the Church's redeeming mission. In this regard, the Pentecostals of today must not forget that their first churches were kerygmatic, inclusive, leveling, destabilizing, and prophetic. These churches, as reconciled and reconciling communities, were also communities of active resistence against institutionalized practices of injustice such as racial segregation and oppression of the poor. They were also communities which identified themselves with the left wing of the Protestant Reformation and made a clear separation between Church and State.

In the same way, the Pentecostal churches were pacifist communities whose missionary focus was upon the social sectors which society treated as disposable items. Our history sinks deeply into this missionary foundation. This 'subversive memory', which is highly uncomfortable for those Pentecostals who have become religious addicts of the values of consumerist society and religious

---

[8] Gutiérrez, *The God of Life*, pp. 14-15.

legitimators of political systems which oppress thousands of human beings, must be the missionary key which motivates us to love and defend life. This 'subversive memory' cannot be renounced by those who have come face to face with the God of life and with the Spirit of life.

Consequently, the Church as redeeming communty which has answered a resounding 'yes' to life, must be concerned with the present and future of all the poor and oppressed of the world who directly suffer the nefarious consequences of institutionalized injustice. And for this same reason, they cannot and should not remain quiet. It must be so, because any form of silence, be it public or enclosed, individual or collective, will be a sign of treason to the God of life who loves and defends the life of all human beings.

The gospel of the kingdom is good news for the poor and oppressed of the world who directly suffer the nefarious effects of institutionalized injustice and it would be treason before the God of life to remain in silence when thousands of human beings are sacrificed daily in order to placate the contemporary idols of technology, nuclear arms, material propersity, or ideologies. To affirm the kerygmatic, inclusive, leveling, destabilizing, and prophetic nature of the Church as redeeming community obliges us to love life and oppose all forms of violence. Furthermore, confessing Christ as incarnated, crucified, resurrected, exalted, and as coming King must force us to live as members of an alternative society from the surrounding society, which is an alternative society with only one Lord. Before no others must it bow.

Jesus of Nazareth is *Kyrios* and *Christos*! This is the message which must be proclaimed and incarnated by the life and witness of the Church as redeeming community, whatever may be the historical reality in which she might be found. The correlation of this countercultural missionary action becomes a direct 'dis-encounter' with the values and practices of death which characterize the surrounding society. This 'dis-encounter' will convert the members of the redeeming community into those who are uncomfortable and dangerous for the system, and the Church into a counterculture which, by her presence and witness, will announce the end of all human empires and all earthly lords. Salvation in Christ, then, breaks all oppressions and liberates us to liberate others from structural violence which completely disfigures the purpose of God: that they live the full and adundant life which He offers us.

PART THREE

THE PENTECOSTAL CHURCH AS SANCTIFIED COMMUNITY

4

THE IMPROVISATIONAL QUALITY OF ECCLESIAL HOLINESS

DANIEL CASTELO[*]

If there is one feature of the fivefold gospel paradigm that has exceptional promise for considering its ecclesiological implications, surely it would be that Jesus is 'sanctifier', for 'holy' has the status of being one of the traditional marks or notes of the Church since the formulation of the Niceno-Constantinopolitan Creed of 381 CE.[1] However, this mark, along with the other three (that the Church is 'one, catholic, and apostolic') stands in significant tension with the experience and perceived reality one beholds with respect to any ecclesial body.[2] The creeds are 'confessions of faith', and it is certainly true that these marks are faith claims in that they are often 'convictions of things not seen'; if one were to broach the question of the Church's holiness, the pressing concern would be: How can one narrate the Church's holiness in light of so many evidences to the contrary? This challenge has been present at the onset of any ecclesiological exercise that attempts to narrate both coherently and faithfully the nature and task of the Church.

---

[*] Daniel Castelo (PhD, Duke University) is Associate Professor of Theology at Seattle Pacific University in Seattle, WA, USA.

[1] According to Jaroslav Pelikan, 'holy' is the most prominent and earliest of the four traditional marks of the church, given the creedal testimony; see his *The Christian Tradition* (Chicago: University of Chicago Press, 1971), I, p. 156.

[2] For a survey of the challenge and promise associated with the traditional marks, see Howard A. Snyder, 'The Marks of Evangelical Ecclesiology' in John G. Stackhouse, Jr. (ed.), *Evangelical Ecclesiology: Reality or Illusion?* (Grand Rapids: Baker, 2003), pp. 77-103 and Thomas C. Oden, *Life in the Spirit* (San Francisco: HarperCollins, 1992), pp. 297-365.

This difficulty would face the onset of any Pentecostal exploration of the Church's holiness as well, for Pentecostals, like all other
Christians, would find it difficult to reconcile their faith in what
God has called us to be and often what we come to realize we really
are. On the surface one may think that Pentecostals, as a group that
emerged from the womb of the 19th century Holiness Movement,
would have ample biblical and theological support for understanding themselves as a holy community, but this heritage, helpful as it is
in understanding the movement's theological orientation, does little
to inform present-day Pentecostal self-understandings and self-
projected trajectories. As a symptom of the tension involved with
documenting the links between the Holiness and Pentecostal
Movements, one sees that the element in question between those
folks who advocate a 'fourfold' and 'fivefold' gospel is precisely the
notion that Jesus is sanctifier.[3] Throughout Pentecostalism's history,
the quest for power, and not purity, has been 'at the core of Pentecostal yearnings',[4] and this tendency potentially corresponds to
Snyder's belief that throughout Christian history charisma and holiness have been considered oppositional within ecclesial life; he
stipulates, 'The Spirit gives gifts to whom he pleases, not always to
whom official leaders would prefer (1 Cor. 12:4-11). Leaders tend to
focus on holy or sacred doctrine, tradition, or office and to deny or
limit charisma, while newly gifted believers may rely on charisma
and be lax in ethical holiness (1 Cor. 3:1-3; 13:3).'[5] I tend to disagree
with this assessment on a number of scores,[6] but its coherence rests

---

[3] In advancing a preference for the fourfold pattern in his *Theological Roots of
Pentecostalism* (Peabody, MA: Hendrickson, 1987), Donald W. Dayton remarks,
'These four themes are well-nigh universal within the [Pentecostal] movement,
appearing ... in all branches and varieties of Pentecostalism, whereas the theme
of entire sanctification is finally characteristic of only the Holiness branch' (pp.
21-22).

[4] Peter Althouse, 'The Ideology of Power in Early American Pentecostalism',
Journal of Pentecostal Theology 13.1 (2004), pp. 97-115 (p. 98).

[5] Snyder, 'The Marks of Evangelical Ecclesiology', p. 86.

[6] For instance, I disagree with the assumption that holiness is the property of
the ecclesial establishment; perhaps a more common model is the way that institutions are pitted against charisma, and yet this antagonism also falls short, as the
following quote of Albert the Great by Yves Congar shows: 'This article (of the
church's holiness) must therefore be traced back to the work of the Holy Spirit,
that is, to "I believe in the Holy Spirit", not in himself alone, as the previous arti-

on the perception that purity and power stand in tension with one another.

Despite these challenges, I wish to contend that a way of considering the Pentecostal fellowship as a holy community rests on an account of what it does, whom it knows/experiences, and subsequently what it is coming to be. The order is intentional: Pentecostals were and continue to be 'doers' before they are 'thinkers'. When they do self-identify, Pentecostals usually opt for considering themselves as a 'movement' on the go rather than an institution that is self-reflective and maintenance-oriented. Second, Pentecostalism generates this self-understanding because of whom it comes to know within a particular understanding of religious experience. Pentecostals are convinced that through their doxological experience they encounter the holy triune God. Finally, through the interplay of what its constituents do and whom they know/experience, one can say that Pentecostals have the task to be a certain kind of fellowship.[7] Through the interplay of these factors, I hope to avoid the pitfalls associated with the faith-reality dichotomy associated with the four marks of the Church by depicting Pentecostal ecclesial holiness as a collective task that is to be intentionally embodied *coram deo* and *coram hominibus*.

---

cle states, but I believe in him also as far as his work is concerned, which is to make the Church holy. He communicates that holiness in the sacraments, the virtues and the gifts that he distributes in order to bring holiness about, and finally in the miracles and the graces of a charismatic type such as wisdom, knowledge, faith, the discernment of spirits, healings, prophecy and everything that the Spirit gives in order to make the holiness of the Church manifest' (as quoted in Congar, *I Believe in the Holy Spirit* [3 vols.; New York: Crossroad Herder, 2000], II, p. 6).

[7] Perceptive readers will notice that I am employing another form of the typology of 'knowing—being—doing' or, as some Pentecostals would narrate it, '*orthodoxy—orthopathy—orthopraxy*.' The order by which I set these, however, should be acknowledged: Traditionally, 'knowing' or 'orthodoxy' is considered as first in the typological sequence, but that ordering runs the risk of privileging the cognitive over other forms of knowing, including the affective and praxis-oriented dimensions. For a helpful guide that elaborates features of this typology, see the essays in Richard B. Steele (ed.), *'Heart Religion' in the Methodist Tradition and Related Movements* (Lanham, MD: Scarecrow Press, 2001).

I. Pentecostal Fellowship is Holy in What Its Participants Do

Pentecostals have always been 'doers', that is to say, they have made the connection between hearing/believing and embodying the faith quite naturally and intuitively. Historically, it has been argued that Pentecostals were quite pragmatic in their thinking and reasoning,[8] that they were willing to employ a variety of means and methods by which to get their message across. Such strategies included using the latest publishing technologies and transportation mediums available so that relatively shortly after revivals, whether these occurred in the Unicoi Mountains of Eastern Tennessee/Western North Carolina; Topeka, Kansas; or Los Angeles, California; Pentecostals were up and about witnessing of their deep and life-changing experiences of the triune God. The evangelistic and missionary zeal of the early Pentecostals must have been a sight to behold, for it is difficult to imagine how quickly and readily folks moved from a particular re-vivalist setting to the outer reaches of the world in what seemed to be one fell swoop.

Largely stemming from their eschatological self-understanding, the Pentecostal tendency to self-identify as a 'movement' rather than a 'church' and to think often of their activity as over and against ecclesial bodies makes for a challenging task when reflecting ecclesiologically about Pentecostalism. The prominence of 'move-ment' language led to a certain 'improvisational' quality about Pen-tecostal identity and practice. With their self-understood place within unfolding history, early Pentecostals demonstrated a certain freedom in starting 'anew' in relation to ecclesial minutia:[9] the lan-guage of 'ordinances' has been more predominant than 'sacra-ments', and the understanding of sacramentality (although not ex-

---

[8] Their pragmatism was often veiled, if Grant Wacker's reading is to be fol-lowed; see *Heaven Below: Early Pentecostals and American Culture* (Cambridge, MA: Harvard University Press, 2001), pp. 13-14.

[9] My quotes here attempt to show that the proclivity by Pentecostals to think of themselves as occupying a vital role in the denouement of history is inherently a modern sensibility. As R.G. Robins has stated with regard to the holiness pre-cursors of the Pentecostal movement, 'Those who flocked to holiness churches, tents, and camp meetings were drawn to the movement not because it resisted some overarching process of "modernization" but because it spoke to their mod-ern needs and aspirations in a language with which they were familiar' (*A.J. Tom-linson: Plainfolk Modernist* [Oxford: Oxford University Press, 2004], p. 24.

plicitly stated as such) has been understood to include both the worshippers' bodies and other quasi-sacramental rites.[10] Additionally, those who could preach and instruct were those who had the Spirit baptism and so the anointing, and these folks were welcomed often without regard to race, sex, and age. Furthermore, baptismal services were sometimes impromptu wherever a body of water was available (rivers, lakes, pools, and even bathtubs served the purpose). In all of this activity, there was a sense of 'making it up' as one went, especially with regard to ecclesial practices.

Inevitably, when traditional formulations, practices, and understandings are suspended or reconfigured, great potential exists for both peril and promise. That which has been 'passed' down often is purposefully so, having been shaped and tried through different agonistic and tension-laden contexts; as many are prone to say, orthodoxy emerges within the precarious and contested context of formulating and discerning what is faithful from what is heretical. Lamentably, these tried and contested accomplishments were often neglected by Pentecostals when they understood themselves as over and against ecclesial institutions; such posturing not only saw them fail to offer the peace of Christ to fellow sisters and brothers but in turn miss the continuity of the Spirit's work in the world; an unfair disparagement of others and an aggrandized view of themselves were sometimes the results.[11] In this regard, Pentecostals failed to be a holy fellowship, and their actions and motives are worth scrutinizing in a probing, transparent, and contrite way.

And yet, tradition can also be reifying and stifling, and the advantage Pentecostals had in beginning 'anew' ecclesiologically was the vision and implementation of what seemed to them to be marks of God's kingdom. Rather than being led by 'man-made creeds' and customs, early Pentecostals enacted certain practices that were grounded in God's word and prompted by God's Spirit in such a

---

[10] Cf. Amos Yong, 'Ordinances and Sacraments', in Stanley Burgess (ed.), *Encyclopedia of Pentecostal and Charismatic Christianity* (New York: Routledge, 2006), pp. 345-48.

[11] As a case in point, Peter Hocken notes that early in the Movement's history certain groups believed that only those who had experienced Spirit-baptism were members of the church; see 'Church, Theology of the', in Stanley M. Burgess (ed.), *New International Dictionary of Pentecostal and Charismatic Movements* (Grand Rapids: Zondervan, rev. and updated edn, 2002), pp. 544-51 (p. 544) (hereafter *NIDPCM*).

way that they imagined a 'new order' for reality. Within this new order, it was understood that the lame could walk, the blind could see, and daughters could prophesy. In a hermeneutical move that had vast theological ramifications, Pentecostals believed that the God who was at work in revealing Godself on Mount Sinai and on Calvary was the same God who was working in the context of Pentecostal worship. In this regard, Pentecostals demonstrated themselves to be a holy fellowship when they embodied and put in motion the implications of encountering this holy God.

The Pentecostal penchant for 'doing' suggests that holiness was not simply an attribute of God that solely marked the ineffable and unique Creator of all that is. Quite the contrary, Pentecostals (even those of a more Reformed persuasion)[12] were inclined, given their robust approach to Scripture and the prominence of Jesus' life and ministry for their vision of reality, to think in terms of embodying and performing holiness. Performing holiness, of course, stands in tension with many Christian traditions and approaches that would think of holiness as the true essence of God, that feature of God's existence that makes God who God is; when pushed, this logic would find problematic or at least worrisome the claim that we participate or demonstrate holiness since agency in such a schema would shift the focus from the theological to the anthropological realm.[13] Scripture, however, supports a multi-tiered approach to ho-

---

[12] Paul Alexander makes this case with regard to shifting views of the Assemblies of God in relation to military service and pacifism more generally; as he notes, 'Pentecostals said, "Military service is incompatible with the gospel of Jesus Christ." Since Christians were and are followers of the Christ, the teachings and example of Jesus the Christ were central to their understanding of their place in the world' (*Peace to War: Shifting Allegiances in the Assemblies of God* [Telford, PA: Cascadia, 2009], p. 46). Alexander further states, 'The early Pentecostals tried to take the Bible so seriously and follow Jesus so well that they believed and accepted teachings even when they went against the grain of conventional Christianity' (p. 108).

[13] One sees this cautiousness in John Webster, *Holiness* (Grand Rapids: Eerdmans, 2003), especially Chapter 3. Webster depends significantly on the Epistle to the Ephesians, the notion of election, and the wisdom of considering the church's sanctity as an 'alien sanctity' (p. 56) for his work on holiness. He is explicitly aware and attempting to avoid extremes, but his perspective is easily detectable: 'The Church is holy; but it is holy, not by virtue of some ontological participation in the divine holiness, but by virtue of its calling by God, its reception of the divine benefits, and its obedience of faith. Like its unity, its catholicity and its apostolicity, the Church's holiness is that which it is by virtue of its sheer contingency upon the mercy of God' (p. 57).

liness; on a plain-sense reading, instances occur within the holy canon where holiness is attributed to those who engage in various practices associated with covenant-keeping.[14] Usually stemming from non-Pauline sources, the collective testimony of this witness suggests that holiness is not simply something that characterizes believers on the basis of the effects of God's work in Christ extended to believers but also a moral category that reaches into all of one's life as an implication of being transformed in, through, and by Christ. The tendency by many Pentecostals to think of their faith in terms of a spirituality further underscores the Pentecostal penchant to think of holiness not as something simply to be recognized of God's very self but a possibility to be enacted in the common life of the worshiping community.

Of course, what it means to purify our hearts, souls, or very selves is an open question in part because that which contaminates us by living in the world is so sinister. Because the filth of the world makes us impure in so many ways, embodying holiness must also take shape in multitudinous ways. Reifying the practice of holiness only has the potential for leading to a Pharisaical works-righteousness; there has to be a certain communal liberty and dynamism involved in discerning what does not conform to God's purposes, both in the community's praxis and its collective affectional life. Additionally, whereas purifying oneself implies the 'negative' connotation of 'giving up' certain practices and habits, it also implies the 'positive' corollary of 'picking up' other habits and practices. Both in discerning that which does not conform to God and in the practices of 'putting aside' and 'picking up,' embodied holiness demonstrates an improvisational quality, one that is both coherent and yet free.

---

[14] Three examples from the Catholic Epistles give us a specific view of the matter: James 4.8 (*'Cleanse* [your] hands, sinners, and *purify* [your] hearts, double-minded ones'), 1 Pet. 1.22 ('You *have purified* your souls by obedience to the truth'), and 1 Jn 3.3 ('And everyone who has this hope *purifies oneself* on the basis of [God] just as [God] is pure'). I was directed to these canonical instances through conversations with my colleague Robert W. Wall; he will lay out a formal treatment of 'practicing holiness' from the New Testament witness in the upcoming volume *Holiness as a Liberal Art* (ed. Daniel Castelo; Eugene, OR: Pickwick Publishers, forthcoming); biblical citations in the body of this paper are my translations.

Samuel Wells has done much to introduce and argue for a notion of improvisation as a theological category. According to Wells, 'Improvisation in the theater is a practice through which actors seek to develop trust in themselves and one another in order that they may conduct unscripted dramas without fear.'[15] Wells sees this practice as analogous to the ethical task of the Church, for he hopes to show 'how the church may become a community of trust in order that it may faithfully encounter the unknown of the future without fear.'[16] The value of thinking of Christian ethics as improvisation is that it assumes both a ruled-account of tradition and yet a certain freedom in its performance. Wells continues: 'There is a dimension of Christian life that requires more than repetition, more even than interpretation—but not so much as origination, or creation de novo…. When improvisers are trained to work in the theater, they are schooled in a tradition so thoroughly that they learn to act from habit in ways appropriate to the circumstance.'[17] The task of being 'faithful improvisers', i.e. faithful disciples of Christ, requires a way of life that both shapes its members so that they are thoroughly ingrained into the tradition and yet that shaping constitutes a certain *habitus* by which the future, with all of its vicissitudes and uncertainties, can be faced with confidence and hope.

Three features of Wells' use and exploration of the notion of improvisation for Christian ethics stand out for the present task. First, faithful improvisation beckons an ecclesial framework rather than an individualist approach. Wells has in mind a cadre of performers/improvisers on the grand stage of redemptive history who learn from one another how to embody the practice of faithful discipleship; he cites Jeremy Begbie's reading of the book of Acts as being 'a stream of new, unpredictable, improvisations'.[18] From this

---

[15] Samuel Wells, *Improvisation: The Drama of Christian Ethics* (Grand Rapids: Brazos Press, 2004), p. 11.

[16] Wells, *Improvisation*, p. 11.

[17] Wells, *Improvisation*, p. 65.

[18] Wells, *Improvisation*, p. 66, citing Jeremy Begbie, *Theology, Music, and Time* (Cambridge: Cambridge University Press, 2000), pp. 222-23. As its title suggests, Begbie's approach to improvisation is through the lens of musicology whereas Wells opts for the context of the theatre. In this section, Begbie has some very suggestive remarks about the way the Spirit improvises in our midst out of what Jesus has done by 'hooking into' our realities and anticipating the age which is to come.

testimony one sees that the early church faced a number of new and unforeseen circumstances in which they had to demonstrate covenant-fidelity, yet there was no precedent for much of what these early believers were facing, making the task of discernment ever so crucial for their life together. Second, improvisation grants a certain 'freedom within boundaries' that is necessary for the enactment and embodiment of holiness. If holiness is assumed to be the way the Church embodies the reign of God in such a manner that it both demonstrates to the world 1) what it means to be the world and 2) what it means to be the Church, then a conceptual alternative is needed that can accommodate the need of a Christian community to maintain borders/distinctives in an open-ended way. Improvisation, when considered an ecclesial practice that involves both habituation and skill,[19] can help overcome the way the institutional and charismatic dimensions of ecclesial life are thought to be antagonistic to one another by allowing for both an objective (Pauline) as well as a subjective (Catholic Epistles) feature of performance for the understanding and enactment of holiness. Finally, the process of improvisation is inherently and necessarily pneumatological. Wells does mention this feature of ecclesial improvisation, but he could have made it even more explicit: Ecclesial improvisation does not simply rest on the talents, habits, and gifts of improvisers, but in a more determinative way, this process occurs in the Church by the shaping, discipline, promptings, and beckonings of the Holy Spirit. This pneumatological feature is intrinsically tied to the modality of worship, one which Wells does emphasize: 'For Christians the principle practice by which the moral imagination is formed, the principal form of discipleship training, is worship.'[20]

When Pentecostals were truly operating under the direction of the Holy Spirit, I believe something was at play akin to Wells' vision of theological and ecclesial improvisation. Pentecostals had a heightened sense of the possibilities for the future stemming from

---

[19] Wells, *Improvisation*. Chapter 5 is very helpful in elaborating improvisation in terms of a virtue or skill that is fostered by the church's worship and performance over time.

[20] Wells, *Improvisation*, p. 82 (the theme of worship is further extended in pp. 82-85). See also Wells' co-authored chapters with Stanley Hauerwas in Wells and Hauerwas (eds.), *The Blackwell Companion to Christian Ethics* (Oxford: Blackwell, 2004), Chapters 1-4.

both their restorationist primitivism and their modified dispensational premillennialism. They desired the kingdom and believed that the kingdom was on display in their lives and worship services as the Spirit gave witness. They believed this inbreaking kingdom to be a holy order, one that recreated, reconfigured, and called for a re-imagining of social arrangements, ecclesial practices, and individual piety.

One demonstration of this kind of ecclesial improvisation among Pentecostals was the enactment of footwashing. The ancient church, as well as the broader Mediterranean world of the first few centuries, practiced footwashing for varying reasons,[21] and during medieval times the practice came to be associated with Maundy Thursday, the day of Holy Week in which the 'command' of Jesus for his disciples to love one another (Jn 13.34) is recognized for all of its implications regarding servitude and humility. However, the rite of washing the saints' feet has had a variegated history; Alister McGrath points out a rather telling example of this rite's practice over time:

> In England, a particularly interesting ceremony has come to be associated with this day. As an affirmation of humility, the monarch would wash the feet of a small number of his or her subjects. This has now been replaced by the ceremony of the 'Maundy Money,' in which the monarch distributes specially minted coins to the elderly at cathedrals throughout England.[22]

Now, there may be some very good reasons for this transition that I am not aware of, but the move from washing someone's feet to giving him or her coins is certainly, by all appearances and with all due respect, one of theological incoherence and inconsequence. Stated

---

[21] For some background to the practice, see the summary piece by John Christopher Thomas, 'Footwashing Within the Context of the Lord's Supper', in Dale R. Stoffer (ed.), *The Lord's Supper: Believers Church Perspectives* (Scottdale, PA: Herald Press, 1997), pp. 169-84 and his more extensive treatment in *Footwashing in John 13 and the Johannine Community* (JSNTSup 61; Sheffield: JSOT Press, 1991).

[22] Alister E. McGrath, *Christianity: An Introduction*, second edition (Oxford: Blackwell, 2006), p. 309. The practice of footwashing in the Anglo-Saxon world has had a long tradition that endured for centuries until the actual practice fell out of favor in the 1700s; cf. G.A. Frank Knight, 'Feet-Washing', in James Hastings (ed.), *Encyclopedia of Religion and Ethics* (Edinburgh: T & T Clark, 1912), V, pp. 814-23 (818-20).

pointedly, giving coins fails to recognize the 'moral miracle'[23] that was on display in Jesus' acts toward his disciples as portrayed in John 13. I suspect that my own North American context would be no different: It is hard to escape the conviction that the majority of churchgoers would most likely prefer to write a check than wash another person's feet. The rite of footwashing is no easy undertaking.

Pentecostals were not unique in the practice of footwashing;[24] however, that the practice of footwashing was even adopted by Pentecostals is suggestive of another dimension of the Pentecostal ecclesial ethos. Historically, Pentecostals have tended not to be very self-consciously sacramental; as noted above, many Pentecostals feel more at ease to talk about 'ordinances' rather than 'sacraments', the former term suggesting to Pentecostals acts of faithfulness undertaken by the command of Jesus to remember and imagine the implications of Christ's work rather than (as the latter term suggested to them) acts that by their execution are efficacious (*ex opere operato*). And yet, these believers managed to see this practice of footwashing in John 13 as one meriting obedience and imitation, a move that had important theological ramifications for demonstrating what in fact the Spirit was doing in their midst.[25] For all the anti- or non-

---

[23] I am borrowing this language from Frank Macchia, who recounts a time when a group of Chinese pastors were gathered and asked to recount what was most impressive for them about Jesus' life, to which they replied the washing of the disciples' feet. Cf. 'Is Footwashing the Neglected Sacrament? A Theological Response to John Christopher Thomas', *Pneuma* 19.2 (1997), pp. 239-49 (240).

[24] For a survey of the different Pentecostal contexts in which footwashing was practiced among early adherents, see John Christopher Thomas, 'Footwashing', *White Wing Messenger* 78 (November 2000), pp. 10-13.

[25] I find it peculiar that Harold Hunter denies this improvisational feature of Pentecostal fellowship on the basis of normative assertions: 'Some pentecostal groups have practiced footwashing as an ordinance. Such an insistence wrongly infers a moral necessity in Jesus' actions that should be applied only to water baptism and the Eucharist. This object lesson in humility, as portrayed by Christ, is not an extraneous rite' ('Ordinances, Pentecostal,' *NIDPCM*, pp. 947-49 [948]). The language of 'moral necessity' as well as 'object lesson' does not accurately reflect the role and function of footwashing among those Pentecostals who practiced it. When coming to the text 'anew', Pentecostals saw matters differently; to use the language of Begbie, Pentecostals tended from time to time to particularize the 'cultural restraints' within broader Christian expressions in the face of the 'occasional restraints' that they enacted through their worship and reading practices. It is no surprise, then, that a Pentecostal scholar could observe, 'When

sacramental stereotypes circulated about Pentecostals, Frank Macchia believes that they have traditionally and consistently found such rites as footwashing and the laying on of hands for healing as those encounters of God that manifest the 'greatest power'.[26] If this observation is true, then what is the significance of the practice of footwashing for Pentecostal ecclesiology?

I wish to argue that the practice of footwashing by some Pentecostals took shape initially as an ecclesial activity of an improvisational kind, one that marked a holy kind of fellowship as indicated by the leveling and empowering work of the Holy Spirit surrounding such a rite. Pentecostal fellowship purifies itself and demonstrates the holy reign of God in such practices as footwashing where structures of privilege, power, and difference are called into question in doxologically impromptu ways before the Lamb who was slain, the one who showed us the nature and character of God through this one's acts of self-giving, renunciation, and solidarity. Pentecostals are not alone in appropriating footwashing as a quasi-sacramental rite, but what is remarkable about the Pentecostal context is that this practice was appropriated by a fellowship that traditionally emphasizes power. That a movement like Pentecostalism can employ a practice like footwashing within a setting like Pentecostal worship suggests that Pentecostals had a keen sense from whom and in what setting they were empowered.[27]

Pentecostals stumbled upon a practice that they had paltry few theological resources to narrate for its full implications within their common life; however, it is also true that the impression is often more powerful than the narration. Jean Vanier, the founder of l'Arche communities, seems to agree:

---

compared with the words of institution associated with water baptism and the Lord's Supper in the New Testament, the commands to wash feet appear to be the most emphatic of the three' (Thomas, 'Footwashing Within the Context of the Lord's Supper', p. 174). New possibilities open up when dominant restraints are suspended for a time.

[26] Macchia, 'Is Footwashing the Neglected Sacrament?' p. 242.

[27] In following Jesus' practices, Pentecostals were engaging in a form of *imitatio Christi* that John Howard Yoder believed was the only form such a task could take: 'There is thus but one realm in which the concept of imitation holds ....
This is at the point of the concrete social meaning of the cross in its relation to enmity and power. Servanthood replaces dominion, forgiveness absorbs hostility.
Thus—and only thus—are we bound by New Testament thought to "be like Jesus"' (*The Politics of Jesus* [Grand Rapids: Eerdmans, 2nd edn, 1994], p. 131).

At special moments in l'Arche and in Faith and Light, we wash each other's feet as an expression of our love. It is always very moving for me when someone with disabilities washes my feet or when I see a person wash the feet of their mother or father. It is the world turned upside down. In 1998 the Central Committee of the World Council of Churches in Geneva asked me to animate a day on spirituality. I suggested that after my talk, all the members of this Central Committee, representing some 230 different Christian churches, be invited to wash each other's feet during a special liturgy. It was particularly moving to witness an Orthodox bishop kneeling down and washing the feet of an American woman who was a Baptist minister. Gestures sometimes speak louder and more lastingly than words. It was a moment of both grace and unity.[28]

And, I would add, by virtue of being one in which the 'world was turned upside down' because of the example of Jesus and the leading of the Holy Spirit, this enactment of footwashing was an improvisational moment of embodied and practiced holiness.[29]

The Pentecostal movement 'turned the world upside down' because it typified a kind of fellowship in which the lot of humanity is considered hungry, poor, and needy before God, and in that acknowledgment of human deficiency and divine sufficiency, holy power was thought to be available to all who would heed the call to follow Jesus. This dialectic of purity and power, of *mortificatio et vivificatio*, is at the heart of what was at work when social convention was particularised and radical arrangements were proposed, be they in relation to different kinds of human identifiers (e.g. race, gender, and age) or corporate institutions (e.g. established churches and the state).

---

[28] Jean Vanier, *Drawn into the Mystery of Jesus through the Gospel of John* (New York: Paulist Press, 2004), p. 230.

[29] In elaborating the dynamics of tradition and freedom in light of musical improvisation, Begbie remarks, 'What of paintings, missionary activity, the testimonies of prisoners, Bible-study groups in remote churches? These improvisations are potentially as fruitful and liberating as anything issuing from a committee of priests, and *they themselves will often prove their worth by repeated particularisation in radically different situations*' (*Theology, Music and Time*, p. 217; emphasis added).

II. Pentecostal Fellowship is Holy because of Whom Its Participants Know/Experience

The dialectic of purity and power is on display quite vividly in the Johannine depiction of Jesus washing the disciples' feet. One who attends to the context of Jesus' world would not be surprised of Mary anointing Jesus' feet in John 12; John 13, however, presents another matter altogether. Given the coarseness of the activity because of its association with one of the most exposed parts of the body, footwashing took place in a number of specific circumstances. Sometimes, family members engaged in the activity, which demonstrated a level of trust and intimacy. At other moments, the host would wash the feet of a guest in an act of hospitality. Most often, slaves would engage in this activity, although Jewish slaves were not required to participate in such a practice on behalf of their masters. All in all, the activity functioned in a dual way: either as a sign of grace and love or as a needed obligation that those lower on the social scale would have to perform. Both dynamics, footwashing as a sign of intimacy or social stratification, pivot off of this act being one of cleansing; only select people under select circumstances and arrangements come into contact with one's filth.[30]

That Jesus chose to wash the disciples' feet during and not before the supper suggests that he was intentionally showing them something of significance,[31] and given Peter's reaction, the incident was quite unusual. From one perspective, Peter's initial refusal of Jesus' act of cleansing suggests that he had in mind the stratification that marks human relationships as a whole; after all, here is Peter's rabbi, his *kurios* who wishes to wash his feet.[32] Jesus' response is telling: 'If I do not wash you, you have no part with me' (Jn 13.8).

---

[30] Thomas remarks, 'Due to its humble nature, the performance of such an act demonstrates tremendous affection, servitude, or both' (*Footwashing in John 13 and the Johannine Community*, p. 42).

[31] When taking into account the canonical witness, the incident may be related to the internal strife on display in Luke 22 regarding who among the disciples was the greatest.

[32] One should not ignore what a revolutionary act this was: According to Thomas, 'Jesus' action is unparalleled in ancient evidence, for no other person of superior status is described as voluntarily washing the feet of a subordinate' (*Footwashing in John 13 and the Johannine Community*, p. 59).

Obviously, Jesus had something in mind other than 'propriety' or social convention. Through this single act of holy improvisation, Jesus called into question both what intimacy and authority mean in the Kingdom of God.

Pentecostal fellowship is holy to the degree that it knows and experiences this Jesus as the Lord and Giver of life. Holiness is an ecclesial possibility because the Holy One of Israel 'went out into the far country' and dwelt among us and extended and opened his very self to us. If Jesus is the truest and most accessible demonstration of who God is and what God is like, then one could argue that in Christ we see the truest and most accessible expression of God's holiness.[33] We see in him the dynamic of *mortificatio* and *vivificatio*, both in his life and in the order that he proclaims and initiates.

God's character is on display in a radical way through Jesus' act of washing the disciples' feet. Jesus acknowledges that there is a vast difference between the disciples and him: 'You call me Teacher and Lord—and you speak rightly, for I am' (Jn 13.13). He claims his authority in this passage but does so in order to call it into question in a very crucial way: Jesus' authority rests not on the exercise of power or might according to conventional human standards but through the enactment of servitude, humility, and yes, washing another's filth. Rather than perpetuating the social, philosophical, and theological patterns of the day in which holiness, privilege, and all that is deemed sacrosanct must be preserved and so separate from that which is dirty, fleeting, and coarse, Jesus shows something altogether different. This act is not simply an 'object lesson'; it is a sign of God's holy, in-breaking reign in the world, one in which the kenotic quality of all that is involved with incarnation is on display in a scandalizing and 'turning-the-world-upside-down' kind of way.

Pentecostals have intuitively sensed that power from God stems from what Jesus has promised and done, including his work as sanctifier. The repeated emphasis on anointing and power by Pentecos-

---

[33] Jason Goroncy reminds us that to speak of the holy in a thoroughly Christian way is 'to speak of none other than One who has bared his holy arm in Jesus Christ and by the Holy Spirit as the "Holy One in our midst", as our Redeemer and Sanctifier. In other words, we must never think of God's holiness (or human holiness) in abstraction from the action of the Triune God who elects, judges, saves and sanctifies humanity in Jesus Christ' ('The Elusiveness, Loss and Cruciality of Recovered Holiness: Some Biblical and Theological Observations', *International Journal of Systematic Theology* 10.2 [2008], pp. 195-209 [201]).

tals rests on a 'full gospel' that hinges on the identity and work of Christ. Sadly, this understanding tends to quantify and commodify power as a 'something' we have. Such inclinations are brimming with a number of threatening dangers, including an unhealthy sense of independence and individuality that can allow us to think of ourselves as powerful apart from God. It is here where the push by some to consider Pentecostalism as a spirituality is key. The source of power is not from ourselves but from the triune God, and participating in this life, a possibility which Christ has offered, is the only way to partake of such power. And the shape of this power matters: In the case of Jesus' example in John 13, the power is 'other-directed'; as Barth notes, 'How emphatically the [Fourth Gospel's portrayal of the footwashing] emphasises the fact that the service of Christ is His true power and majesty and therefore the grace by which man receives his life.'[34]

Staying on the vine (John 15) implies a continual attentiveness, one in which the whole body need not be washed but certainly the feet as one peregrinates in a vile world (Jn 13.10). This imagery of continual dependence in knowing and experiencing God is repeated throughout the Johannine literature in its *meno* or 'remaining/abiding' language. The implication of such imagery within the broader call of discipleship is that 'remaining' in Jesus is both an embarrassingly intimate and personally and socially disarming reality, one that implies continual 'pruning/cleansing' (Jn 15.2-3) on God's part to sanctify us in the midst of a hostile world. It is in this dynamic of vulnerability and dependency that Christ can be wondrously apprehended and powerfully proclaimed as the one who makes holy, i.e. the sanctifier.

III. The Ontological, Moral, and Ultimately Doxological Question

Pentecostals in the past have struggled mightily with how to define and sustain a holy fellowship. Because of the complexity of the issues involved, sometimes it was easier to appeal to a standardized list in order to make the task more manageable and assuring. The

---

[34] Karl Barth, *Church Dogmatics*, III/4 (eds. G.W. Bromiley and T.F. Torrance; Edinburgh: T & T Clark, 1961), p. 476.

point of Pentecostal fellowship, however, is not to codify its collective life but to 'encounter the life of this crucified and risen Christ in the power of the Spirit.'[35] Such an encounter will entail following Christ in improvisational and yet faithful ways: 'If you know these things, blessed are you if you do them' (Jn 13.17); the performance of holiness is a Christ-enabled possibility and command (cf. Jn 13.14) that is required for us to grow in grace. In this growth, we follow and attend to the Holy One of Israel, our master, the one who has sent us (cf. Jn 13.16), and ultimately the one who loves us 'until the end' (Jn 13.1).

The holiness that marks Pentecostal fellowship can never be reified or codified, for doing so would compromise a fruitful and innovative (i.e. a Spirit-empowered and Spirit-led) future. When early Pentecostals practiced footwashing, advocated pacifism, allowed women to be in ministry, and held services of diverse racial backgrounds, they did so not on the basis of maintaining a level of relevance by their observance of the status quo; quite the contrary, their apparent irrelevance to the conventions of their day was the bedrock of their alarming relevance, one that has become increasingly apparent to those of us who study the movement's history; they 'did not understand' what they were doing (cf. Jn 13.7), but at present we are coming to understand more and more the way the Spirit was leading this fellowship in the ways of holiness.

These believers improvised in a holy way as they caught a glimpse of God's kingdom and in turn attempted to live in conformity with it when they encountered the practice of footwashing as depicted in John 13. It would seem that the future for the holiness of Pentecostal fellowship rests on its ability to 'remain' in the presence of Christ through the Spirit in such a way as to see and enact this holy reign in scriptural and yet unscripted ways. This dynamic of 'scripturally-unscripted improvisation' could mean anointing somebody with oil or washing another's feet; it could mean providing aid to relief organizations at the time of a natural disaster or refusing to bear arms in a war-crazed nation-state; it could mean reaching out to the pariahs or 'untouchables' of a given society or seeking those who are lost in a specific region. Whenever Christians are prompted, quickened, and led by the Spirit to engage in the

---

[35] Macchia, 'Is Footwashing the Neglected Sacrament?' p. 243.

work of the Kingdom in a scriptural, timely, and prophetic way, there is enacted holy Christian fellowship. As Jonathan R. Wilson remarks, 'We must learn properly to confess in word and deed that the church is one, holy, catholic and apostolic. But what those marks mean in particular times and places requires discernment under the guidance of the Spirit.'[36]

To conclude, the holiness of Pentecostal fellowship is both a moral task and an ontological reality, and both features are subsumed and sustained within the modality of Pentecostal worship. Unfortunately, it is not a given that within a particular Pentecostal fellowship people will be continually and in a sustained way 'encounter[ing] the life of this crucified and risen Christ in the power of the Spirit.' Wherever this encounter is occurring in such a way that 'worship absorbs the world',[37] the improvisational and spiritual implications of *being* a holy people will come to bear; a truly Pentecostal fellowship is called to nothing less.

---

[36] 'Practicing Church: Evangelical Ecclesiologies at the End of Modernity' in Mark Husbands and Daniel J. Treier (eds.), *The Community of the Word: Toward An Evangelical Ecclesiology* (Downers Grove, IL: InterVarsity Press, 2005), pp. 63-72 (71).

[37] This phrasing is a variant of George Lindbeck's famous remark of the 'text absorbing the world' in *The Nature of Doctrine* (Philadelphia: Westminster, 1984), p. 118.

5

THE CHURCH AS SANCTIFIED COMMUNITY

MATTHIAS WENK*

Introduction

Pentecostalism and holiness are often referred to almost synony-mously, whereas ecclesiology and Pentecostalism are not as close relatives; Pentecostalism has frequently been accused of its indi-vidualistic tendencies. However, the very notion of the Fivefold Gospel with one emphasis being on Jesus as sanctifier assumes otherwise: the existence of a sanctified community. Therefore, the focus of this paper is on how a theology of holiness may help either overcome or foster such individualistic inclinations within Pentecostalism.

In order to do so I shall first outline Pentecostal approaches to holiness and their implications for the understanding of the Church as a sanctified community before looking at the New Testament evidence on this matter. Special attention shall be given to the role of rites as a way to express a community's values and (re)definition of reality.[1]

---

* Matthias Wenk (PhD, Brunel University) is Pastor of the BewegungPlus in in Hindelbank and Burgdorf and Head of the Theology Department at the Insti-tutPlus in Liestal, Switzerland.

[1] Since the works of Victor Turner, in which he analyzed especially the roles of rituals in times of transition and uncertainty (the liminal phase of a per-son/group of people), much has been said and written on the theory of rituals that cannot be reflected in this paper (V. Turner, *The Ritual Process: Structure and Anti-Structure* [New Brunswick, NJ: Aldine Transaction, {1997} 2008]. For a more

Pentecostal Approaches to a Holy Community

The rise of Pentecostalism is inseparably linked with the 19th century holiness movement. This inherited emphasis on sanctification soon led to a conflict within the young movement, both in the United States as well as in Europe; the finished work debate.[2] Since the emphasis of this paper is on Pentecostal ecclesiology, no attempt shall be made to present a detailed historical/theological overview on the roots and the development of the issue of sanctification within the various Pentecostal traditions,[3] neither shall the debate be recapitulated, nor shall the different arguments be expounded.[4] In regard to the nexus between Pentecostal ecclesiology and its emphasis on holiness, two other issues appear to be more significant and shall be addressed briefly:

A Renewed Community Filled by the Spirit

From its very beginning Pentecostalism was known for its inclusive power, its potency in overcoming ethnic, gender, and social barriers

---

complete overview on his works, cf. the bibliography in C. Strecker, *Die liminale Theologie des Paulus. Zugänge zur paulinischen Theologie aus kulturanthropologischer Perspektive* [Göttingen: Vandenhoeck & Ruprecht, 1999]).

[2] This debate is centring around the question of sanctification as a finished work accomplished by Christ on Calvary on behalf of the believer. Cf. R.M. Riss, 'Finished Work Controversy', in S.M. Burgess and G.B. McGee (eds.), *Dictionary of the Pentecostal and Charismatic Movements* (Grand Rapids: Zondervan, 1988), pp. 638-69; W.K. Kay and A.E. Dyer, *Pentecostal and Charismatic Studies: A Reader* (London, SCM Press, 2004), pp. 127-43. For a European perspective on the issue see: 'Pastor Jonathan Paul, "The Work of the Cross"', *Confidence* (June 1909), p. 135, as quoted in Kay and Dyer, *Reader,* pp. 131-32.

[3] For such an overview cf. Donald W. Dayton, *Theological Roots of Pentecostalism* (Metuchen: Scarecrow Press, 1987); C.E. Jones, 'Holiness Movement' in S.M. Burgess *et al.* (eds.), *The New International Dictionary of Pentecostal and Charismatic Movements* (Grand Rapids: Zondervan, rev. and expanded edn, 2002), pp. 726-29.

[4] The entire issue of *Pneuma* 21.2 (1999) is dedicated to the Wesleyan and Pentecostal Dialogue on power and sanctification. For the more 'Baptist' (Keswick) oriented positions, cf. D. Leggett, 'The Assemblies of God Statement on Sanctification (A Brief Review by Calvin and Wesley)', *Pneuma* 11.2 (1998), pp. 113-22; Mark Cartledge, 'The Early Pentecostal Theology of *Confidence* Magazine (1908-1926): A Version of the Five-Fold Gospel?', *Journaal of the European Pentecostal Theological Association* 28.2 (2008), pp. 120-25. For an overview on the more contemporary discussion, cf. F.D. Macchia, *Baptized in the Spirit. A Global Pentecostal Theology* (Grand Rapids: Zondervan, 2006), pp. 28-33.

between people.[5] Some aspects of this dynamic spirituality have received due weight among contemporary scholarship on Pentecostalism, such as the role of women,[6] the attitude towards war and pacifism,[7] as well as the general concern for the poor.[8] Although in the USA and in Western Europe the movement may have lost some of its prophetic dynamics in becoming more and more middle-class oriented from the middle of the 20th century onward, it never lost the social dimension of its spirituality entirely, as evidenced in David Wilkerson's outreach to young drug addicts in New York and the subsequent founding of Teen Challenge (late 1950s, early 60s),[9] or in the strong emphasis on social work among Swiss Pentecostals during the 1970s and 80s.[10] The social-ethical relevance of Pente-

---

[5] Cf. C.M. Robeck, *Azusa Street—Mission and Revival. The Birth of the Global Pentecostal Movement* (Nashville: Thomas Nelson), pp. 129-86. For a detailed overview of and bibliographical references regarding contemporary Pentecostal scholarship on social ethics, see K. Warrington, *Pentecostal Theology: A Theology of Encounter* (London: T & T Clark, 2008), pp. 226-45. For an appraisal of the social relevance of a pneumatological spirituality of the charismatic/pentecostal churches in Brazil, without explicitly addressing such issues, cf. R. Shaull and W. Cesar, *Pentecostalism and the Future of the Christian Churches* (Grand Rapids: Eerdmans, 2000).

[6] J.E. Power, '"Your Daugthers Shall Prophecy": Pentecostal Hermeneutics and the Empowerment of Women' in M.W. Dempster *et al.* (eds.), *The Globalization of Pentecostalism. A Religion Made to Travel* (Carlisle: Paternoster, 1999), pp. 313-37; *idem*, 'Recovering a Woman's Head with Prophetic Authority: A Pentecostal Interpretation of 1 Corinthians 11.3-16', *Journal of Pentecostal Theology* 10.1 (2001), pp. 11-37; D. Chapman, 'The Rise and Demise of Women's Ministry in the Origins and Early Years of Pentecostalism in Britain', *Journal of Pentecostal Theology* 12.2 (2004), pp. 217-46; *idem*, 'The Role of Women in Early Pentecostalism 1907-1914', *Journal of the European Pentecostal Theological Association* 28.2 (2008), pp. 131-44.

[7] R. Robins, 'A Chronology of Peace: Attitudes toward War and Peace in the Assemblies of God: 1914-1918', *Pneuma*, 6.1 (1984), pp. 3-25; M.W. Dempster, '"Crossing Borders": Arguments Used by Early American Pentecostals in Support of the Global Character of Pacifism', *EPTA Bulletin* 10.2 (1991), pp. 63-80; Joel Shuman, 'Pentecost and the End of Patriotism: A Call for the Restoration of Pacifism among Pentecostal Christians', *Journal of Pentecostal Theology* 9 (1996), pp. 70-96; Paul N. Alexander, 'Spirit Empowered Peacemaking: Toward a Pentecostal Peace Fellowship', *Journal of the European Pentecostal Theological Association* 22 (2004), pp. 78-102.

[8] Dempster, 'Pentecostal Social Concern', pp. 129-53; David Bundy, 'Social Ethics in the Church of the Poor: The Cases of T.B. Barratt and Lewi Pethrus', *Journal of the European Pentecostal Theological Association* 22 (2002), pp. 30-44.

[9] David Wilkerson, *The Cross and the Switchblade* (New York: Pyramid Books, 1964).

[10] Rossel, *Erinnerungen*, pp. 94-99.

costal spirituality is also reflected in Hollenweger's report of a Mexican Indian woman's baptism in which he concludes that in her baptism as well as through her testimony in front of two thousand people, she, who had so far no voice and no face in society, was given a voice and dignity within a community.[11] Behind this inclusive and community building power of Pentecostal spirituality were various influences such as the church's understanding of scripture, eschatology and the work of the Spirit.[12]

In explaining the prominence of women in the holiness movement, Nancy Hardesty and Donald Dayton mention six factors that seem also to be applicable to Pentecostalism's inclusive tendencies in general, since they reflect aspects of a Spirituality that is closely related to Pentecostals' experience of the Spirit:

1. The emphasis on the sanctification experience to which both women and men were to testify, which often led women to perceive a call for preaching in their lives.

2. Scriptural truth (the doctrine of holiness) was illustrated by personal experience that freed people from a literalist interpretation of Scripture.

3. The emphasis on the work of the Spirit and the experience of spiritual gifts led to a charismatic concept of leadership as well as to the awareness of a person's 'call' or anointing for service.

4. Freedom to be experimental; if the 'method' was successful in winning people and in encouraging holiness, it was approved.

---

[11] W.J. Hollenweger, *Charismatisch-pfingstliches Christentum. Herkunft. Situation, ökumenische Chancen* (Göttingen: Vandenhoeck & Ruprecht, 1997), p. 283.

[12] Analyzing, for example, the motivation for the concern of the Assemblies of God with regard to war and peace, Robins concludes that the argument 'in favour of pacifism … is biblically rooted, eschatologically informed, and it frequently appeals to the work of the Spirit in sanctification…. That is to say that the argument is characterized by qualities which are central to our self-understanding as Pentecostals. Conversely, argumentation against pacifism is characterized by political considerations, rationalism and humanism' (Robins, 'Chronology of Peace', p. 24).

5. The call to perfection challenged the status quo[13] and gave way for reform and new ideas.

6. The emergence of informal groups with female leadership.[14]

Reading Hollenweger's report of the Indian's baptism in Mexico and comparing Robins' with Hardesty's and Dayton's conclusions regarding the motivation for this inclusive character of holiness, it is evident that the 'social side' of Pentecostalism's stress on sanctification is more pneumatologically (the experience of the Spirit within the Church) and eschatologically motivated, and its appeal to Scripture is less literalist as in its emphasis on personal purity.[15]

The Emphasis on Personal Purity and Its Potential to Encourage Individualistic Tendencies

Although there was no common agreement on the doctrine of sanctification among the various early (and contemporary) Pentecostal groups, they all shared to some degree a mutual concern for personal purity.[16] One argument being that the power and the gifts of the Holy Spirit can only operate in purified vessels.[17]

---

[13] This corresponds in part with Blumhofer's observation that early Pentecostals were a subculture, shaped by convictions and values that often opposed the views of their time (E. Blumhofer, *The Assemblies of God: A Chapter in the Story of American Pentecostalism* [Springfield: Gospel Publishing House, 1989], p. 19.

[14] N. Hardesty, L.S. Dayton, D.W. Dayton, 'Women in the Holiness Movement: Feminism in the Evangelical Tradition', in R. Ruther and E. McLaughlin (eds.), *Women of Spirit: Female Leadership in the Jewish and Christian Traditions* (New York: Simon & Schuster, 1979), pp. 241-48.

[15] This is not unlike the ethics of the Old Testament prophets, who also stresses more Israel's social responsibility than individual virtues. Hence, it does not surprise that Dempster's article on a 'biblical mandate' for Pentecostal social concern almost exclusively builds upon Old Testament texts (Dempster, 'Pentecostal Social Concern', pp. 129-53).

[16] This concern is reflected both in the more 'Baptist oriented' definition of the Assemblies of God that sanctification is 'separation from sin and dedication to God' (cf. the Assemblies of God (USA) statement from 1916 and 1961 as quoted in Kay, *Reader*, p. 129), and in the more Wesleyan formulation of the International Pentecostal Church of Holiness that sanctification 'delivers from the power of sin [and] is followed by a life-long growth in grace and knowledge of our Lord and Saviour Jesus Christ'. (The International Pentecostal Church of Holiness' statement on sanctification, as quoted in Kay, *Reader*, p. 139).

[17] Cf. Robert Willenegger, 'Gemeinde des Neuen Testaments' in Johann Widmer (ed.), *Im Kampf gegen Satans Reich* (Selbstverlag: 1942), II, p. 18.

On the one hand this striving for purity often had positive influences in the lives of families (overcoming anger,[18] various kinds of addictions,[19] newly found joy,[20] etc.), and freed people from the sense of 'being trapped in their biographies'; a new beginning was possible.[21]

On the other hand, this emphasis on personal purity had also the potential of fostering individualistic and exclusive tendencies, nurtured with lists of do's and don't's. In his book on early Pentecostals and American culture, Grant Wacker gives several examples of such outward expressions of personal purity; taboos related to a person's mouth (certain food and drinks, lying, swearing, etc.), to the ear and the eyes (reading novels, comic books, worldly music such as ragtime, classical violin, etc.) and focusing on a dress code (mainly relating to women) as well as jewellery.[22] Such lists were not only a North American phenomenon but flourished also in Europe.[23] In the *Gemeinde für Urchistentum,* Switzerland (today called *BewegungPlus*) such lists not only were pronounced in sermons and church magazines but also in prophecies during church services or national conventions; specific sins, and sometimes also specific people, were thereby publicly addressed and exposed.[24]

Needless to say, such an approach to sanctification often led to legalism and gave way to power and control mechanisms within churches. It further encouraged an individualistic concept of holiness with an emphasis on personal virtues or duties. It also fostered a climate of fear (not complying with the high standards of holiness

---

[18] Cf. the report in Johann Widmer, *Im Kampf gegen Satans Reich* (Selbstverlag, 1952), III, p. 131.

[19] Widmer, *Im Kampf gegen Satans Reich*, III, pp. 216-17.

[20] Widmer, *Im Kampf gegen Satans Reich*, III, p. 147, 168.

[21] Widmer, *Im Kampf gegen Satans Reich*, III, pp. 196-99.

[22] G. Wacker, *Heaven Below: Early Pentecostals and American Culture* (Cambridge: Harvard University Press, 2001), pp. 122-26.

[23] They included tobacoo (cf. Johann Widmer's 'attack' against tobacco, as quoted in A. Rossel *et al.* (eds.), *Erinnerungen an die Zukunft. Das Buch zum 80. Geburtstag der BewgungPlus* [Bern: Berchtold Haller Verlag, 2007], p. 26) women's hairstyles and dress code (cf. Minutes of the executive committee meeting of the Gemeinde für Urchristentum [BewegungPlus], 1951, as quoted in Rossi, *Erinnerungen*, p. 81).

[24] Some are preserved in Johann Widmer, *Im Kampf gegen Satans Reich* (Selbstverlag, 1952, 2nd edn), III, pp. 26-30.

and thereby not being ready at the return of Jesus) as well as a sense of separation from the rest of society.[25]

Pentecostalism's emphasis on holiness and the emergence of an alternative, inclusive community are interrelated: It positively influenced and transformed the lives of individuals as well as of families; people were no longer 'bound' to their familiar patterns of behaviour and social interaction, which in turn brought about a new quality of community life and fostered integration and the overcoming of social barriers both in a horizontal (crossing beyond one's peer group) as well as on a vertical level (uniting people from different social 'levels'). At the same time this very same emphasis had the potential to encourage individualistic and exclusive tendencies and create a rigorist, and at times exclusivist, atmosphere within a community.

This difference between the more exclusive, at times almost elitist approach to holiness ('we' against the world) and the more inclusive one ('we' with and for the world) is almost perfectly illustrated in the 'political excursion' of two of the early leading figures of the *Gemeinde für Urchristentum*, Switzerland, and their respective political programmes. One was exclusively concerned to oppose homosexuality and so-called moral issues, combined with a strong anti UNO and anti EU position. The other one also addressed subjects like social justice, materialism, corruption and speculation with real-estate.[26] In this case, as in the Assemblies of God's attitude towards war and peace, a more individual stress on holiness and moral issues seems to correspond with a more literal approach to scripture and with certain political positions.

Hence, Pentecostals' accent on sanctification always had an impact on their ecclesiology; either in cultivating a certain individualism and a rigorist atmosphere within the community, or in fostering integration and the overcoming of social barriers both in a horizontal (crossing beyond one's peer group) as well as on a vertical level (uniting people from different social 'levels').

---

[25] Cf. the reports in Rossel, *Erinnerungen*, pp. 38-39; 44.

[26] Rossel, *Erinnerungen*, pp. 88-89.

The New Testament Vision of a Holy Community

Turning to the New Testament the leading question will be to what extent the concept of holiness disseminated by Jesus or one of the New Testament authors encouraged community, and thereby contributes towards a Pentecostal ecclesiology, and what was perceived as stimulating both holiness as well as community. Special attention will also be paid to the rites enacting the values and the self-understanding of the early church as a holy people of God.

Jesus, a Renewed Community and Purity

Gerd Theissen has argued that in Israel an ethics of solidarity was developed, contrary to the Greek approach of an ethics of self-control. Hence, at the centre of biblical ethics is not the emphasis on a person's virtues, duties, or self-discipline, but rather the care for one's neighbour expressed in acting love.[27] Biblical ethics thereby is primarily social ethics, focusing on interpersonal relationships with the aim to guarantee a successful living together.

Based on Lev. 19.17-18, Theissen further argues that the Jewish understanding of love went beyond an ethics of social behaviour as evinced in antiquity, since the command to love includes the enemy and the renunciation of status, hence, Jewish ethics actually contradicts any ethics of autonomy and assertion of status as endorsed in antiquity. Based on Lev. 19.17-18, love overcomes social barriers on a horizontal level between those that are inside and outside the peer group, and by renunciation of status it overcomes the barrier between groups of 'higher' or 'lower' social status.[28] Thereby the aim of biblical ethics is nothing less than the realisation of a renewed community. A community of people pursuing holiness thus is a reconciled community, as is evidenced in the Old Testament eschatological hopes for a messianic age (Joel 3.1-5; Isa. 2.1-5; 11.1-9; 32.15-20, 65.25; etc. See also 1 En. 52; 2 Bar. 73).

---

[27] G. Theissen, *Erleben und Verhalten der ersten Christen: Eine Psychologie des Urchristentums* (Gütersloh: Gütersloher Verlagshaus, 2007), pp. 408-409.

[28] Theissen, *Erleben und Verhalten der ersten Christen*, pp. 412-19. For a more detailed argument, cf. G. Theissen, 'Nächstenliebe und Statusverzicht als Grundzüge christlichen Ethos', in W. Härle, H. Schmidt, M. Welker (eds.), *Das ist christlich: Nachdenken über das Wesen des Christentums* (Gütersloh: Mohn, 2000), pp. 119-42.

This inclusive approach to holiness is reflected in all four of the Gospels,[29] and if there is any agreement in contemporary scholarship regarding Jesus, it is that he radically promoted a renewed community characterised by such inclusiveness and acceptance of those formerly marginalised and excluded.[30] Luke, more than the other evangelists, has illustrated this in his account of Jesus' anointing by a sinful woman (Lk. 7.36-50, *par.* Mt. 26.6-13; Mk 14.3-9; Jn 12.1-8): Simon's self-righteousness seems to be the greater obstacle in coming close to Jesus than the woman's sins. This may explain why all four Gospels rarely depict Jesus as confronting people with specific sins, other than religious self-righteousness (i.e. Jn 8.21-46) or trust in one's wealth (i.e. Lk. 12.16-21).[31] It seems that a lack of love (Lk. 5.36-50) and trust in money (Mt. 19.23, *par.* Mk 10.23-25; Lk. 18.24-25) as well as in one's religious achievements (Mt. 15.1-20, *par.* Mk 7.1-23, Lk. 11.37-41; Jn 8.7) have been by far the greater problems addressed by Jesus than any other moral issues.

Jesus' inclusive approach to holiness is paralleled with his lack of interest in ritual purity, as reflected in all four Gospels: Mk 7.1-23 (*par.* Mt. 15.1-20; Lk. 11.37-41); Mk 7.19; Mt. 23.25 (*par.* Lk. 11.39); Jn 3.25.[32] This lack of interest in ritual purity is also evidenced in the evangelists' use of καθαρίζω ('cleanse') and its derivatives:

---

[29] In the Gospel of Mark one of the first things Jesus does is to call the tax-collector Levi (Mk 2.13-17; *par.* Mt. 9.9-13; Lk. 5.27-32), in Matthew the gentile magicians are the first ones to worship Jesus (Mt. 2.1-11), in Luke the crippled woman is called 'a daughter of Abraham' (Lk. 13.16), the Gospel of John tells us about Jesus' talk with a Samaritan woman, the result being 'many of the Samaritans from that town believed in him' (Jn 4.39) as well as the Greeks that came to Jesus (Jn 12.20-23), and both in Matthew and in Luke Jesus was called by his opponents 'a friend of tax-collectors and sinners' (Mt. 11.19; Lk. 7.34).

[30] Cf. R.A. Burridge, *Imitating Jesus: An Inclusive Approach to New Testament Ethics* (Grand Rapids: Eerdmans, 2007), pp. 73-78; F.M.J. Borg, *Conflict, Holiness and Politics in the Teachings of Jesus* (Lewiston: Edwin Mellen Press, 1984), pp. 125-27.

[31] Most references to ἁμαρτία and its derivates are fairly general, or, as in Mt. 1.21, have a 'positive' connotation in the sense that Jesus will save his people from their sins.

[32] The references to Jewish rites regarding purification/defilement in the Fourth Gospel may even imply a 'Christological' statement and thereby underline John's (Jesus') critical attitudes to ritual purity (Jn 2.6; 18.28). Schnelle argues that 2.6 may also signal the replacement of Jewish religion by the Christian faith, and in 18.28 the reference to the cultic rite serves to indicate that in keeping with the ritual law the Jewish religious leaders prevented themselves from access to the true Passover lamb (U. Schnelle, *Das Evangelium nach Johannes* [ThHK, Leipzig: Evangelische Verlagsanstalt, 1998], pp. 60, 271).

Other than in conflict situations with the religious leaders, the synoptic Gospels apply the verb almost exclusively for healings from leprosy[33] (i.e. Mk 1.40-44; Lk. 5.12-14; Mt. 8.2; 10.8, etc).[34]

The references to ἅγιος or ἁγιάζω ('holy') in the Gospels are also rare and mainly refer to God, the temple (Mt. 4.5; 24.15), to Jewish rites (Mt. 7.6; 23.17-19; Lk. 2.23) or as title of honour to special God-fearing and righteous people (i.e. Mt. 27.52; Mk 6.20). Since a number of these passages are part of redactional glosses, one can conclude that 'ἅγιος-language' seems not to have been at the centre of Jesus' ethical discourse, surprisingly neither μετάνοια-language ('repentance/conversion'). In John's Gospel it's entirely absent, and in the synoptics it is clearly part of the Baptist's preaching (Mk 1.4, *par.*) and used to summarise Jesus' proclamation (Mk 1.14, *par.* Mt. 4.17; but not Luke). Since these passages are redactional summaries, they say little about Jesus' use of μετάνοια terminology. Other references are in connection with the

- woes on the unrepentant cities (Mt. 11.20-21, *par.* Lk. 10.13);
- reference to the people of Nineveh (Mt. 12.41, *par.* Lk. 11.32);
- summary of the message of the twelve sent out by Jesus (Mk 6.12);[35]
- Galileans killed by Pilate (Lk. 13.3);

---

[33] 'The cleansing or healing of leprosy involved religious, physiological, and sociological implications. Since leprosy was regarded as defilement and hence made a person ritually unacceptable, it also meant excommunication from social life.' (J.P. Louw and E.A. Nida, *Greek-English Lexicon of the New Testament based on Semantic Domains* [New York: United Bible Societies, 2nd edn, 1989], p. 535).

[34] Further occurrences are in Luke's birth narrative (Lk. 2.22); in Mt. 5.8 where the adjective καθαρός is not associated with ritual purity but rather with the person as a whole; and in Mt. 23.26-27 (Luke's parallel account [Lk. 11.41] shall be discussed below), where it is applied in a polemic way. John's unique reference to καθαρός shall be discussed later.

[35] Matthew and Luke omit this reference in their respective reports on the commissioning of the twelve. Luke's emphasis on conversion as 'being embraced by God's love' might explain why Luke did not write that the disciples 'preached repentance' (Mk 6.12) but that they rather 'proclaimed the Good News and healed many' (Lk. 9.6) (M. Wenk, 'Conversion and Initiation: A Pentecostal View of Biblical and Patristic Perspectives', *Journal of Pentecostal Theology* 17 [2000]), pp. 58-66.

- parables of the lost coin and the lost sheep (Lk. 15.7, 10);[36]
- interpersonal forgiveness and the restoration of community (Lk. 17.3-4).

In Luke 5.32 Jesus' call to repentance is in sharp contrast to the self-righteous religious people and comes close to signifying Jesus' love and concern for the marginalized,[37] similar to Lk. 24.47. It seems that among the evangelists Luke had the greatest interest in μετάνοια ('repentance/conversion') language,[38] perhaps because in his parables of the lost sheep and the lost coin he had given 're-pentance' a slightly different slant.[39]

The evidence runs across all four Gospels that Jesus' vision of a holy community was inclusive and not characterized by fear of associating with the ungodly and sinners, nor by anxiety of becoming defiled because of the neglect of certain food and purity laws. Jesus seems to have shown no interest in ritual purity, including long lists of do's and don't's, nor was he preoccupied in his preaching with moral issues. Neither did his proclamation lack sharpness (Mt. 8.28-

---

[36] Wenk, 'Conversion and Initiation', pp. 63-64.

[37] Whereas the saying is also found in Mark (Mk 2.17), Luke has reworked it: 'It is not the healthy who need a doctor, but the sick. I have not come to call the righteous, but the sinners *to repentance*.' The statement 'to repentance' is Lucan and gives the analogy an interesting twist. In the case of sickness the doctor is to cure a person who cannot cure her/himself. In the same way Jesus is stimulating people to repentance who cannot repent on their own. The emphasis of the parabolic saying clearly falls on what Jesus is doing, and as a result thereof, what people are experiencing. Like a doctor who 'brings healing' to a sick person, Jesus brings repentance to sinners.

[38] Surprisingly he did not follow Matthew and Mark in summarizing Jesus' message by applying such terminology.

[39] The 'passivity' of both the sheep and the coin in repenting has led E.P. Sanders to conclude that the sheep did not repent. Sanders further argues that the Lucan statement about repentance clashes with the original parable of Jesus. The original intent is still reflected in the Matthean version (E.P. Sanders, *The Historical Figure of Jesus* [London: Penguin Books, 1993], p. 232-34, cf. *idem, Jesus and Judaism*, [Philadelphia: Fortress Press, 1985], pp. 106-13; 203-205 where he argues that most passages depicting Jesus as calling for repentance are inauthentic). Concerning the lost sheep, I think Sanders had to come to his conclusion because he did not grasp the Lucan definition of repentance. While Witherup emphasises the passive dimension of conversion, being found (R.D. Witherup, *Conversion in the New Testament* [Collegeville: Liturgical Press, 1994], pp. 47-59), he misses the point of being carried home, being re-united with 'the community'. This last aspect is also true for the third parable; however, precisely in the parable stressing more the active return of the one lost, the reference to the joy in heaven about a sinner who has repented is missing.

29) for it constantly aroused opposition (Mk 2.1-3.35; Lk.14.26; Mt. 10.34-39; Lk. 12.51; Jn 9.13-34).

Regarding holiness and community, we may thus far conclude that all the evangelists present Jesus as accepting all people and assuring them of divine forgiveness. One may argue that his acceptance and assurance of forgiveness demonstrate divine and human acceptance and forgiveness and thereby replaced the purification rites at the temple.[40]

How Jesus' approach to a holy community impacted the New Testament authors shall be analyzed by looking at the three that placed most weight on the Holy Spirit in their writings. This selection makes it possible to perceive more clearly the role of the Spirit in the process of sanctification and community building as they understood it. Special attention shall also be paid to the role of rites in that process in order to elucidate how Jesus' rites of acceptance and forgiveness were 'ritualised' in the early church when he was no longer physically present. Or simply asked: Were Jesus' rites of interaction that communicated divine and human acceptance and forgiveness replaced by rites of representation?

Corpus Paulinum

General Observations on Holiness and Ecclesiology in Paul

Paul frequently addresses his readers or refers to the church as ἅγιοι ('holy ones' or 'saints'), thereby denoting their (new) identity as Christians (Rom. 1.7; 8.27; 12.13; 15.25, 31; 1 Cor. 6.1-2, etc.). Another favoured term of Paul in referring to the believers is 'those being called' (κλητοῖς).[41] In Rom. 1.7 he combines the two definitions by entitling his readers as 'those called to be holy' (κλητοῖς ἁγίοις). Applying such terminology, Paul stresses that God is the one who calls (i.e. Rom. 9.12, 24; 1. Cor. 1.9, etc.) and who sanctifies the believers (Rom. 15.16; 1 Cor. 1.2; 6.11; Eph. 5.26; 1 Thess. 5.23, etc.). On other occasions Paul addresses his readers as 'the

---

[40] According to Gerhardt's differentiation between rituals of representation and of interaction, these would clearly fall in the latter category of rites of interaction (Gerhardt, 'zwei Gesichter', p. 50).

[41] Sometimes qualified with 'by God', or 'by Jesus Christ', or 'to be holy' (Rom. 1.6; 1 Cor. 1.2), and sometimes without any further qualifications (i.e. 1 Cor. 1.24).

sons of God' or the 'children of God' (i.e. Rom. 8.14-17: 2 Cor. 6.18; Gal. 3.26; 4.6-7, etc.). All these definitions are firmly rooted in the Old Testament description of Israel as a people of God[42] and all three connote the idea of separateness; Israel's, and thereby the Church's identity as a people singled out from the rest of the world and thereby especially belonging to God. Thereby it becomes evident that for Paul 'being holy' is foremost a matter of belonging. As will be noted later, the issue of purity or morality is secondary and results from the believers' status of 'belonging to God'. It shall further be argued that according to the writings of Paul it is impossible to be holy, in the sense of belonging to God, without belonging to the community of believers; one cannot be 'with Christ' without being with one's fellow believers.[43]

It comes as no surprise that for Paul the Spirit is associated with the Church's identity as 'holy' (i.e. Rom. 15.16) as well as 'son(s) of God' (i.e. Rom. 8.14-17), for according to Paul the Spirit is both the origin and the 'norm' of the believers' new life (Rom. 8.4-6; 8.4; 1 Corinthians 12–14; Gal. 3.2; etc.).[44] While the Church's identity as a 'holy community' that is called out by God to be son(s) of God marks a certain separation of the Church from the rest of the world, two basic observations are decisive for our further study: 1) Paul does not foster an exclusive understanding of the Church as holy over against the world based on any virtues or moral qualities evidenced in the Church but rather on the inclusive presence of the Spirit in the Church,[45] and 2) it is surprising that Paul does not promote a 'progressive' model of holy within the Church; there are

---

[42] Cf. Holy, Lev. 11.44; called, Gen. 3.9; Isa. 42.6; 43.1; son(s) of God: Isa. 43.6; Jer. 3.19; Wisd. 18.13.

[43] This is not only evidenced in Paul's body-metaphor for the church (1 Corinthians 12), but also in his exhortations in 13.8-14 that he introduces with the call to love. Only thereafter does he summon his readers to put aside the deeds of darkness, described as orgies and drunkenness, sexual immorality, dissension and jealousy. In contrast, they shall put on the armour of light, which Paul does not define in terms of virtues but in terms of love and the knowledge of Christ (2 Cor. 4.6; 6.14), because living in the light is, like being holy, described by the apostle primarily in terms of belonging (1 Thess. 5.5).

[44] The description of the church as 'those being called' is used by Paul only in connection with God (i.e. Rom. 9.12; 1 Cor. 1.9, 1 Thess. 2.12; etc.).

[45] Cf. P. Oakes, 'Made Holy by the Holy Spirit: Holiness and Ecclesiology in Romans' in K.E. Brower and A. Johnson (eds.), *Holiness and Ecclesiology in the New Testament* (Grand Rapids: Eerdmans, 2007), pp. 167-83.

not various degrees of 'being holy' within the Church.[46] Hence, Paul's understanding of the Church as a holy people is both exclusive and inclusive; exclusive in contrast to the rest of the world (2 Cor. 6.14-7.1), inclusive based on the presence of the Spirit in the Church (1 Corinthians 12; 2 Cor. 7.2). Four further observations are important in regard to Paul's inclusive understanding of holiness within the Church:

1. His understanding of the Church as a holy people is not static, for Paul summons his readers frequently to live in accordance with their status as a holy people (1 Thess. 4.3). This is traditionally defined as Paul's indicative-imperative approach to ethics.

2. In his argument for the Church's separation from the world, Paul rarely refers to moral categories, but rather to the indwelling of the Spirit in both the Church and in each believer (Rom. 8.5, 14-21; 1 Cor. 2.12; Gal. 3.3). For Paul, people are not holy because they live morally correct, but rather because the Holy Spirit indwells them, which, as a result thereof, will influence their ethical life.[47] Hence Paul's argument in Galatians 5: The contrast between a sinful and a godly person is not one between an immoral and a moral person, but between a selfish person and one in whom the Spirit of God lives (Gal. 5.16-18) and as a result thereof evidences the fruit of the Spirit.[48]

3. The designation of the Church as 'holy', 'called by God', and 'son(s) of God' builds upon the concept that the characteristics of God are to be the characteristics of his people (Lev. 11.44). This explains Paul's strong emphasis on love (i.e. Rom. 13.8, 10; 1 Corinthians 13; 14.1; 2 Cor. 9.9; 1 Thess. 3.12) and on recon-

---

[46] What Oakes has pointed out for Paul's concept of 'holy' in Romans applies also to the other Epistles: People are either 'holy' or 'not holy', and there are then no varying degrees to it (Oakes, 'Made Holy', p. 177). Winter has argued similarly regarding 1 Cor. 1.2-3.30 that in this section 'holy' refers to the believers' new status in Christ and not to a process of moral change; it designates a rank bestowed to them (B.W. Winter, 'Carnal Conduct and Sanctification in 1 Corinthians' in *Holiness and Ecclesiology in the New Testament*, p. 193.

[47] For a discussion on how the Spirit is to influence the ethical life of the believer, cf. V. Rabens, *The Holy Spirit and Ethics in Paul: Transformation and Empowering for Religious-Ethical Life* (Tübingen: Mohr Siebeck, 2010).

[48] The terms used to define the fruit of the Spirit are all relational ones and define of social interaction/behaviour.

ciliation/forgiveness: The Church is a community of reconciliation and peace (2 Cor. 2.5-11;[49] Eph. 2.11-22; 4.32; Col. 3.13), for these are the characteristics of God (Rom. 5.5, 8; 14.7; 1 Cor. 14.33; 2 Cor. 13.11-13; Phil. 4.7, etc.). Hence, holiness is always a matter of and realized in relationships (cf. Gal. 5.16-26). This is also evidenced in the call 'not to grieve the Spirit', for to grieve the Spirit is to desecrate the community (Eph. 4.17-32).

4. Paul's inclusive understanding of the Church as a 'holy community' is also manifest in his call 'to accept each other' (παρα-λαμβάνω; 1 Cor. 11.23; 15.1-3; Gal. 1.9, 12; Col. 4.17; Phil. 4.9; προσλαμβάνω Rom. 14.1, 3; 15.7). His strong emphasis on mutual acceptance explains why Paul defends at length his action of church discipline in 1 Corinthians 5. But even in this case, the aim of the church's discipline in the 'name of the Lord Jesus' is the salvation of the person's spirit at the day of the Lord (1 Cor. 5.3-5). In light of Paul's inclusive approach to holiness and community, the expulsion of the immoral person from the community seems to be almost contradictory to his call to 'accept each other as Christ has accepted us' (Rom. 15.7). In turn, Paul's final aim of the offender's salvation contradicts any understanding of church discipline that is purely exclusive, for the ultimate aim of 'being turned over to Satan'[50] is not the destruction of the flesh (ὄλεθρον τῆς σαρκός) but the salvation of the spirit.[51] In spite of all uncertainties in understanding this passage, the one thing that is clear—and thereby causes difficul-

---

[49] For holiness as forgiveness and restoration as well as reconciliation, cf. J.A. Adewuya, 'The People of God in a Pluralistic Society: Holiness in 2 Corinthians', in *Holiness and Ecclesiology in the New Testament*, pp. 207-209.

[50] Most likely referring to the 'world' as the sphere of Satan's influence (cf. in G.D. Fee, *The First Epistle to the Corinthians* (NICNT; Grand Rapids: Eerdmans, 1987), p. 209; W. Schrage, *Der erste Brief an die Korinther* (EKK; Zürich: Benzinger Verlag, 1991), I, p. 375.

[51] Although it is disputed what Paul meant here in referring to the πνευμα, it surely does not represent anything like a dualistic view of a person, referring to the soul that 'survives' physical death (cf. the discussion in Fee, *The First Epistle to the Corinthians*, pp. 208-14; Schrage, *Korinther,* vol. I, pp. 369-78). More plausible is Fee's argument that Paul is applying here his typical 'flesh—spirit antithesis', implying that by putting this man outside the Christian community that which was carnal in him should be destroyed so that he may be saved (Fee, *The First Epistle to the Corinthians,* pp. 212-13).

ties in understanding it—is that Paul's aim is the final inclusion of this man into communion with God, and not his exclusion.[52]

Based on the introductory assumptions made on rituals, Paul's theology of holiness and community should be reflected in the two major ecclesial rites the apostle is referring to: baptism and Eucharist.

Baptism, holiness, and community in Paul

For Paul the rite of baptism is associated both with the believer's new life with Christ as well as with the new community of the people of God (Rom. 6.1-14; Gal. 3.26-29). Because of the argument in Romans 6, baptism is often, and almost exclusively, associated with purification and the elimination of sin.[53] However, in Gal. 3.26-29 Paul refers to baptism for the sake of developing his argument that the Church is a new community in which former social, gender, and ethnic barriers are no longer applicable. Hence, baptism cannot be adequately understood as merely an individual's religious rite of initiation (purification of sins), without considering its social implications because in Galatians the reference to baptism serves Paul's ecclesiological argument.

There is an on-going scholarly debate with regard to the aptness of calling baptism 'a rite of passage'.[54] DeMaris has argued that 'Paul's language of participation with Christ's dying and rising does not refer exclusively and unambiguously to the baptismal rite of initiation'—baptism represents just one aspect of Paul's language of participation.[55] Therefore he would rather call baptism a 'boundary-crossing-ritual': 'For rites, past or present, affect not only the subject of the rite but also the broad web of social relations in which the subject is embedded',[56] or as Catherine Bell argues: 'ritual practices are themselves the very production and negotiation of

---

[52] The whole thought that for Paul there is no Eucharist with God without the Eucharist with his people still needs to be tackled in this difficult passage.

[53] 'Most obviously it symbolizes cleansing from sin' (G.R. Beasley-Murray, 'Baptism' in G.F. Hawthorne, R.P. Martin and D.G. Reid (eds.), *Dictionary of Paul and his Letters* (Downers Grove: IVP, 1993), p. 61; cf. U. Wilckens, *Der Brief an die Römer* (EKK; Zürich: Benziger Verlag, 3rd edn, 1993), II, p. 23.

[54] Similarly Strecker, *Liminale Theologie*, pp. 311-13.

[55] DeMaris, *The New Testament and its Ritual World* (London: Routledge, 2008), p. 19.

[56] DeMaris, *The New Testament and its Ritual World*, p. 24.

power relations'.[57] In light of the above discussion on rituals, the questions are: 1) What values and what form of action does Paul perceive to be communicated in the rite of baptism, and 2) do these values and actions relate in any way to his concept of the Church as a holy community?

These questions are best answered by briefly looking at Paul's reference to baptism in Gal. 3.26-29 in order to substantiate his claim for the newness of relationships within the Church: Through faith in Jesus Christ the Galatians all are sons of God (see above); they are in Christ (ὑμεῖς Χριστοῦ) and as such 'seed of Abraham' (Gal. 3.29). This is equal to being clothed with Christ (Gal. 3.27), which in turn implies that the former social, ethnic, and gender categories dividing them are now overcome by their participation in Christ through baptism. Paul's holiness language (sons of God = belonging to God) as well as his reference to the believers 'being in Christ' is made in the context of ecclesial relationships which thereby enlightens his understanding of the Church as a holy community:[58] the rite of baptism creates, so to speak, a new community. At the same time this new and inclusive community 'in Christ' is in stark contrast to the larger world of which it is part, and thereby lives in tension to it;[59] a world that is characterized by social, ethnic, and gender divisions. For Paul baptism signifies the believers' 'being in Christ' and 'being Abraham's seed' (Gal. 3.29), yet this communion with Christ, this belonging to God, cannot be separated from its ecclesial dimension,[60] for to be in Christ implies to live in an inclusive community as Christ initiated a new community of acceptance, reconciliation, and peace. The purification of sins, signified with baptism, includes more than simply the washing away of an indi-

---

[57] Cathrine Bell, *Ritual Theory, Ritual Practice* (New York: Oxford University Press, 1992), p. 196.

[58] As noted above, the reference to 'sons of God' is holiness language and therefore it is appropriate to argue that Gal. 3.26-28 is part of Paul's vision of the church as a holy community.

[59] For a discussion that rites engender an idealized situation that may not always match with reality, and thereby stand in tension with it, see DeMaris, *The New Testament and its Ritual World*, pp. 30-31.

[60] While Strecker also emphasises that in Gal. 3.26-29 baptism is of social and ecclesial importance, he does not highlight clearly enough that the soteriological and the social ecclesisal aspect of the rite are interdependent (Strecker, *Liminale Theologie*, pp. 354-58).

vidual's immorality; it includes the washing away of social, gender, and ethnic barriers that separate people from each other; it thereby creates a community of acceptance, love, forgiveness, peace, and reconciliation. Sin is not merely defined in moral but in social categories.[61] At the heart of Paul's theology of holiness is the idea of belonging to God and as a result thereof his understanding of the Church as a renewed community.[62] And baptism is the rite that enacts both of these aspects.[63] In conclusion we may say that baptism as a ritual 'is a means of performing the way things ought to be in conscious tension to the way things are';[64] it signifies a departure from former social identity to a new communal identity which is 'in Christ', or 'with Christ' and thus holy, belonging to God; it is a rite of interaction.[65]

---

[61] Further research needs to be done on Paul's understanding of sin in Romans 6, for in this passage he does not apply moral categories either for defining sin, but rather defines it more in terms of 'belonging'.

[62] Robeck and Sandige have demonstrated the individual tendencies in mainly North American Pentecostal theologies of baptism and have called for a theology of baptism that is more considered of the 'koinonia dimension' of the rite: 'We are required to die to self (Gal. 2:20) and live as sisters and brothers together, as children of the reign of God. The implications of this are both social and ethical. At each baptism the question must be asked again: Do we accept them as our brothers and sisters? Are we willing to be responsible for them?' (C.M. Robeck and J.L. Sandige, 'The Ecclesiology of Koinōnia and Baptism: A Pentecostal Prerspective', *Journal of Ecumenical Studies* 27.3 [1990], p. 528).

[63] In 1 Cor. 12.12-13 Paul argues also for he unity of the church by applying baptismal language. However, there is some debate as how to understand his reference to 'having been baptized by the Spirit'; some take it as a reference to water baptism, some more in a metaphorical sense. For an overview of the discussion, cf. Fee, who then argues for a metaphorical understanding of the expression, *The First Epistle to the Corinthians,* pp. 603-606; similarly, W. Schrage, *Der erste Brief an die Korinther,* III, pp. 217-18.

[64] J.Z. Smith, *To take Place: Toward Theory in Ritual* (CSHJ; Chicago: University of Chicago Press, 1987), p. 109.

[65] Dale Coulter has suggested that Pentecostals, Catholics, and Methodists share a common soteriological substructure that would allow these three traditions to have more appreciation—if not even recognition—of each other's rite of baptism (D.M. Coulter, 'Baptism, Conversion and Grace: Reflections on the "Underlying Realities" between Pentecostals, Methodists, and Catholics', *Pneuma,* 31 (2009), pp. 189-212. His whole and well-taken argument builds, however, entirely on baptism as a rite of initiation and neglects the aspect of baptism as a rite to create a renewed and inclusive community. This whole aspect could be of vital importance in the ecumenical dialogue on baptism.

Eucharist, Holiness, and Community in Paul[66]

The idea of community is at the centre of Paul's concern in 1 Cor. 11.17-34, hence his opening statement: 'In the first place, I hear that when you come together as a church, there are divisions among you' (1 Cor. 11.18). Only after having set the agenda, divisions within the Church, he now addresses the Corinthians' Eucharist services and states right at the beginning what he thinks thereof: 'When you come together, *it is not* the Lord's supper you eat, for as you eat, each of you goes ahead without waiting for anybody else' (1 Cor. 11.20-21a).

Paul's statement that whatever the Corinthians may be doing during their meetings does not qualify as celebrating the Lord's Supper, enhances Gruenwald's argument that a ritual is successfully done only when the rules and the conditions to perform the rite are followed.[67] Concerning the Lord's Supper Paul is explicit about what cannot be done in any other way without nullifying the rite: celebrating the Lord's Supper as the unified body of Christ in which each part is considered of the other one.[68] In Paul's theology the rite of Eucharist and the call for unity are interdependent.[69]

It is only after having defined the parameters for the rite of the Eucharist that Paul gives some formal instructions on how they should proceed when they are all together. The apostle then con-

---

[66] The discussion of Paul's reference to the Eucharist in 1 Cor. 11.17-34 builds upon Theissen's observation that this ritual comprises both aspects found in ritual sacrifices: The exclusion of what threatens a community (guilt offering) as well as a meal representing a renewed community. He further argues that it is quite possible that the Eucharist as commemorating the death of Jesus was celebrated only once a year in the church and served as a way to violate the taboo of eating and drinking blood and 'human flesh', hence, the Eucharist was both celebrated to commemorate the death of Jesus, as well as an eschatological meal of joy, centring on the idea of a reconciled community (Theissen, *Erleben und Verhalten*, pp. 366-84; *idem*, 'Ritual Dynamik und Tabuverletzung im Abendmahl' in D. Harth and G.J. Schenk (eds.), *Ritualdynamik. Kulturübergreifende Studien zur Theorie und Geschichte rituellen Handels* (Heidelberg, Synchron Publisher, 2004), pp. 275-90).

[67] Gruenwald, *Rituals*, p. 10-14.

[68] Verses 21-22 seem to indicate that in the Corinthian church there were not only divisions among various groups centring on their favoured apostle (1 Cor. 1.12), but also among people from various social strata within society.

[69] Regardless of how one understands v. 21 exactly, Paul obviously addresses a conflict between the wealthier and the poorer members of the Corinthian church. For a discussion of the various interpretations of v. 21, see Fee, *The First Epistle to the Corinthians*, pp. 540-41.

cludes his instruction concerning the Eucharist by once more underlying its social inclusiveness: 'So then, my brothers, when you come together to eat, wait for each other' (1 Cor. 11.33). For Paul it is also clear that everyone who eats or drinks unworthily, which means not recognising the community character of the Church, will bring judgement upon himself or herself (1 Cor. 11.28-33). With regard to Pauline ecclesiology it is noteworthy that the exclusive aspect of the Church (judgement) is precisely stressed when its inclusive character is violated. And when its inclusive character is violated, the rite celebrated by the Church no longer qualifies as the Eucharist.

Applying Gerhard's concept of rites of interaction or of representation, the Eucharist as understood by Paul, is a rite of interaction and creates a community of shared interest and reflects its values and attitudes—in this case the equality and worth of every individual believer, regardless of his or her social status:[70] 'Whatever is involved in "the Lord's Supper, … involves a process that is intended to bring about a ritual transformation of a group of believers into a community of believers"'.[71]

At the end of this section we conclude that both baptism and the Eucharist are directly related to Paul's ecclesiology and theology of holiness. The initial overcoming of social, ethnic, and gender barriers in baptism is constantly re-actualised in the Church's celebration of the Eucharist.[72] Although Paul clearly addresses issues of immorality within the churches and frequently exhorts his readers to live a holy life, his inclusive understanding of the Church is never at stake in these discussions. While sin and immorality are real problems for Paul, it is separation and divisions that actually damage the Church and grieve the Holy Spirit (cf. Rom. 14.1–15.13; Eph. 4.30). According to Paul the Church as a holy community is more than the absence of sin and immorality, it is the presence of the Spirit, it is unification with Christ and thus it is the presence of peace, mutual acceptance, and reconciliation among those that are 'with Christ'.

---

[70] Gerhardt, 'Zwei Gesichter', pp. 52-68.

[71] Gruenewald, *Rituals,* p. 249.

[72] Cf. Strecker, *Liminale Theologie*, p. 450.

Luke–Acts

The Announcement of John's Ministry in Luke 1.16-17

Luke, probably more than any other Gospel writer, has emphasised Jesus' inclusive approach to holiness and community. In chapter 1 he narrates the episode of the angel's announcement to Zechariah about the birth of his son, who

> ... will be filled with the Holy Spirit even from birth. Many of the people of Israel will he bring back (ἐπιστρέψει 'turn') to the Lord their God. And he will go on before the Lord, in the spirit and power of Elijah, to turn (ἐπιστρέψαι) the hearts of the fathers to their children and [to turn] the disobedient to the wisdom of the righteous—to make ready a people prepared for the Lord (Lk. 1.15-17).

John's future ministry, introduced with 'he will turn (ἐπιστρέψει) many of the people of Israel to God',[73] is defined in a twofold way: to turn the hearts of the fathers to the sons and the disobedient to the wisdom of the righteous. This whole process of turning is finally equated with 'making ready a people prepared for the Lord'. Hence, to turn many to God (bring them back to God) is equated with to make them prepared for the Lord, and this whole process is defined as a twofold reconciliation; reconciliation among people that are ostracized from each other, specified as fathers who turn to their sons,[74] and reconciliation of those that are alienated from God by turning to the wisdom of the righteous. The statement about the fathers turning to their sons is a partial quote from Mal. 4.6, omitting the second part of Malachi, 'and the hearts of the children to their fathers; or else I will come and strike the land with a curse'. Thereby Luke may indicate that he perceives the far greater problem in the hearts of the fathers not turning to their sons, than in the sons not turning their hearts to the fathers.

---

[73] The two well-known Lukan parables of the lost coin and the lost sheep (Lk. 15.1-10) may reflect this aspect of the restoration of Israel; they both were found and brought back into the Eucharist. The last parable, Lk. 15.11-31 differs from the previous ones in that there is no reference to the joy in heaven about a sinner who repents. Cf. M. Wenk, 'Conversion and Initiation', pp. 58-66.

[74] Luke's parable of the father and his two sons (15.11-31), waiting for and staying with them, may serve as a positive example for all fathers in their relationship with run away and heart hardened children.

Luke later identifies the fathers, together with the scribes and Pharisees, as those who have rejected God's prophets and message (6.23, 26, 11.47-48). Therefore it may be appropriate to conclude that Lk. 1.17 has the religious leaders in view. There is also a reference to the 'sons' (τέκνα) in the Baptist's conflict with the religious leaders: 'Do not say that we have Abraham as our father. For I tell you that out of these stones God can raise up children for Abraham' (Lk. 3.8). While Luke shares this saying with Matthew, only he narrates the episode of the crowd,[75] the tax collectors, and the soldiers responding positively to John's proclamation. One of these 'raised up children of Abraham' is Zacchaeus, who is explicitly identified as son (υἱός) of Abraham (Lk. 19.9). Therefore, it may be best to assume that a people prepared for the Lord (Lk. 1.16-17) is one in which the religious leaders will turn towards those that are marginalised and ignored within the community of faith.[76]

The second part of defining John's ministry, obedience to God, is not defined in legal but in relational terms and described as 'turning to the wisdom of the righteous'.[77] If one understands, as Bovon does, the 'righteous ones' as the faithful ones who were waiting for God,[78] the entire process of 'turning towards God' is even more community of faith oriented: the religious leaders shall turn towards

---

[75] Luke uses the term 'crowd' (ὄχλοι) mainly to refer to the poor masses that are neither known as particularly religious nor as completely marginalised within society (cf. Lk. 4.42; 5.1-3; 23.48, etc.). They are the people in need, for in 6.19 they are those who came to touch Jesus. One may almost assume that the crowd is in contrast to the religious leaders, for immediately after having been touched by these people, Luke lets Jesus begin to pronounce the blessings and the woes (6.20-26).

[76] J. Green notes that in Lk. 1.16-17 the *fathers* are in the company of the disobedient, and the *children* in the company of the righteous (J. Green, *The Gospel of Luke* [NICNT; Grand Rapids: Eerdmans, 1997], pp. 76-77). While it is correct that the *fathers* play an ambivalent role throughout Luke's Gospel, he misses the point that in John's proclamation (Lk. 3.1-20) the children too are called to repent. It seems better to understand the two statements in Lk. 1.16-17 simply as the two sides of reconciliation and not as strict parallelisms.

[77] Green argues that this unusual terminology may allude to Mal. 2.6 as well as to the wisdom tradition in which wisdom is identified with Torah obedience (Green, *Luke*, p. 77).

[78] F. Bovon, *Das Evangelium nach Lukas* (EKK; Zürich: Benzinger Verlag, 1989), I, p. 58. Bovon's reading of 'the righteous' as those waiting for God is also plausible 'from within the Lukan narrative', for in Lk. 2.25 Simeon is identified as devout and righteous, a man who was waiting for the consolation of Israel.

those they marginalize and the disobedient shall turn towards the wisdom of those that were faithfully waiting for God, for there is wisdom in waiting for the 'consolation of Israel' (Lk. 2.25).

Thus, Luke spells out his understanding of a 'sanctified community' right at the beginning of his Gospel: it is an inclusive community that embraces both the obedience to God and each other.

John's call to Repentance in Luke 3.10-14

Later in his Gospel, Luke clearly defines the Baptist's ministry as evolving around the issues of repentance and purification,[79] which further enlightens Luke's understanding of holiness and community. He is the only Gospel writer to describe the various responses to John's call proclamation. The reactions of three particular groups are singled out: the crowd, the tax collectors, and the soldiers. Each group responds with the typical Lukan terminology towards the proclamation of repentance: what shall we do? (cf. Acts 2.37; 16.29). The Baptist's answers to each group define Luke's understanding of repenting:

- Those who have two tunics shall share with those who have none, likewise should those who have food shall share with those who have none.
- The tax collectors should not misuse their position to enrich themselves in an unjust manner.
- The soldiers should not abuse their power nor should they accuse people falsely to enrich themselves.

Each answer serves as a definition of what it means to repent, or, what is implied in turning towards God: a renewed form of social behaviour. John's 'baptism of repentance and forgiveness of sins' (Lk. 3.3) will lead to a community where those who have will share with those who do not,[80] and those who are in positions of power will not abuse it for their own benefit and at the expense of others.

---

[79] I have argued elsewhere that Luke depicts the Baptist's ministry as the fulfilment of the angel's announcement: M. Wenk, *Community Forming Power: The Socio-Ethical Role of the Spirit in Luke-Acts* (JPTSup 19; Sheffield: Sheffield Academic Press, 2000), pp. 175-82.

[80] Cf. the account of the life of the first church in Jerusalem, Acts 2.42-47, as well as Luke's characterization of Barnabas as a man full of the Spirit and full of faith (Acts 11.24), who is first introduced into the narrative when he sold his property in order to help supporting those who were needy among the church (Acts 4.32-37)

Whereas in many contemporary Pentecostal circles repentance is described in terms of a person's 'becoming right with God' and is also often associated with emotions of sorrow for one's guilt, in this text Luke outlines repentance exclusively in terms of renewed social interactions (cf. Lk. 19.8).

Table Fellowship, the Rite of an Inclusive Community of Faith in Luke-Acts

At the heart of Luke's inclusive understanding of the Church and holiness is the motive of table fellowship. This, more than anything else, has received a lot of attention in the scholarly discussion and shall, therefore, not be repeated here at length. Throughout the Gospel of Luke and the book of Acts Jesus and his disciples are said to have had table fellowship with sinners, gentiles, and other people that were marginalised from society. The issue of holiness and purity is almost omnipresent in all these passages (cf. Lk. 5.27-39; 11.37-54; 19.1-10; Acts 10.1-11.18).[81] Beyond that, the book of Acts carefully underlines the inclusive character of the people of God and the summary in Acts 2.42-47 depicts a unity among people of the early church that goes beyond the Greek understanding of friendship.[82] Throughout Luke-Acts, to enjoy table-fellowship with Jesus or his disciples is the rite *par excellence* to demonstrate the inclusive character of the community of Christians as well as the rite that re-defines the contemporary Jewish definition of purity.

In the two passages that are of pivotal significance in Acts (Acts 2.38-41; 10.47-48, but also 16.15, 33-34), the rite of table fellowship is found in proximity to baptism, the other rite that demonstrates participation in the promise of God. In one instance baptism is referred to as the sole rite to demonstrate the inclusion into the community of faith (Acts 8.36-38),[83] and the passage is of special

---

[81] For a detailed discussion of holiness, ecclesiology, and the meals in Luke's Gospel, see R.P. Thompson, 'Gathered at the Table: Holiness and Ecclesiology in the Gospel of Luke' in *Holiness and Ecclesiology in the New Testament*, pp. 76-94.

[82] A.C. Mitchell, 'The Social Function of Friendship in Acts 2.44-47 and 4.32-38', *Journal of Biblical Literature* 111 (1992), pp. 255-72; B.J. Capper, 'Reciprocity and the Ethics of Acts', *The Book of Acts in its First Century Setting* (Carlisle: Paternoster Press, 1993), VI, pp. 76-106.

[83] Ananias' table fellowship with Saul (most likely implied in Acts 9.19) was no problem with regard to the Jewish purity regulations; hence the emphasis on his baptism (Acts 8.18). Saul's difficult process of being accepted into the Christian community is narrated in Acts 8.20-31.

interest, since it is the only account in Acts where the initiative to baptism comes from the newly converted, which may be a way to demonstrate Philip's reluctance towards the full inclusion of a gentile eunuch into the Christian community.[84]

According to Luke, what made the new community most exclusive in regard to its environment was precisely its inclusive character (Lk. 19.1-10; Acts 2.42-47), demonstrated in the rites of table fellowship and baptism. And since this inclusive community was of pneumatic origin,[85] people 'full of faith and of the Holy Spirit' (Acts 6.5; 11.24; Stephen and Barnabas) were people that cared for the poor (Acts 6.1-7); forgave those who killed them (Acts 7.59); shared their possessions with those who had none (Acts 4.36); helped those finding their way into the community that were confronted with rejection (Acts 8.26-28); were mediating between churches that were endangered to part ways (Acts 11.22); and finally gave those who failed a second chance (Acts 15.36-39).[86] In his two volumes Luke has defiantly redefined purity and what it means to be the people of God.

The Johannine Writings[87]

Although the fourth Gospel shares with the Synoptics Jesus' inclusive approach to the new people of God (Jn 4.1-42; 12.20-23), its vision of a holy community is in some sense unique. Part of this uniqueness is the absence of metanoia-language[88] on the one hand

---

[84] For a more detailed discussion, cf. Wenk, *Community forming Power*, pp. 294-98; Wenk, 'Reconciliation and the Spirit in Acts', pp. 17-33.

[85] For the argument that this new and inclusive community is of pneumatic origin, cf. Wenk, *Community Forming Power*, pp. 257-308; Wenk, 'Community Forming Power: Reconciliation and the Spirit in Acts', *Journal of European Pentecostal Theological Association* 19 (1999), pp. 17-33.

[86] Although Barnabas is afterwards not mentioned anymore in the book of Acts, the New Testament canon proves him right in his support Mark (2 Tim. 4.11). Most likely our first Gospel goes back to this Mark that was given a second chance by Barnabas.

[87] The following observations shall be limited to the Fourth Gospel and the three epistles.

[88] Jesus' call to the adulteress woman in Jn 8.11 comes probably closest to a call for repentance. However, preceding it is Jesus' act of forgiveness (not condemning her) towards this woman that neither sought the closeness to Jesus nor forgiveness herself.

and its apparent ethical dualism on the other hand.[89] This basic observation raises some questions because for many Pentecostals the two are almost interdependent: an explicit ethical dualism seems to be the very foundation for the call to repent. In order to address this tension, I shall first look at the footwashing pericope (Jn 13.1-17) and at Jn 15.1-4, before elucidating the role of the Spirit in John's understanding of a 'holy community'. The main focus will be on purity and the forgiveness of sins and less on sanctification as consecration for ministry.[90]

Footwashing as a Rite of Assurance and Purity

In the footwashing pericope (Jn 13.1-17) the disciples are assured that they are clean (13.10), but no word is said about them seeking to be cleansed or even repenting; their state of being clean is simply ascribed to them by the presence of Jesus. Therefore one may conclude that footwashing 'serves as a sign of continued fellowship with Jesus and additional cleansing in the disciples' lives'.[91] It clearly represents a rite of interaction, focusing on the sanctity of a person; her or his dignity shall be preserved.[92] It is a rite to assure each other cleanness in the presence of God (cf. 1 Jn 2.1-2).

In the parabolic saying of Jn 15.1-4 the issues of bearing fruit, being cleansed and remaining in Jesus are interrelated. While Schrage correctly points out that the lack of fruit becomes the very reason for any branch to be cut off (cf. 15.6), and that the whole passage represents the dialectic of 'indicative and imperative',[93] he does not fully come to terms with the dynamic of the passage. Verses 1-3 are all indicative statements and the saying that 'every

---

[89] Interestingly enough, while often referring to the 'commandments' in the plural (Jn 10.18, 11.57, etc.), John actually only shows interest in the brotherly love, which in turn is predominantly Christologically sustained (Jn 13.34, 15.9-14; 17.23).

[90] Bauckham has argued convincingly that one needs to differentiate in the Johannine writings between purity and consecration; purity referring to the past sins and consecration to the service to God (R. Bauckham, 'The Holiness of Jesus and His Disciples in the Gospel of John' in *Holiness and Ecclesiology in the New Testament*, pp. 95-113).

[91] J.C. Thomas, *Footwashing in John 13 and the Johannine Community* (JSNTSup 61; Sheffield: JSOT Press, 1991), p. 116. Similarly Bauckham, 'Holiness of Jesus', p. 98.

[92] Gerhardt, 'Zwei Gesichter', pp. 52-68.

[93] Schrage, *Ethik*, p. 305,

branch that does bear fruit[94] he trims clean (καθαίρει)' (15.2) is immediately afterwards differentiated by the assurance: 'You are already clean because of the word I have spoken to you'. The disciples (readers) are not clean because of their repentance or their moral lifestyle but simply based on the word spoken to them. In the following imperative one would expect a call to bear fruit; however, what follows is the call to remain in Jesus (15.4). This imperative is emphatically underscored in the following double metaphorical saying of the inability to bear fruit without remaining in Jesus. Hence, the main paranetic concern of the passage is to emphasise the necessity of remaining in Jesus. Being clean and bearing fruit are the natural consequences thereof and, to some degree, do not have to worry the disciples.

John 15.1-4 confirms Theissen's assessment, that the fourth evangelist is more pessimistic about human abilities in regard to salvation and purity; all initiative comes from God;[95] forgiveness and cleanness are given to the disciples. This does, however, not discharge those cleansed by the word from 'the imperative': 'Stop sinning or something worse may happen to you' (Jn. 5.14). As reluctant as the author is about human ability with regard to establish relationship with God, as optimistic is he about God's initiative and gift: The disciples are clean simply because of the word spoken to them (15.1-4; cf. 8.1-11). In light of this assurance, the preceding warning about cut off branches is, at least for the disciples, almost an impossible possibility.

The fourth evangelist may have a pessimistic view with regard to humanity's capacity to take the initiative in the divine-human relationship but he paints a very bright picture of God (Jn 1.7-9) in whose presence there is an overflow of grace (Jn 1.16).[96] Both Jesus and later his disciples are to assure each other of this continuous overflow in the rite of footwashing. Footwashing thus creates a community of people that are equally clean because their purity is

---

[94] For a discussion of 'fruit' as keeping the law and doing good works, cf. H. Sahlin, 'Die Früchte der Umkehr: Die ethische Verkündigung Johannes des Täufers nach Lk. 3:10-14', *Studia theologia* 1 (1947), pp. 54-68; Petra von Gemünden, 'L'Arbre et son Fruit', *Etudes théologiques et religieuses* 69 (1994), pp. 315-28.

[95] Theissen, *Erleben und Verhalten,* pp. 72-75.

[96] In light of this emphasis on the abundance of God's grace and light, it is best to understand καταλαμβάνω in Jn 1.5 as 'overcoming'.

not defined in moral terms but in their common encounter with Jesus through the rite performed.[97] The mere rite further assumes that the disciples need continuously to be assured of Jesus' continual cleansing presence; being defiled by sinning after baptism was an issue in the Johannine community which he addressed both with the 'imperative' (Jn 5.14) as well as with the rite of assurance (Jn. 13.1-17). The prominence in his writings seems to fall on the latter and thereby his emphasis on the community of faith as a purified people always remained inclusive.

The Role of the Spirit

Although the Johannine writings represent a pneumatological wealth, the Spirit is not closely linked with the issue of purity and community. This may have to do with the fact that John's ethic is predominantly Christologically motivated; the Spirit will reveal Christ, remind the disciples of all that Jesus taught (Jn 14.15-31, cf. 1 Jn 2.15, 17, 26-27), and enable them to continue the ministry of Christ (Jn 20.21-23).

In this programmatic passage (Jn 20.21-23) the author ties all of the Gospel's main themes together: as the word spoken by Jesus cleansed the disciples, their word spoken as people who have received the Spirit[98] as the continuing presence of Jesus in their lives, will forgive sins—or withhold the forgiveness.[99] John's community of those that are clean truly is christocentric. The word spoken by Jesus cleansed the disciples (Jn 15.3); faith in Jesus who became flesh will overcome this world (1 Jn 5.1-12); and the word spoken through the community that has received the Spirit will assure peo-

---

[97] There is no doubt that John understands the community of believers to live in sharp contrast and distance to the world (Jn 15.19; 17.14-16; 1 Jn 2.15-17) which they will overcome (1 Jn 5.4). In 1 Jn 5.1-12 they are, surprisingly, not summoned to overcome the world but they are assured that they do so. By their mere faith in Jesus, the God who became human, the community of disciples is to overcome a world that has become inhuman. The entire passage is again characterised by a strong dualism—but there are no imperatives, only indicatives.

[98] For the argument that the reference to the Spirit is to guarantee that the words spoken by a person are actually God's words, cf. Wenk, *Community forming Power*, pp. 120-48.

[99] It seems to be best to read the participle of ἀφίημι in Jn. 20.23 as a perfect participle; both participles (ἀφέωνται and κεκράτηνται) implying that through the Spirit the disciples speak what has already been spoken by God (cf. Jn 8.26; 16.13-15); they assure their audience of divine forgiveness—or the lack thereof.

ple of their forgiveness—or the lack thereof. In regard to the community it means that the purified community always is a consecrated community[100] that continues to speak 'the word' which causes people to be 'clean'.[101]

The Johannine writings reflect a strong—also ethical—dualism, but its contrast is never one of 'moral vs. immoral' but of darkness vs. light in which the light will effect its purpose of cleansing, forgiving and overcoming a world that is inhuman because of its greed (1 Jn 2.17) and lack of love (1 Jn 2.7-11; 3.1-3). According to John a holy community is clean because of the word spoken by Christ, and it is consecrated by the Spirit to speak the word it heard from Christ to this world.

Summary and Conclusion

The history of the Church in general and of Pentecostalism in particular shows that the emphasis on holiness and purity has the potential both to encourage the rise of a healing community as well as to cause separation which may at times foster an individual's impression of exclusive elitism. A careful look at the New Testament may help to find ways to emphasise holiness (and the imperative related to it) and at the same time have an inclusive ecclesiology. This inclusive understanding, however, demands that holiness and purity is not defined in terms of virtues and issues of morality, but primarily in categories of divine acceptance of all people (Paul's παραλαμβάνω language; Luke's emphasis on shared meals and John's assurance of being clean through the word)—without downplaying the imperative aspect of it either. This acceptance is enacted in the Church's rites (baptism, Eucharist, footwashing or ecclesial meals).

Further, for all three, Paul, Luke, and John, the presence of the Spirit in the Church is essential for its understanding as a holy community, a people belonging to God that reflects his character for this world.

---

[100] Cf. Bauckham, 'Holiness of Jesus', pp. 95-113.

[101] John 16.4-15 indicates that rejecting Jesus and his word spoken (also through the disciples) makes it impossible to become clean, for the sin of this world is that it does not believe 'the incarnated word' of God. The centre of Jn 15.4-15 (the sin of this world) is Christological argument and not a moral one.

For Paul the Church as a holy community represents an alternative reality that by its inclusiveness is in sharp contrast to the rest of society. For Luke the Church is a holy community because it embraces those that are marginalised both by the Jewish religious leaders of his time and by society in general, and for John the Church is holy, consecrated to speak the word of forgiveness and assuring each other of ones cleanness in the presence of God.

This brief survey of the New Testament and its ecclesiology as it relates to a theology of holiness raises some issues:

1. For all three authors, as for Jesus, the Church lives in sharp contrast to the world. But this contrast is its very inclusiveness by which social, ethnic, and gender barriers are overcome. Whenever these barriers find their way back into the Church, the world has infiltrated it.[102] Hence issues like racism, social prejudices or injustice, and limitations placed on people based on their gender, ethnic, or social background are more 'worldly' than the reading of certain books, or wearing certain clothes.

2. Sin and immorality are clearly addressed by all New Testament authors. However, the Church's status as a holy community never is defined on the presence or absence of such issues but on the presence of the Spirit in its midst. This raises the question how to address sin, brokenness and failure in the Church, a) without violating its inclusive character and b) without endorsing a cheap grace? The rite of footwashing may help us in this regard more than anything else.

3. Any form of the Eucharist and baptism,[103] stressing mainly an individual's interaction with God, does not do justice to the rites as they are presented in the New Testament and thus do not qualify as the Eucharist or baptism. Any celebration of these rites of interaction needs to reflect the inclusive character of the Church.[104]

---

[102] It is almost tragic when division comes into the church by way of separating on lists of do's and don't's, as was often the case in Pentecostalism.

[103] This is less possible in footwashing for it always needs at least two people.

[104] For a discussion of both the ecumenical as well as the social and ethical implications of a theology of baptism cf. Robeck and Sandige, 'Ecclesiology, Koinõnia, Baptism', pp. 526-29.

4. Footwashing, the Lord's Supper, and baptism properly celebrated may enhance the Church's understanding as an inclusive, holy community that is to assure each other of divine and humane acceptance. By the very fact that these rites assure the participants of divine acceptance and cleansing, cheap grace is ruled out. For if there is no sin, there is no need to assure each other of divine forgiveness and cleansing.

5. Further work needs also to be done on a 'theology of failure and brokenness' as well as on grace. This is especially important for Pentecostals with their emphasis on holiness and perfection.

6. The issue of the interaction between divine and human agency in the sanctification process still needs further research.[105]

7. There is no greater gift that the Church can give to the world than being a holy community,[106] for such an inclusive people will bring healing to a world that suffers from divisions, conflicts and envy among ethnic, gender, and social groups, as well as among families or in the work place.

---

[105] For a good introduction to this topic, cf. J.G. Samra, *Being Conformed to Christ in Community: A Study of Maturity, Maturation and the local Chruch in the undisputed Pauline Epistles* (JSNTSup 320; London: T & T Clark, 2006); J.M.G. Barcley and S.J. Gathercole, *Divine and Human Agency in Paul and his Cultural Environment* (London, T & T Clark, 2007); Rabens, *Holy Spirit and Ethics in Paul.*

[106] For the argument that discipleship as well as the church's experience of God's restoring power is its light for the world, cf. M. Wenk, 'Light: A Pentecostal Reading of a Biblical Metaphor', *Journal of the European Penetcostal Theological Association* 26.2 (2006), pp. 168-83.

PART FOUR

THE PENTECOSTAL CHURCH AS EMPOWERED COMMUNITY

6

JESUS AS SPIRIT-BAPTIZER: ITS SIGNIFICANCE FOR PENTECOSTAL ECCLESIOLOGY

SIMON CHAN[*]

Although I have been tasked to present a paper on the subject of 'the empowered community' under the third aspect of the fivefold gospel, I would like to expand the frame of reference of Spirit-baptism beyond that of power. I agree with Frank Macchia that Spirit-baptism should be considered 'the crown jewel of Pentecostal distinctives'. It is not just one of the five elements of the gospel but the one through which we could make sense of all the others.

I believe that traditional Pentecostals have an implicit grasp of this truth when they identified Spirit-baptism with the Pentecost Event of Acts 2 and made it their distinctive experience. Spirit-baptism was the basis for their claim to have the 'full gospel'. The problem with Pentecostals is that they have hitherto been unable to justify that claim theologically. The traditional explanation that Spirit-baptism is the second work of grace 'distinct from and sub-sequent to the new birth' has been subject to quite justified criti-cisms from evangelicals and even some fellow-Pentecostals. I will argue that Spirit-baptism is far more central to Pentecostal faith and experience than Pentecostals themselves realize, and that it is from its definitive character that a truly Pentecostal ecclesiology could emerge. Further, if we examine the shape of Pentecostal spirituality, we discover that its main features are quite consistent with such an ecclesiology.

---

[*] Simon Chan (PhD, Cambridge University) is Earnest Lau Professor of Sys-tematic Theology at Trinity Theological College in Singapore.

In this paper I will attempt to do three things: First, I will show that Pentecostal ecclesiology needs to be located within the Trinitarian economy. Second, I will show that the distinctive Pentecostal spirituality involving the personal presence of the Holy Spirit is in the main faithful to such an ecclesiology. Finally, I will show, but only briefly, that some of the perennial problems found in Pentecostalism could be better dealt with if Pentecostal spirituality is interfaced with a Trinitarian Pentecostal ecclesiology.

I. The Church and the Trinitarian Narrative

According to Nikos Nissiotis Orthodox theology is essentially 'a commentary on the Trinitarian God'.[1] What he says of the nature of Orthodox theology could be said of any good theology. This is especially true of ecclesiology. The doctrine of the Church cannot be properly understood except in relation to the story of the triune God. It grows directly out of the Trinitarian narrative. The revelation of the triune God in the NT follows a basic story line which could be told in terms of 'two sendings' beginning with the sending of the Son into the world and culminating in the sending of the Holy Spirit *to the Church*. We have a succinct summary of it in Gal 4.4-6.

> [4]But when the time had fully come, *God sent his Son*, born of a woman, born under law, [5]to redeem those under law, that we might receive the full rights of sons. [6]Because you are sons, *God sent the Spirit* of his Son into our hearts, the Spirit who calls out, 'Abba, Father.'

But to cut the long story short, I will focus only on the second sending, the coming of the Holy Spirit. Although the Spirit comes from the Father, he was sent in Jesus' name. What is unique about the second sending is the special relationship that the Holy Spirit bears to Jesus. Jesus is the Spirit-baptizer. This is the concerted testimony of Scripture. Of all the New Testament references to the identity of Jesus, his identity as Spirit-baptizer is perhaps the most widely attested (Mt. 3.11-12; Mk 1.8; Lk. 3.6; Jn 1.26-27, 33; Acts

---

[1] Nikos Nissiotis, 'Interpreting Orthodoxy: The communication of some Eastern Orthodox Categories to Students of Western Church Traditions', *Ecumenical Review* 14.1 (Oct 1961), p. 7.

1.5; 11.16). It was this fact, more than any other that led the Church to a full-orbed Trinitarian doctrine. Its development could be briefly traced as follows. In the OT the outpouring of God's Spirit as the sign of the messianic age is seen as the direct work of Yahweh (Acts 2.17 = Joel 2.28 cf. Ezek. 36.26, 27; 37.14; 39.29). But OT scholars tell us that the Spirit of Yahweh does not refer to a separate identity but to Yahweh in action. We have as yet no clear 'hypostasis' of the Spirit.[2] In the NT Jesus himself makes the claim to send the Spirit from the Father (Lk. 24.49; Jn 15.26).

[49]I am going to send you what my Father has promised; but stay in the city until you have been clothed with power from on high.

[26]When the Counselor comes, whom I will send to you from the Father, the Spirit of truth who goes out from the Father, he will testify about me.

This claim puts him in the position of Yahweh, but unlike the other claims to divinity, this one requires revising the OT identification of the Spirit with Yahweh himself, otherwise Jesus would be seen as 'lord' over the Father. This juxtaposing of God to Jesus as Spirit-baptizer makes it necessary for the Spirit to be differentiated from the Father.[3] In other words, it is primarily in relation to Jesus as Spirit-baptizer that the Spirit is distinguished as the third identity and the full Trinitarian doctrine is revealed for the very first time. Spirit baptism could be said to constitute the dénouement of the Trinitarian narrative. Robert Jenson in his own idiosyncratic way, captures this truth accurately: 'The divine beginning at which the relations of origin focus is acknowledged as the Father's Archimedean standpoint. Equally, the divine *goal* at which relations of *fulfillment* focus should be acknowledged as the Spirit's Archimedean standpoint....'[4] The claim of the early Pentecostals in equating their experience of Spirit-baptism with the 'the full gospel', therefore, contains perhaps more truth than they themselves realized. It is in connection with the second sending that we begin to see a clearer

---

[2] See, e.g., Walther Eichrodt, *Theology of the Old Testament* (trans. J.A. Baker; London: SCM, 1967), II, pp. 46-68.

[3] Max Turner, *The Holy Spirit and Spiritual Gifts* (Peabody, MA: Hendrickson, 1998), pp. 169-78.

[4] Robert Jenson, *Systematic Theology* (New York, NY: Oxford University Press, 1997), I, p. 157 (author's emphasis).

outline of the Holy Spirit as third person and the completion of the revelation of God as Trinity.

Now, the story of the Spirit is about his coming to the Church making the Church an inextricable part of the Spirit-event. The story of the Church is part of the story of the Spirit since the basic identity of the Spirit is spelled out in relation to his coming to the Church. We cannot talk about the Spirit without at the same time talking about the Church and vice versa. The Church, therefore, is part of the Trinitarian narrative because she is part of the story of the Spirit. The Church is thus more than an agent to carry out the mission of the Trinity; she is part of the Trinitarian mission itself. Mission is more than what the Church does but what the Church *is*.[5] How does the Spirit constitute the Church as part of the triune narrative? In what follows I shall outline three main features of what might be called a pneumatological ecclesiology.

The Church as the Spirit's Personal Indwelling
First, the Spirit's coming to the Church is not just about the continuation of the historical mission of Christ through the Church acting as Christ's agent but completes the Trinitarian story by including something *new*. That is to say, Pentecost reveals the Spirit's own proper work (*proprium*). It is essentially the story of the Spirit's constituting the Church by his personal indwelling.[6] The story of the Church is so inextricably linked to the story of the triune God, especially with reference to the third person of the Trinity, that any attempt to de-link the Church from the story simply does not do full justice to the real identity of either the Church or the triune God. Earlier we have seen from the biblical accounts how the second sending identifies the Holy Spirit as the Third Person. It is this sending of the Spirit *to the Church* that clarifies the personhood of the Spirit. His coming to indwell the Church could be called the 'enhypostatization' of the Spirit paralleling Jesus' own enhypostasis

---

[5] Surprisingly, this idea is also endorsed by a Free Church advocate, Miroslav Volf. See Miroslav Volf and Maurice Lee, 'The Spirit and the Church', in Bradford E. Hinze and D. Lyle Dabney (eds.), *Advents of the Spirit* (Milwaukee, WI: Marquette University Press, 2001), pp. 398-99.

[6] David Coffey, *'Did you Receive the Holy Spirit When You Believed?' Some Basic Questions for Pneumatology* (Milwaukee, WI: Marquette University Press, 2005).

as a human person at the incarnation.[7] But unlike Jesus who assumed human nature, the Spirit is not incarnated in the Church; that is to say, the Spirit is not *constituted* by the union of Spirit and Church, but he comes in his *whole person* into the Church, such that in and through the Church the Spirit's personhood is *revealed*.[8]

The intimate relationship between the Spirit and the Church could be also explained in terms of the order of the Trinitarian revelation. Lossky citing John of Damascus notes that 'the Son is the image of the Father, and the Spirit the image of the Son.'

> It follows that the third Hypostasis of the Trinity is the only one not having His image in another Person. The Holy Spirit, as Person, remains unmanifested, hidden, concealing Himself in His very appearing. This is why St. Symeon the New Theologian was to praise Him, in his hymns to the divine love, under the apophatic lineaments of a Person at once unknowable and mysterious.[9]

But in coming to the Church, according to Ralph del Colle,

> The image of the Holy Spirit, not borne by another divine person, becomes actual in created persons ... through his deifying work. In this sense the ministry of the Holy Spirit is associated with ecclesiology; some even make the argument that ecclesiology is best understood when it is a branch of pneumatology.[10]

---

[7] Ralph del Colle sees a 'double enhypostasis of Jesus in the Logos and the Spirit.' In the incarnation the Son 'in his human nature undergoes an inpersoning in the Spirit.' This second enhypostasis is what is usually meant by 'Spirit Christology'. Ralph del Colle, 'The Holy Spirit: Presence, Power, Person', *Theological Studies* 62 (2001), p. 336.

[8] It should be made clear that the Spirit's 'enhypostatization' in the church is, unlike the incarnation, not a hypostatic union. Meyendorff sums up the distinction well: 'The Spirit ... does not en-hypostatize human nature as a whole; He communicates His uncreated grace to each human person, to each member of the Body of Christ. New humanity is realized in the hypostasis of the Son incarnate, but it receives only the *gifts* of the Spirit.... Gregory of Cyprus and Gregory Palamas will insist, in different contexts, that at Pentecost the Apostles received the eternal gifts or 'energies' of the Spirit, but that there was no new hypostatic union between the Spirit and humanity'. *Byzantine Theology: Historical Trends and Doctrinal Themes* (New York: Fordham University Press, 2nd edn, 1979), p. 173.

[9] Vladimir Lossky, *The Mystical Theology of the Eastern Church* (London: James Clarke, 1957), p. 160.

[10] Del Colle, *Christ and the Spirit*, p. 25. Cf. Lossky, *Mystical Theology*, p. 173.

That is to say, the Spirit's personhood is expressed primarily in and through the Church as persons-in-communion; in fact, only through the personal indwelling of the Spirit is it possible to speak of the Church as a communion. As del Colle further notes,

> Only as Person can he recreate persons in community ecstatically oriented to the other. With Christ the Spirit provides the space for their concrete identities to emerge into the maturity of the full stature of Christ (Ephesians 4:13) and into the consummation of God's temple so that all of creation may be filled with the fullness of God (Ephesians 2:20-22; 3:16-19).[11]

An important feature of the Spirit's 'enhypostatization' in the Church is that in the process the Spirit experiences a *kenosis*.[12] He becomes the 'localized' *Shekinah* in the Church just as Yahweh's *Shekinah* was localized in the tabernacle, and just as Jesus is the temple and the localization of God's presence on earth (Jn 1.14; 2.21).[13] Again, in the words of del Colle,

> The triune economy reaches its goal in the economy of the Holy Spirit, who like the Son undergoes his own kenosis in a temporal mission. Just as the Son emptied himself by becoming flesh through the union of his hypostasis to a human nature, so, too, the Holy Spirit empties himself by indwelling human hypostases through the impartation of uncreated grace. The former unifies common human nature in the one hypostasis of the Son; the latter diversifies God's gifts among many human persons or hypostases.[14]

In summary, the Spirit and the Church clarifies each other's identity. The Spirit is the third person precisely in his relation to the

---

[11] Ralph del Colle, 'The Holy Spirit: Presence, Power, Person', p. 334.

[12] Lossky, *Mystical Theology*, pp. 168, 244; Boris Bobrinskoy, 'The Church and the Holy Spirit in 20th C Russia', *The Ecumenical Review* 61.2 (July 2000), p. 334 citing Lossky and Bulgakov. Moltmann, however, sees the Spirit's *kenosis* and Shekinah only in connection with his descent upon Jesus and in his identification with Jesus' suffering. *The Way of Jesus Christ: Christology in Messianic Dimensions* (London: SCM, 1990), p. 174; *The Spirit of Life: A Universal Affirmation* (Minneapolis, MN: Fortress, 1993), p. 62.

[13] Raymond E. Brown, *The Gospel According to John* (Anchor Bible; Garden City, NY: Doubleday, 1970), II, p. 33.

[14] Del Colle, *Christ and the Spirit*, p. 25. The idea that Christ unifies while the Spirit diversifies is also found in Lossky, *Mystical Theology*, pp. 166-68.

Church; and the Church is what it is essentially in relation to the third person of the Trinity: it is the body of Christ indwelled by the Spirit, making it the temple of the Holy Spirit as Eph. 2.18-22 makes clear:

> For through him [Christ] we both have access to the Father by one Spirit. Consequently, you are no longer foreigners and aliens, but fellow citizens with God's people and members of God's household, [20]built on the foundation of the apostles and prophets, with Christ Jesus himself as the chief cornerstone. [21]In him the whole building is joined together and rises to become a holy temple in the Lord. [22]And in him you too are being built together to become a dwelling in which God lives by his Spirit.

As the temple of the Holy Spirit, the Church's chief act is the worship of God, through Jesus Christ, in the power of the indwelling Spirit:

> You also, like living stones, are being built into a spiritual house to be a holy priesthood, offering spiritual sacrifices acceptable to God through Jesus Christ (1 Pet. 2.5).

Church Is Ontologically United to Christ

Second, in coming to indwell the Church, the Holy Spirit unites the Church ontologically to Christ as its head. This establishes the intimate connection between Christology, pneumatology, and ecclesiology. The work of the Spirit vis-à-vis Christ and the Church is always to actualize, to make concrete, to create, and re-create. Just as Christ is pneumatologically conditioned, the Church too is pneumatologically conditioned. The pneumatological conditioning of Christ is seen in the first sending where the Spirit actualizes the coming of the Son in the work of his conception in the virgin's womb, enhypostatizing the Word in human flesh. Further the Spirit anointed the Son at his baptism making him the Christ, the anointed one (Mk 1.9). Through the Spirit Jesus battled and overcame the devil (Mk 1.12) and began his ministry of proclaiming the kingdom of God (Mk 1.14). In the second sending, except for the Incarnation, everything else that the Spirit does in relation to the Son is done in the Church by his personal indwelling. At Pentecost, the Holy Spirit unites the people of God to Christ the Head, making the Church Christ's body.[15] This ontological unity of Christ and the Church is what is meant by the phrase the total Christ (*totus Christus*). If the Spirit is the bond of love between the Father and the Son, the Spirit is now the bond of love between Christ and his body, and within his body, the Church.[16] The Church *is* the unity and communion of the Holy Spirit.[17] Through the indwelling Spirit the Church becomes the 'corporate personality' of Christ, that is, the extension of Christ the Truth. Through the Spirit the Church is christologically shaped into the body of Christ. From this perspective, as Zizioulas puts it, Christ is not just a historical individual who stands externally to us, but 'a relational entity' linked to the Church such that '[b]etween the Christ-truth and ourselves there is *no gap to fill* by the means of grace.'

> When we make the assertion that [Christ] is the truth, we are meaning His whole personal existence …; that is, we mean His relationship with His body, the Church, ourselves. In other words, when we now say 'Christ' we mean a person and not an individual; we mean a relational reality existing 'for me' or 'for us.' Here the Holy Spirit is not one who *aids* us in bridging the distance between Christ and ourselves, but he is the person of the Trinity who actually realizes in history that which we call Christ, this absolutely relational entity, our Savior. In this case, our Christology is *essentially* conditioned by Pneumatology.[18]

The Farewell Discourse provides another way to understand the distinctive role of the Spirit vis-à-vis the Christ of the Church. Many scholars believe that the role of the Holy Spirit portrayed in John 14–16 is to answer the vexing question: what will happen to

---

[15] For a fuller discussion of this see Robert Jenson, *Systematic Theology, II: The Works of God*, pp. 167-88; Simon Chan, *Liturgical Theology* (Downers Grove, IL: IVP, 2006), pp. 31-39.

[16] As Pannenberg puts it, the Holy Spirit is the 'condition and medium' of the fellowship between the Father and the Son and '[o]nly on this basis may the imparting of the Spirit to believers be seen as their incorporation into the fellowship of the Son with the Father'. *Systematic Theology* (Göttingen: Vandenhoeck & Ruprecht, 1988), I, p. 316.

[17] Nissiotis, 'Spirit, Church, and Ministry,' p. 487.

[18] John D. Zizioulas, *Being as Communion: Studies in Personhood and the Church* (Crestwood, NY: St. Vladimir Seminary Press, 1993), pp. 110-11. Emphasis author's.

the Church when the last living witnesses of Jesus have died? Will
the Church lose its last links to Jesus? The presence of the Paraclete
as taking the place of Jesus ensures continuity of the Church with
the apostolic tradition. Subsequent generations of believers are no
farther removed from Jesus because of the presence of the Spirit
who is the Spirit of Truth just as Jesus is the Truth.[19] Through the
Spirit, the Church becomes the 'expanded' Christ or *totus Christus*.
The Spirit does this in his own unique way *as* the Spirit of the
Church. The Church is not only linked to the truth *historically* in a
linear fashion (from Christ to the apostles to bishops and people),
but also *charismatically* by the Spirit who comes from beyond history,
freeing the Church from historical limitations. This is why Jesus
could promise his disciples that they would do 'greater things' because of his ascension to the Father (Jn 14.12). The ascension is the
prerequisite for his sending the Spirit to the Church (Jn 16.7). But
Pentecost is not just a one-time event but a repeated event. The
Spirit has come, but the Church continues to pray for his coming in
the *epiclesis*. Through the Spirit and his gifts, the Church is no longer
restricted in her relation to Christ to just the historical-linear dimension. In this work the Holy Spirit constitutes the Church as the living Tradition. Using the language of Irenaeus, the Church that
holds the precious deposit of faith, the truth of the gospel of Jesus
Christ, is so united with it that it is constantly being rejuvenated by
the Spirit.

The Church Becomes the Temple of the Spirit

Irenaeus' picture of the Church as a precious vessel in which the
Spirit dwells brings out a third feature of ecclesiology. Irenaeus' discussion is in connection with his rebuttal of the Gnostic claim to
have access to esoteric knowledge coming directly from the apostles
apart from the Church. Irenaeus argues that apart from the Church,
which has proof of direct historical links with the apostles, there is
no true knowledge of salvation—a knowledge embodied in the
Church's rule of faith. The Spirit not only links the Church to the
precious deposit of truth so that she is constantly renewed by it, he
is God's gift 'distributed throughout the Church' as the 'communion with Christ' and 'the ladder of ascent to God.... For where the
Church is, there is the Spirit of God; and where the Spirit of God

---

[19] Brown, *John*, II, pp. 1141-42.

is, there is the Church, and every kind of grace.'[20] The Church is the locus of the Spirit's presence and the means of communion; in fact, the Church is essentially communion.

If the Pentecost event must be understood theologically as the coming of the third person to indwell the Church and in so doing reveals God as trinity, then the next question is, are Pentecostals justified in identifying their experience of Spirit-baptism as the experience of the Pentecost event? To answer this question we need to consider the shape of Pentecostal spirituality.

II. The Shape of Pentecostal Spirituality

Pentecostal Particularity

There are a number of important characteristics found in Pentecostal spirituality. Spirit-baptism, for Pentecostals, is an intensely real encounter with the persons of the Spirit and of Jesus. This is a fact that comes through over and over again in Pentecostal testimonies. Pentecostals are not primarily interested in ideas but in persons. We may call this characteristic Pentecostal particularity; that is to say, they are supremely interested in the particular rather than the general. This penchant for the particular is quite central to Christianity. As the Orthodox theologian David Hart observes

> [I]f indeed God became *a* man, then Truth condescended to become *a* truth, from whose historical contingency one cannot simply pass to categories of universal rationality; and this means that whatever Christians mean when they speak of truth, it cannot involve simply the dialectical wresting of abstract principles from intractable facts.[21]

God, for Hart, is revealed as 'transcendently determinate' beauty; that is to say, this beauty or the glory of God resists reduction to the 'symbolic' seen, for example, in Tillich's concept of 'the ultimate'.[22]

---

[20] Irenaeus, *Against Heresies*, III.24.1

[21] David Bentley Hart, *Beauty of the Infinite: The Aesthetics of Christian Truth* (Grand Rapids: Eerdmans, 2003), p. 5.

[22] Hart, *Beauty*, pp. 24-28 cf. p. 177.

The Pentecostal would find this emphasis on particularity quite congenial. For at the heart of Pentecostal spirituality is the focus on the concrete person of Jesus as 'the way, the truth, and the life'. This spiritual instinct explains why the early Pentecostals were suspicious of traditional theology and theological training, especially seminary training. They want to know Jesus as the Truth, not what others say about him, and theology as reflections and generalizations of the concrete is felt to be a step removed from the *real* truth. For at the heart of the Christian faith is the 'transcendently determinate' Truth of the particular person, Jesus Christ. In Jesus truth reaches its most concrete expression—the revelation of the Second Person in human flesh.

The gospel, which is the proclamation of *this* truth, was a scandal to the Greeks and a stumbling block to the Jews. Many people today continue to be scandalized and stumbled. Yet, if Jesus is the concrete Truth by which all other truths must be judged, then any approach that reduces him to an abstraction, be it the 'cosmic Christ' or the 'Christic principle', is a parody of the Truth. If Jesus Christ could be translated into some moral ideal or metaphysical principle, then conversion to Jesus would be unnecessary and any attempt to call people to Christ would be sheer arrogance. All one needs to do is adopt the moral ideal or metaphysical theory Jesus exemplifies. Thus an 'inclusivist' understanding of truth is ultimately contradictory to the deepest Pentecostal spiritual instinct. Here I must add, parenthetically, why I have serious reservations whether Amos Yong's pneumatological approach to other religions could be properly called Pentecostal. In trying to establish points of contact with other religions, he has essentially reduced concrete particularities into abstract principles.[23]

Relation to the Third Person

Pentecostalism is essentially the spiritual impulse driving the Christian towards personal intimacy with God. More specifically, if the Pentecost event is about the Spirit's personal indwelling of the Church, then Pentecostals are correct in making relation with *the person* of the Holy Spirit a distinctive feature of their faith. Pentecostals have been practicing the *epiclesis*, long before that have heard

---

[23] See Amos Yong, *Beyond the Impasse: Toward a Pneumatological Theology of Religions* (Grand Rapids: Baker, 2003).

of that term. However the person of the Spirit is *understood*, Pentecostals are clear that what distinguishes their experience from non-Pentecostals is to be found in the way the presence of the Holy Spirit is operative in their lives. The language they use is particularly revealing. While evangelicals may speak of being 'born again', illuminated, by the Spirit, etc., the person of the Spirit is usually not in the foreground but, as it were, working behind the scene. In the tradition of Reformed theology, the focus is more on the 'secret working of the Spirit'.[24] Pentecostals, by contrast, often use language that suggests a more direct working of the Spirit that impinges upon their senses. The Spirit is referred to not only in terms of powerful and supernatural activities, he is often spoken of as the subject of those activities. The Spirit guides, speaks, empowers, restrains, etc. This is unambiguously the language of Acts (cf. Acts 13.4; 16.6-7; 20.22, 23, 28). This sense of personal presence is frequently encountered in classical Pentecostal preaching and testimonies. We see this, e.g. in David du Plessis' classic *The Spirit Bade Me Go* or David Yonggi Cho's *The Holy Spirit, My Senior Partner*. The title of du Plessis' book itself is taken from Acts 11.12, King James Version. Expressions like the following from du Plessis is commonplace in Pentecostal testimonies: 'I suddenly felt a warm glow come over me. I knew this was the Holy Spirit taking over …'; 'I knew that the Holy Spirit was in control …'; etc.[25] Although their understanding of the relationship between the person of the Spirit and the persons of the Son and the Father may sometimes be problematic, the experience of the Spirit as personally present is the common denominator in all Pentecostals and qualifies it as distinctively Pentecostal. If we are to use scholastic categories, evangelicals tend

---

[24] This and similar phrases are used frequently by John Calvin. See *Institutes of the Christian Religion* 3.1. Interestingly, Eugene F. Rogers, Jr. in an insightful article on the pneumatologies of Calvin, Rahner, and Florensky has shown that the reticence to speak directly about the Spirit and more in terms of his hidden workings—what he calls the apophaticism of the Spirit—is quite pervasive. Rogers suggests that this view spread across diverse traditions may have been due to their common fear of enthusiasm (p. 256). 'The Mystery of the Spirit in Three Traditions: Calvin, Rahner, Florensky Or, You *Keep* Wondering Where the Spirit Went', *Modern Theology* 19.2 (April 2003), pp. 243-60.

[25] David du Plessis, *The Spirit Bade Me Go: The Astounding Move of God in the Denominational Churches* (Oakland, CA: David du Plessis, 1960), p. 16.

to focus more on the 'created graces' of the Spirit while Pentecostals tend to speak in terms of 'uncreated grace.'

Pentecostals are supremely interested in the truth not as an abstraction, but in Truth as a concrete manifestation—as person, specifically the second and third persons of the Trinity, usually with the second person at the center of their devotion.[26] As Steven J. Land puts it, 'Jesus is the center and the Holy Spirit is the circumference' of Pentecostal spirituality.[27] It is their focus on personal intimacy that makes sense of their most distinctive spiritual marker: glossolalia. Glossolalia, as I have pointed out elsewhere, is ultimately about personal relationship with God through the Holy Spirit.[28] Personal intimacy is what Pentecostals treasure. But in ways that they themselves cannot fully explain, personal intimacy is somehow linked to glossolalia. We see this connection often recounted in Pentecostal testimonies.[29] They may not be able to explain the 'initial evidence' *doctrine* satisfactorily, but there is no question that they have an 'initial evidence' *experience*. This is what gives the initial evidence doctrine its particular potency. By saying that glossolalia is the initial evidence of Spirit-baptism, Pentecostals are in effect saying that Spirit-baptism is essentially about personal indwelling—which is what the Pentecost event is theologically.

Personhood and the Miraculous

It is also in terms of personal relationship that the Pentecostal interest in the miraculous could be properly understood. G.K. Chesterton notes that it is in the very character of normal persons to do things sometimes without a particular purpose: 'If any human acts may loosely be called causeless, they are the minor acts of a healthy man; whistling as he walks; slashing the grass with a stick; kicking his heels or rubbing his hands. It is the happy man who does the useless things; the sick man is not strong enough to be idle.'[30] Free-

---

[26] David Reed, *'In Jesus' Name': The History and Beliefs of Oneness Pentecostals* (JPTSup 31; Blandford Forum, Dorset: Deo Publishing, 2008), pp. 32-68.

[27] Steven J. Land, *Pentecostal Spirituality* (JPTSup 1; Sheffield: Sheffield Academic Press, 1993), p. 23.

[28] See Simon Chan, *Pentecostal Theology and the Christian Spiritual Tradition* (JPTSup 21; Sheffield: Sheffield Academic Press, 2000), ch. 2.

[29] E.g., Jack Hayford, *The Beauty of Spiritual Language* (Dallas, TX: Word, 1992), pp. 189-91.

[30] G.K. Chesterton, *Orthodoxy* (New York: Image Books, 1959), pp. 18-19.

dom and unpredictability are one of the most distinctive marks of a healthy person—and a healthy Christian. Only persons are capable of springing surprises, whereas the behavior of other living things ruled by instincts is quite predictable. There is an *intrinsic* connection between the God who works miracles and the fact that He is Person. H.H. Farmer made this astute observation some years ago:

> The religious instinct to cling to the concept of miracle is at bottom not the result of the craving for portends to gape at, or for accommodations on the part of the universe to merely selfish desires, but for personality in God …; it is a protest against an all-inclusive monism which leaves the soul choking for want of air.[31]

In terms of the Trinitarian doctrine of appropriation, this unpredictable feature of personhood could be said to be appropriated to the person of the Holy Spirit. It belongs to the very nature of the Spirit of God to move where he wills (cf. Jn 3.8), to work in ways that often do not conform to human expectations or any predictable pattern. This drive towards personal intimacy through the Spirit who does 'surprising works'[32] is the peculiar strength of Pentecostalism. The intimate, personal knowledge of Jesus Christ through the person and power of the Spirit gives Pentecostals an unparalleled boldness to proclaim the fivefold gospel: Jesus as savior, sanctifier, baptizer, healer, and coming king; further, they do it in a manner that is utterly convincing as only people with a deep familiarity with the persons of Jesus and the Spirit can.

Pentecostal mission and worship

This focus on personhood underlies two other key Pentecostal concerns namely worship and mission. The two most conspicuous features of Pentecostal churches are their spirited worship and boundless energies expended in mission activities. They may not have been practiced in the same way, or in the most appropriate way, but they are always central in the Pentecostal Church. Pentecostal 'pas-

---

[31] H.H. Farmer, *The World and God* (London: Nisbet and Co., 1946), p. 6.

[32] Cf. the title of Jonathan Edwards' account of the Great Awakening: 'A Faithful Narrative of the Surprising Work of God' in *The Works of Jonathan Edwards* (Edinburgh: Banner of Truth, 1987), I, pp. 344-64.

sion for the kingdom' as Land describes its spirituality, is grounded in personal relationship.

Worship draws Pentecostals into a deep personal relationship with God and the proclamation of the gospel is about bringing people into a 'personal relationship with Jesus'. To be sure, mission includes a social dimension, and Pentecostals in recent years are seeking to catch up on the social implications of the Pentecostal message.[33] But getting people to know Christ *personally* has always been and still is the primary focus of Pentecostal mission practice. Ask any Pentecostal for a reason for preaching the gospel and the first thing that we are likely to hear is that people need to know Jesus as *personal* savior.

The traditional Pentecostal *explanation* of its own spirituality may not always be consistent with what is best in its own spiritual experience, and consequently its approach to worship and mission has been adversely affected. Historically, the cultivation of personal relationship has been to focus on *one* of the persons of the Trinity,[34] usually either Jesus or the Spirit resulting in either Christomonism or pneumatomonism, both of which could be amply illustrated in Pentecostal history. The problem could be understood as a misappropriation of the doctrine of persons. The historical context from which Pentecostalism arose was a major contributing factor. David Reed has noted that the early Pentecostals inherited a doctrine of the Trinity from the holiness movement whose concern to defend the deity of Jesus and the Spirit against liberals and Unitarians led to a rather crude conception of the Trinity bordering on tritheism.[35] The problem could be described as the 'over-hypostatization' of the Trinity, in which the Trinitarian persons are treated as 'separate per-

---

[33] See, e.g., Murray A. Dempster, Byron D. Klaus and Douglas Petersen (eds.), *Called and Empowered: Global Mission in Pentecostal Perspective* (Peabody, MA: Hendrickson, 1991).

[34] The separation of Father, Son, and Holy Spirit has its precedent in Joachimism which links them to three successive epochs of human history. See Yves Congar, *I Believe in the Holy Spirit* (trans. David Smith; 3 vols., New York: Seabury, 1983), I, p. 127. Some Pentecostals entertain a similar idea by identifying the 20th Century outpouring of the Spirit as the coming of the age of the Spirit. But the separation of the Trinitarian persons occurs not only eschatologically, but also thematically as the following makes clear.

[35] Reed, *'In Jesus' Name': The History and Beliefs of Oneness Pentecostals*, chap. 3, esp. 49-50.

sonalities.' This has resulted in a tendency to view relationship with the Trinity in a highly individualized way. Yet at its best this individualizing impulse creates a spirituality that draws Pentecostals into a very vital relationship with the persons of Jesus Christ and the Holy Spirit. However, without grounding it in a stable Trinitarian structure which includes a theology of the Church as part of the Trinitarian narrative, the relationship with Jesus and the Holy Spirit threatens to become either christomonistic or pneumatomonistic.

III. The Interface of Pentecostal Ecclesiology and Spirituality

What might constitute a stable Trinitarian structure on which an adequate Pentecostal ecclesiology could be built? Time would only allow me to state rather than elaborate on a few proposals:

1. Not any Trinitarian theory would do. Thomas Smail, one of the early leaders of charismatic renewal within the Anglican Church has correctly noted that Pentecostal-charismatics are enamored of Christomonism and pneumatomonism because they have forgotten the Father who 'is the integrating factor within the Godhead and the gospel'.[36] Pentecostals, therefore, need to retrieve the doctrine of the Father. In particular I would like to suggest the Orthodox doctrine of the Trinity focusing on the *monarchy of the Father*. The monarchy of the Father implies a certain irreversible order or *taxis* in the Church which transcends both egalitarianism and authoritarianism, both of which have bedeviled Pentecostalism throughout much of its history. What a Trinitarian order does imply is a *differentiated* communion. This communion could be described as hierarchical. It is necessary if the all too fluid nature of Pentecostal spirituality is to be stabilized.

2. A Trinitarian order in the Church is best preserved in the liturgy. This is because the liturgy is the faithful enactment of Trinitarian theology. The liturgy is shaped by and around the Gospel. It is the Word, i.e. the story of the triune God culminating in the Eucharist, i.e. its actualization in communion with the Father, through the Son, in the Spirit. This means that if there is to be a

---

[36] Thomas A. Smail, *The Forgotten Father* (London: Hodder and Stoughton, 1980), p. 17.

stable Pentecostal ecclesiology ordered around the monarchy of the Father, Pentecostals need to consider seriously the place of a *normative* liturgy in their worship.

3. An ecclesiology linked to the Trinity means that the Church is first, a spiritual corporate reality and only secondarily a social reality. In Catholicism, these two aspects correspond roughly to the *ecclesia congregans* and *ecclesia congregata* respectively. *Ecclesia congregans* is the Church in her wholeness: the pure Bride in relation to Christ, and the Mother who gathers and sustains the faithful through her gifts. *Ecclesia congregata* is the faithful as a gathered community, the 'great multitude' gathered from every nation, tribe, people, and language (Rev. 7.9). Although in recent years Pentecostals and evangelicals are recognizing the need to move beyond an individualistic concept of spirituality, yet failure to understand the Church as a spiritual entity has resulted in an understanding of the corporate life of Christians as largely a matter of social dynamics. For a more adequate ecclesiology to emerge, we need to go beyond *my* faith and even beyond *our* faith to *the* faith of the Church. A spiritual-corporate understanding of the Church means that the Church is governed by spiritual resources, primarily word and sacraments, with which Mother Church nourishes her children. In other words, a robust Pentecostal ecclesiology requires, among other things, a strong sacramental theology.

A Trinitarian ecclesiology juxtaposes three basic elements: church order, liturgy, and sacrament. These elements are basic to Catholicism and Orthodoxy. But can these elements shape a Pentecostal ecclesiology as well without compromising its spirituality? This is the subject for another paper.

Conclusion

Pentecostal spirituality conforms in the main to the theology of the Pentecost event which I have outlined in the first part of my paper. But it has been hampered to a great extent by its excessive individualism; and even if it has been able to move beyond individualism, it is still hampered by a merely sociological understanding of the Church. To be fair, this is a problem Pentecostals share with their evangelical counterparts. The problem goes beyond the failure to understand the person as a relational being as opposed to Cartesian individualism; it is also the failure to appreciate the nature of the Christian as an *ecclesial* being: a member of the body of Christ through baptism by the Spirit and united with one another through the indwelling Holy Spirit, a son who has God for his Father and the Church for his mother.[37] This understanding of the Christian as ecclesial being can only be realized if there is an adequate Trinitarian theology of the Spirit which juxtaposes the hierarchical, liturgical, and sacramental nature of the Church. I do not believe that the Pentecostal spiritual instinct at its deepest level is inherently opposed to these elements. I am, therefore, hopeful that a truly Pentecostal ecclesiology can be built on these premises without compromising anything that is true of Pentecostal faith and experience.

---

[37] Cf. Cyprian: 'He can no longer have God for his Father, who has not the Church for his mother' (*On the Unity of the Catholic Church*, §6).

7

THE EMPOWERED CHURCH:
ECCLESIOLOGICAL DIMENSIONS OF THE
EVENT OF PENTECOST

DANIELA C. AUGUSTINE[*]

The confession of Christ as Spirit-Baptizer and the corresponding sacramental practice of speaking in tongues are one of the focal points of Pentecostal theology and spirituality. The Christocentricity of the Fivefold Gospel as the distinct template of Pentecostal theological inquiry highlights this confession as essential for the Church's understanding of her identity and mission. Therefore, the event of Pentecost serves as contextual origin, dialogical anchor, and continual source of inspiration and challenge within Pentecostal theological reflection.

It is not accidental that the Day of Pentecost described in Luke's account of the Acts of the Apostles has been identified as the birthday of the Christian Church.[1] It establishes her demarcations as the charismatic *koinonia*[2] of the ones who have received God's Word of Life and have been transformed into the living Body of Christ on earth through the agency and empowerment of the Holy

[*] Daniela C. Augustine (DTh, University of South Africa) is Scholar in Residence at the Centre for Pentecostal Theology in Cleveland, TN, USA and a Member of the Center of Theological Inquiry in Princeton, NJ, USA.

[1] Keith Warrington, *Pentecostal Theology: A Theology of Encounter* (London, England: T & T Clark, 2008), p. 107.

[2] For an overview of the Pentecostal/Charismatic view of the church as a charismatic *koinonia* see Veli-Matti Kärkkäinen, *An Introduction to Ecclesiology: Ecumenical, Historical & Global Perspectives* (Downers Grove, IL: InterVarsity Press, 2002), pp. 74-76.

Spirit. The Church is the teleological creation of the Triune God and as such exhibits the synergistic presence and work of Christ (the eternal, incarnated Word) and the Spirit according to the will of the Father. Therefore, the work (*leitourgia*) of the Body of Christ is the work of God on earth.[3]

The event of Pentecost ushers on the stage of salvation history the community of faith as the *One, Holy, Catholic* and *Apostolic* ecclesia—the anointed and empowered Body of Christ representing, in its mystical union with the Redeemer (Eph. 5.32), the eschatological fusion of heaven and earth (Eph. 1.10). This is the Body that, in the power of the Holy Spirit, continues the ministry of the resurrected Christ in this world as the living extension of His character and mission.

The marks of the Church are visibly outlined in the Pentecost narrative: The disciples are 'all together in one place' (Acts 2.1) and their unity anticipates the outpouring of the Spirit, the promise of the Father (Lk. 24.49), that reaffirms their identity in Christ as God's children. The oneness of the Church is established through her organic unity with the One Christ as being His Body on earth (Eph. 1.22-23), anointed by the Holy Spirit in accordance to the will of the Father (2 Cor. 1.21-22). As Frank D. Macchia points out, the unity of Pentecost is 'not abstract and absolute, but rather concrete and pluralistic'.[4] It embraces the other in their ethnic, socio-economic, and gender diversity (Acts 2.17-18), and affirms their human dignity 'as bearers of the divine image'.[5]

---

[3] The present theological reflection is rooted in the context of Eastern-European Pentecostalism which, by virtue of its geographical location and spiritual heritage, has developed its theological content in continual dialogue with the Eastern Orthodox tradition. Therefore, the Eastern European Pentecostal view of the event Pentecost and its ecclesiological significance does not emphasize Pneumatology over or against Christology and holds a continual focus on the work of the Trinity, with all three persons simultaneously present in all events of salvific history. For more on the Eastern Orthodox ecclesiological perspective, cf. Timothy (Bishop Kallistos) Ware, *The Orthodox Church* (New York, NY: Penguin Books, 1997), pp. 239-63.

[4] Frank D. Macchia, *Baptized in the Spirit: A Global Pentecostal Theology* (Grand Rapids, MI: Zondervan, 2006), p. 218. The scope of the present essay does not allow for an in-depth analysis of the classical marks of the church. Macchia's work offers an inspiring Pentecostal theological reflection on the marks of the church (pp. 204-41) and the sacramental life of the faith community (pp. 241-56).

[5] Macchia, *Baptized in the Spirit*, p. 218.

The divine origin of the Church's inauguration and her identity as the Body of the resurrected Christ emphasize her holiness 'in' and 'through' her ontological and eschatological union with God. The believers are positioned 'in' and united 'with' Christ as the Holy Spirit saturates them with the divine presence (Acts 2.4) making them 'partakers (*koinonoi*) of the divine nature' (2 Pet. 1.4). There is one flame that distributes itself as tongues of fire upon each one of the believers (Acts 2.3), giving the reader a visualization of the simultaneous oneness and catholic diversity of the Body. The catholicity of the Church is further articulated by the assertion of the presence of representatives 'from every nation under heaven' (Acts 2.5) who after the proclamation of the Good News in their native tongues (Acts 2.6-11) become constituting members of the Pentecost faith community. It upholds the Church's unity of sustained diversity, as oneness that celebrates personal identity in all of its complex beauty, worshiping the creative Trinity as its icon on earth[6] and reflecting God's presence in His community. The Trinity, as the proto-community, is the very model of this catholicity expressed in love—the identifier of the Trinitarian relationships and of the community of believers as authentic disciples of Christ (Jn 13.35). The catholicity of Pentecost reveals the radical hospitality of God welcoming all nations under heaven into the life of the Trinity through His self-giving in the Holy Spirit. It also simultaneously forecasts the eschatological unveiling of the cosmic lordship of the resurrected Christ before whom 'every knee shall bow, in heaven and on earth and under the earth, and every tongue confess that Jesus Christ is Lord, to the glory of the Father' (Phil. 2.10).

The Apostolicity of the Church is established by placing her birth in the context of the apostolic witness and teaching as articulated by Peter and the rest of the disciples at the event of Pentecost (Acts 2.14-40). Their first-hand witness of the risen Christ, through the voice and acts of His Body in the power of the Holy Spirit,

---

[6] The Eastern Orthodox tradition has given us the vision of the church as the icon of the Trinity on earth. Both personal human sociality and the church's *koinonia* find their origin in the intersociality of the Trinity and its mystical unity in diversity as the proto-community of love. Vladimir Lossky, *Introduction to Orthodox Theology* (Crestwood, NY: St. Vladimir Seminary Press, 1978), p. 67. Timothy (Bishop Kallistos) Ware, pp. 240-42.

spreads from Jerusalem throughout Judea and Samaria and to the uttermost parts of the world (Acts 1.8).

The radical Christocentricity of the event of Pentecost which shapes and marks the ecclesia as the Body of Christ, is consistent with the work of the Spirit as the agent who mediates, articulates, and leads all redemption history towards its eschatological fulfillment and summation in Christ. 'As the historical community of Christ, therefore, the Church is the eschatological creation of the Spirit.'[7] In the ecclesia, human history is met with its eschatological unfolding. Raptured and transfigured by the Spirit into the Kingdom of God, the Church becomes the sacred space where history is faced with its own future as the demand for and inevitability of transformation. The Church is the embodiment of this future on earth and as such faces the world with the face of Christ as the ultimate destiny of all existence.[8]

The Pentecost event authenticates Christ's presence with and in His Body as the Baptizer with the Holy Spirit (Mk 1.8). The coming of the Spirit witnesses the completion of the redemptive work of Christ and transforms the community of faith into what it is truly called to be—a mission (Jn 15.26). For where Christ is, there is the Spirit through whom the Word becomes flesh and dwells among us—redeeming, healing, and renewing the world. And where the Spirit is, there is the *koinonia* of the Trinity extending its loving embrace in invitation to humanity to partake in the divine communal life and be transfigured into its likeness.

In view of the above, the present work offers a look at the event of Pentecost as the moment of birthing, anointing, and empowering the Body of Christ on earth to be a living extension of its resurrected Lord. The text further examines the significance and liturgi-

---

[7] Jürgen Moltmann, *The Church in the Power of the Spirit* (Minneapolis, Minnesota: Fortress Press, 1993), p. 33.

[8] Both Miroslav Volf [*After Our Likeness: The Church as the Image of the Trinity* (Grand Rapids: Eerdmans, 1998), p. 128] and Frank Macchia (*Baptized in the Spirit*, pp. 209-11) affirm that the marks of the Spirit-baptized church are not drawn from the local or global dimensions of the ecclesia, but from the eschatological fulfillment of the gathering of the people of God in the new creation. Through the presence of the Spirit, this eschatological reality is experienced here and now. As Macchia asserts, this 'priority of the eschatological Spirit in determining the marks of the church explains why a local body can be filled with the Spirit with all grace' (p. 210).

cal function of speaking in tongues and the translatability of languages. It offers an understanding of *xenolalia* and *glossolalia* as an eschatological audible sign of the call to community with one another, and of heaven and earth in the Triune God, pointing to our ultimate eschatological destiny in Christ as the *omega* of all existence. Finally, the text offers an understanding of speaking in tongues as a form of liturgical *askesis*—of fasting from oneself on behalf of the other and the different from us. The practice of this spiritual discipline unites us with our eschatological *telos* in a prophetic proclamation of oneness with Christ as our personal and communal destiny. It asserts the advent of God's future in the midst of the Body of Christ as being the entrance to the new *aeon* of the fullness of God's Kingdom on earth and marking the prophesying community of faith as the embodiment of the very future of the world.

The Event of Pentecost as the Birthing, Anointing, and Empowering of the Body of Christ on Earth

The event of Pentecost could be viewed as the incarnation of Christ in the community of faith, a moment brought about through the agency of the Holy Spirit.[9] As the third person of the Trinity pours Himself over the hundred-and-twenty in the upper room, they become both Christ-bearers and a living extension of His resurrected Body on earth. Sergius Bulgakov has given us the image of Jesus' conception as being 'the Pentecost of the Virgin'.[10] As the Holy Spirit descends on Mary in response to her willingness and readiness for service (Lk. 1.38), she is transformed into an instrument of God's Word becoming flesh in our midst (Jn 1.14). For Bulgakov, it takes a willing human instrument to authenticate the humanness of Christ in the incarnation.[11]

---

[9] Some of the content and insights of this particular section in the present essay originated with my work on 'Pentecost as the Church's Cosmopolitan Vision of Civil Society', in William Storror, Peter Casarella and Paul Metzger (eds.), *A World for All? Global Civil Society in Political Theory and Trinitarian Theology* (Grand Rapids: Eerdmans, forthcoming).

[10] Sergius Bulgakov, 'The Virgin and the Saints in Orthodoxy', in Daniel B. Clendenin (ed.), *Eastern Orthodox Theology: A Contemporary Reader* (Grand Rapids, MI: Baker Books, 1995), p. 67.

[11] Bulgakov, 'The Virgin and the Saints in Orthodoxy', p. 67.

In a similar manner, as the Spirit descends upon the disciples, Christ is conceived in them and they are empowered (Acts 1.8). Individually and corporately, they become Christ-bearers and bear forth an embodied Gospel as a hope realized in the midst of a destitute humanity. The proclamation of the Good News is an announcement of God's providential presence with the hearers of the Word. It is an invitation to partake in the life of God and ultimately in the future of the world. The witness of the disciples on the day of Pentecost, 'speaking of the mighty deeds of God' (Acts 2.11), reminds us of Mary's Magnificat (Lk. 1.46-55). In both cases, it is the voice of the socially marginalized, ostracized, and persecuted. They announce the just socio-political reality of God's Kingdom, adventing among humanity in Jesus Christ, in whom the fulfillment of the divine covenantal promises of salvation (Lk. 1.54-55; Acts 2.33, 38-40) has been extended to all, even 'to the ends of the earth' (Acts 1.8).[12]

The Christocentrism of this event is associated further with the transference of the messianic anointing from Christ to the community of faith. The community is His Body present in the world; they are thereby called and empowered to continue His mission and ministry outlined in the programmatic citation of Isaiah in Lk. 4.18-19.[13] In a manner similar to that in the narrative of Jesus' inauguration (Lk. 3.21-22), the Spirit of Pentecost descends upon His own—the incarnated Christ empowering the Body for the fulfillment of the messianic task. Therefore, the prophetic, royal, and priestly dimensions of Christ's ministry become a part of the charismatic reality of His body, and the community of disciples is transformed into a royal priesthood and prophethood of all believers.[14] As such, the Body represents a new Christ-like consciousness. This

---

[12] Beverly Roberts Gaventa, *The Acts of the Apostles* (Abingdon New Testament Commentaries; Nashville, TN: Abingdon Press, 2003), p. 80.

[13] Roger Stronstad (*The Charismatic Theology of St. Luke* [Peabody, MA: Hendrickson, 1984]) draws the parallel between Pentecost and the transfer of the Spirit from Moses to the seventy elders (Num. 11.10-30). As Stronstad notes: 'Both narratives record the transfer of a leadership from a single individual to a group.... In both cases the transfer of the Spirit results in an outburst of prophesy' (p. 59).

[14] On the prophethood of the Pentecost Community see Roger Stronstad, *The Prophethood of All Believers* (JPTSup 16; Sheffield: Sheffield Academic Press, 1999), pp. 65-70.

global and cosmic consciousness of the Kingdom is expressed in a redemptive relationship with the other—as love for God and neighbor (Mt. 27.37-40). Since Christ's messianic mission is fulfilled in self-giving to the other, the consciousness formed by the Spirit in His Body is an antidote to that of empire. While the imperial consciousness commodifies, consumes, marginalizes, and even eliminates the other for its own benefit, the messianic consciousness of Christ's Body prioritizes the other and the other's wellbeing.

This incarnationalist view of Pentecost also allows us to consider the possibility of looking at the remainder of Acts as rooted in Christ's extended presence on earth in His Body. Therefore, if the Gospel of Luke represents the first volume of 'all that Jesus began to do and teach' (Acts 1.1), the book of Acts can be seen as the second volume outlining 'the continuation and fulfillment of what Jesus did and thought'.[15] Being a living extension of the risen Lord and continuation of His ministry in this world, the Body follows the extroverted orientation of Christ's mission, namely, from oneself towards the other. Therefore, for the community of faith, Pentecost is also a literal crossing of the bridge from the private to the public. As the Church moves beyond the enclosure of the Upper Room into the public space of the city and begins to participate in the public discourse about the welfare of its citizens, it becomes a distinct factor of social change. This movement is also a crossing from the zone of mediation on the incarnated Christ to an incarnation of His presence. It is a transition from reflection (prayer) to interaction (witness) to action (transformation). It is a movement from 'the innermost being' (Jn 7.38) to the 'ends of the world'. Incarnation is the mode of this extroverted movement, and the Spirit is its agent, engine, and navigator. The Spirit's mission (in continuity with the character and nature of God) is realized through self-

---

[15] Matthias Wenk, *Community-Forming Power: The Socio-Ethical Role of the Spirit in Luke-Acts* (JPTSup 19; Sheffield: Sheffield Academic Press, 2000), p. 242. The author points to the outpouring of the Spirit at Pentecost as a clear example that the ministry of Christ (the Baptizer with the Holy Spirit) continues in Acts (p. 243) He mentions also the passages of Acts 9.5, 10; 13.39; 7.55-56; 17.7; 18.10; 19.15 and 25.19 as indicative of Jesus' acting upon the disciples. Another example is the healing of the beggar in Acts 3.1-16 'presented as a continuation of Jesus' healing ministry (Acts 4.30)' (p. 245). Beverly Gaventa's work also supports the view of the book of Acts as presenting a continuation of the ministry of Jesus. See her commentary *The Acts of the Apostles*, pp. 34, 62-63.

sharing—God pours Himself upon all flesh. In sharing His life, He becomes the source of life that sustains the spiritual ecology of the faith community.

The fact that Christ is the Truth (Jn 14.6) that sets people free (Jn 8.32) brings into view the image of the prophetic Pentecost community as a truth-embodying and truth-proclaiming social reality that unites the story of the Kingdom with its praxis. The community's voice in the life of the city calls all civic dimensions to moral responsibility and discernment between good and evil. Once again, the incarnation is essential for exercising discernment, for each spirit is known by its fruit (Mt. 7.16, 1 Jn 4.2), and the fruit of the Holy Spirit is revealed within the human *socium* through the prioritization of the other in one's social interactions (Gal. 5.22-23).

This aspect of the Kingdom is an outcome of the Spirit's dialectic of liberation. This new human consciousness is not a result of social evolution (Hegel) or revolution (Marx). Rather, as Nikolai Berdyaev has stated, the Kingdom of God is an outcome of a 'marvelous transfiguration'.[16] Marx's saint and hero was Prometheus, who stole fire from the gods in order to give it to humanity and meet the human need of light, illumination, and the freedom to chart one's own journey. In contrast, the fire of the Spirit is a divine act of self-giving, an expression of divine hospitality. In this fire a self-pouring God meets all human needs. God's Spirit invites humans into His light, gives them dreams and visions, and empowers them to prophesy a just socio-political reality beyond the order of empires. Herein lies a true actualization of human freedom in covenantal community with the Trinity and with one another. The light of the Spirit illuminates and initiates the dialectic of true human freedom beginning with a clarity of vision—'you shall know the truth and the truth shall set you free' (Jn 8.32). This is a different kind of knowing than that of the Marxist revolutionary consciousness emphasizing one's self-interest as a representative of the proletarian class. Illuminated by the Spirit, the liberating epistemology is that of knowing Christ in the other (Mt. 25.31-46)—or knowing otherwise.[17] First of all, knowing the truth is being in a covenant

---

[16] Nikolai Berdyaev, *Philosophy of Inequality* (Sofia: Prozoretz, 1923), p. 220.

[17] James H. Olthuis (ed.), *Knowing Other-Wise: Philosophy at the Threshold of Spirituality* (New York: Fordham University Press, 1997), p. 8.

with the One Who is the Truth and then seeing Him in the other even in their 'most distressful disguise' (Mother Teresa). Knowing the Truth gives us His perspective towards the other, informing and constructing our actions. The other is known otherwise than in the imperial consciousness. We come to know the other as Christ knows him or her, a knowing in which human dignity and wholeness are restored. It is the knowing of love in flesh—knowing in Christ-likeness.

The event of Pentecost also ushers 'the revealing of the sons (and daughters) of God' for which creation longs and groans (Rom. 8.20-23) in anticipation of justice, healing, and restoration. The Holy Spirit descended upon Jesus in His water baptism as a public statement of His identity as the Son of God—a statement of the love and approval of the Father for His only begotten Son (Mt. 3.17). The descent of the Spirit upon the Messiah was the identifier given to John the Baptist who proclaimed publicly Jesus' divine identity and mission (Jn 1.32-33).

In the same manner, the descending of the Holy Spirit upon the hundred-and-twenty on the Day of Pentecost is a public statement from the Father to His children of love and affirmation. They are indeed the sons and daughters of God and are, therefore, the recipients of the promise of the Father (Acts 2.39). This is the long anticipated eschatological unveiling of the identity of those who in their corporate existence as the Body of Christ on earth become the instruments of God's justice, healing, and restoration not only to human society but also to all the rest of creation. Through them the consequences of the life of God, in-fleshed in the community of faith, are translated to the rest of the created cosmos. The first Adam was responsible for the curse that permeated creation and its consequent pollution and distortion that has progressively intensified with humanity's multi-generational distance from Eden. The last Adam set free from the curse not only humanity, but also the rest of the created reality. The embodiment of this liberating truth in the Body of Christ on earth mandates it to carry forth the distributive justice of God towards creation. Thus, the ministry of reconciliation and its effects encompass not only the human socium, but also the rest of the created order—all material existence is brought in the redemptive embrace of the Trinity. Therefore, as Frank Macchia points out, Spirit baptism 'recalls God's Trinitarian openness to the world and the drama of how God would eventually pour the divine presence out in order to indwell all things through the role of the Son as the Spirit Baptizer.'[18] Pentecost marks the revealing of the children of God, and their presence on earth is manifested through God's therapeutic justice exercised through them toward all creation summoned by the eschatological vision of the Cosmic Christ. Therefore, on the Day of Pentecost Spirit Baptism exhibits the teleological tension of the 'already' and 'not yet' of the Kingdom reality and points to its apocalyptic 'culmination with the Day of the Lord'.[19] As God subjects all things to Christ (1 Cor. 15.28), He delivers creation from death unto eternal life, by indwelling it with His own life in the Spirit and 'making all things new' (Rev. 21.5).

This redemptive eschatological union with God in the Cosmic Christ is both experienced and anticipated in the 'liturgical anamnesis'[20] of the community of faith. The anamnesis of Christ (1 Cor. 11.24-25) is not a mental recollection, but an enacted likeness. It is choosing 'to be' and 'to do' like Him, becoming His extension on earth through the incarnational agency of the Holy Spirit. Through the Body of Christ, heaven descends on earth and restores the unity of the Creator with His creation as the liturgical celebration translates the foretaste of the divine fullness of life in and through the Spirit-baptized *koinonia*.

Speaking in Tongues and the Translatability of Human Language

Babel and the Eruption of the Language of the Other

Christian Theology has a long-standing tradition of viewing the event of Pentecost as an overcoming or a reversal of Babel.[21] The connection between the two events, however, can be also seen in the continuity of God's prophetic deconstruction of every imperial

---

[18] Macchia, *Baptized in the Spirit*, p. 125.

[19] Macchia, *Baptized in the Spirit*, p. 102.

[20] Margaret R. Pfeil, 'Liturgy and Ethics: The Liturgical Asceticism of Energy Conservation', *Journal of the Society of Christian Ethics*, 27.2 (2007), pp. 127-49, [136].

[21] On the view of Pentecost as a reversal of Babel see Avery Dulles, *The Catholicity of the Church* (Oxford: Oxford University Press, 1987), p. 173.

consciousness that is inherently homogenizing and violently marginalizing of those who are other and different.[22]

The account in Genesis 11 describes the architectonic of an empire suppressing all differences that attempt to destabilize its own grand project for self-immortalization. The text contrasts the speech and action of the empire (vv. 2-4) with the speech-act of God (vv. 5-8). The imperial project looks for shortcuts to its goal of totalizing uniformity. Substituting 'brick for stone and tar for mortar' (v. 3), the architects of empire hurry to mark a territory and establish dominion. In order to assume superiority over the 'plain of Shinar', they use imperial propaganda that cultivates in the populace a fear of the future and of the other. The boundaries of empire are presented as the demarcations of safety (v. 4). Beyond them is 'the face of the whole world' (v. 4), which is a special designation for the location of *the face of the other*.[23] 'Heaven' (v. 4) is the ultimate goal of the project; the empire has identified itself with the final, undisputed authority. With that move nothing remains beyond its scope. Sacred space collapses in its grip and leaves humanity with no exodus from the totalitarian order.

As God comes down in the plurality of personhood expressed by the divine speech ('let us'—v. 7), He acts in conformity with His nature of creating and affirming diversity. He extends self-giving by opening space and time for the other and thereby creates the possibility of an authentic human community, one in which life can be shared together in a multiplicity of forms and locations. In view of that, the destruction of the empire's project is an act of deconstructing a world order that has eliminated the possibility of the other. God induces this imperial collapse by bringing the language of the other forth within the homogeneity of human space. The monotone superiority of imperial culture is challenged by the polyphony of human speech as the inaugural address of a multicultural human reality (vv. 7, 9). The demanding immediacy of the

---

[22] Miroslav Volf, *Exclusion and Embrace: A Theological Exploration of Identity, Otherness and Reconciliation* (Nashville: Abingdon Press, 1996), pp. 226-31.

[23] The immediate association of this phrase is with the work of Emmanuel Levinas and his emphasis on the other as the focal point of ethics, and of ethics as being the first philosophy. The face of the other, as an expression of their presence, summons us to responsibility and justice becomes defined as our relationship to the other.

other's presence brings about the demolition of the empire's boundaries, as the formerly homogenized population overflows and spreads 'abroad over the face of the whole earth' (v. 9). The new accomplishment of human community after Babel demands accepting the other and making the effort to learn his or her language. This is God's response to the self-perpetuation of imperial consciousness and is inseparable from His providential plan for the salvation of humanity.

The confusion following the eruption of the other (v. 9) will accompany humanity in its journey after Babel. Fallen human nature continues to gravitate to the homogenizing shortcuts of empire, offering its dehumanizing patterns of association as a substitute for the need of sociality in the diversity of authentic human community. God's alternative, designed to bring the restoration of His communion with humanity (and of authentic human sociality as a reflection of the restoration of His image in human beings) situates salvation within the relationship to the other (Exod. 20.12-17). From the midst of 'the thunder and lightening flashes and the sound of the trumpet and the mountain smoking' at Sinai (Exod. 20.18), God establishes in a creative speech-act a covenant with His people. The divine utterance unites the aural and visual dimensions of human communication, and His flaming words become visible to the multitude (similar to the burning bush experience of Moses in Exod. 3.2-5, and later to the flames of Pentecost in Acts 2.3).[24] He brings the other into the center of personal and corporate social redemption (Deut. 5.16-21; Exod. 20.12-17). The appropriation of the covenant bond with God demands the establishment of covenantal bonds with the other—the immediate other (one's mother, father, neighbor) as well as the distant other (the stranger, the foreigner, the gentile). God remains in our midst as the omnipresent Other in whom we move and live and have our being (Acts 17.28).

---

[24] In his commentary on Acts, Luke Timothy Johnson points to the symbolism utilized by Philo Judaeus, 'who explicitly attaches the giving of the Law by God to the communication of speech by flame.' Johnson offers the following quotation of his work (*On the Decalogue*): 'Then from the midst of the fire that streamed from heaven there sounded forth to their utter amazement a voice, for the flame became articulated speech in the language familiar to the audience, and so clearly and distinctly were the words formed by it that they seemed to see rather than hear them.' *The Acts of the Apostles* (Collegeville, Minnesota: A Michael Glazier Book, The Liturgical Press, 1992), p. 46.

Therefore, we see in the Sinai event the establishment of a communal covenant as an immediate embodiment and extension of the salvific covenant with God.

God's words have the unique quality of embodying a creative force that bespeaks reality. As such, they stand before the people not only as a covenantal demand (or a command) but also as a promise. The hearers of the words can love God and neighbor as the Holy Spirit engraves the law on their hearts, and they are thereby transformed into His likeness.[25] The fulfillment of the promise is already initiated in the moment of its impartation, for God and His Word already inhabit the future. In the immutability of the divine presence, the proclamation of the promise becomes an articulated preview of its fulfillment.

The event of Pentecost could be understood in relation to the promised fulfillment of a renewed covenant with God and neighbor (Jer. 31.33) that is brought about through God's transformational self-giving.[26] The covenant has been established in God's self-giving in Christ and sealed with His self-giving in the Spirit that

---

[25] Leonid Ouspensky, 'The Meaning of and Content of the Icon', pp. 33-63 in D.B. Clendenin (ed.), *Eastern Orthodox Theology* (Grand Rapids, MI: Baker Books, 1995), pp. 37-38.

[26] Reflecting on the connection between the giving of the Torah and the celebration of Pentecost, Luke T. Johnson states that: 'After the destruction of the temple in C.E. 70, it is clear that Pentecost was universally understood by the Jews to be the celebration of the giving of the Torah on Mt. Sinai' (*The Acts of the Apostles*, p. 46). Roger Stronstad points out that the feast of Pentecost was historically celebrated as 'the second of three pilgrim festivals in Israel's liturgical calendar' (*The Prophethood of All Believers: A Study in Luke's Charismatic Theology*, p. 54). Regarding the possibility of Luke's account on Pentecost to be influenced by the rabbinic tradition equating the feast of Pentecost with the giving of the Law, Stronstad suggests that it is unlikely, since this rabbinic tradition developed later than the Pentecost narrative in Acts (*The Charismatic Theology of St. Luke* [Peabody, MA: Hendrickson Publishers, 1984], p. 58). The rabbinic tradition eventually developed the belief that when the law was given, it was heard not only by Israel but by the 72 nations listed in Gen. 10.2-31. In his commentary on Acts, F.F. Bruce cites the Midrash Tanchuma 26 C, that at Sinai the voice of God divided into 'seven voices and then went into seventy tongues'. *Commentary on the Book of Acts* (The New International Commentary on the New Testament; ed. F.F. Bruce; Grand Rapids, MI: Wm. B. Eerdmans Publishing Co., 1979), p. 60. In opposition to Stronstad, Johnson points out that 'Luke certainly could have made the connection' between the Pentecost feast and the giving of the Torah, on his own, in spite of the existence or not of such a tradition prior to his account of Pentecost in Acts.

brings the believers into the *koinonia* of the Trinity and makes them partakers of the divine nature.

Therefore, as outlined in Peter's sermon (Acts 2.14-39), the incarnation, crucifixion, resurrection, and ascension of Christ are central to the Pentecost theophany of the Spirit. Pentecost authenticates the redemption accomplished by God on behalf of humanity in Christ Jesus. Christ is the new Adam (1 Cor. 15.45), the perfect icon and representation of God (Col. 1.15, 2 Cor. 4.4). In Him humanity is thus restored to its proper position in relation to the divine and the rest of creation. Human sociality is redeemed in communion with the other as a reflection and extension through the Holy Spirit of the trinitarian life of God.[27] Therefore, the charismatic *koinonia* of the believers represents a renewal of the communal covenant within the context of the restoration in Christ of the salvific covenant between humanity and the Redeeming Trinity.

As Pentecost marks the moment of the historical realization of the promise of covenantal renewal with God and neighbor, language and its translatability becomes once again the symbolic center of the event as an audible manifestation of God's *telos* for humanity and the rest of creation.

The Translatability of Language as a Call to Community

It is no accident that the language of the other stands at the center of the Pentecost event as an expression of the prioritization of the other in the Kingdom of a new humanity. In the words of Mikhail Bakhtin, '… language, for the individual consciousness, lies on the borderline between oneself and the other'.[28] Language participates in the composition of one's personal and corporate identity and therefore could be viewed as being 'constitutive to reality and not just a reflection of it'.[29] Jean-François Lyotard reminds us that the

---

[27] For an in-depth discussion on the Trinitarian sociality as expressed in the human socium, see: Miroslav Volf, *After Our Likeness: The Church in the Image of the Trinity* (Grand Rapids, MI: Wm. B. Eerdmans Publishing Co., 1998). Also see Владимир Соловьёв, 'Троичное Начало и его Общественно Приложение', pp. 243-334 in *Чтения о Богочеловечество* (Санкт-Петербург: Азбука, 2000), esp. in chapter 10, Soloviov's passage on the Social Trinity.

[28] Mikhail Bakhtin, 'Discourse in the Novel', in *The Dialogic Imagination* (ed. Michael Holquist; Austin, TX: The University of Texas Press, 1981), p. 293.

[29] Maria Teresa Morgan, 'Tongues as of Fire: The Spirit as Paradigm for Ministry in a Multicultural Setting', in *The Spirit in the Church and the World* (ed. Bradford E. Hinze; New York: Orbis Books, 2004), p. 107.

translatability of language points to the fact that all human beings are called to one speech community.[30] The translation of language is not a mere tool for transforming an obscure sound into a coherent thought. It is a path to convergence of contents and identities into a dialogical whole which takes a life of its own. In this new mutual conversational identity there is a purpose and a destiny shared by the participants. The participation in the language of the other becomes a participation in their identity and future as our own.

Bakhtin's idea of *heteroglossia* is a useful concept in exploring the corporate and personal social effects of dialogization. Bakhtin points out that words are not neutral and impersonal.[31] Language is historically and ideologically specific.[32] Yet, his view of the dialogization of languages reaches further than the Socratic debate or the Hegelian dialectic. Dialogical *heteroglossia* creates a multi-dimensional unity of oneself with the other while preserving the distinctiveness of each one. On the one hand, the word we speak is always 'half someone else's'.[33] On the other hand, the words we speak become populated with the intentions of the other (as well as with our own), for language is always directed towards understanding of the other.[34] Since language is a historically charged reality, dialogical unity with the other involves our participation in the story of the other. However, this co-habitation of the story of the other gives us, at the same time, an-other perspective on our own language and story.[35] We are able to see ourselves through the eyes of the other.

Jacques Derrida makes the important observation that: 'Language resists all mobilities because it moves about' with us. 'It is the least immovable thing, the most mobile of personal bodies which

---

[30] J.-F. Lyotard, 'The Other's Rights,' in S. Shute and S. Hurley (eds.), *On Human Rights* (New York: Basic Books, 1993), pp. 140-41.

[31] Bakhtin, *The Dialogic Imagination*, p. 294.

[32] Bakhtin, *The Dialogic Imagination*, p. 294.

[33] Bakhtin, *The Dialogic Imagination*, p. 293.

[34] Bakhtin, *The Dialogic Imagination*, p. 282.

[35] Bakhtin, 'Response to a Question from Novy Mir Editorial Staff', in Caryl Emerson and Michael Holquist (eds.), *Speech Genres and Other Late Essays* (trans. Vern W. McGee; Austin, TX: The University of Texas, 1986), pp. 1-7. See also James P. Zappen, 'Mikhail Bakhtin' in Michael G. Morgan and Michelle Ballif (eds.), *Twentieth-Century Rhetoric and Rhetoricians: Critical Studies and Sources* (Westport: Greenwood Press, 2000), pp. 7-20.

remains the stable but portable condition of all mobilities.'[36] Therefore, displaced people—'exiles, the deported, the expelled, the rootless, the stateless, lawless nomads, absolute foreigners, often continue to recognize the language, what is called the mother tongue, as their ultimate homeland, and even their last resting place.'[37]

If the mother-tongue is our mobile habitat—our home away from home, then it is essential to the act of welcoming the other in unconditional hospitality. When the other encounters their mother-tongue in us, they enter their homeland. Our space becomes their space, and they are finally at home.

The event of Pentecost offers a paradigmatic vision of the incarnation of God's self-giving hospitality in the community of the believers as an extension of Christ's Body on earth. The outpouring of the Spirit upon the Body manifests God's self-sharing in welcoming all nations under heaven (Acts 2.5), through submitting His Word to the form and sound of their ethnic tongues (v. 6). Therefore, the proclamation speech of the faith community on the day of Pentecost embraces the language of the other. The divine embrace is no mere rhetorical strategy. It is a gift of divine hospitality. The Spirit invites all humanity to make its habitat in the inter-sociality of the Trinity. This invitation implies the host's self-giving (or surrender) to the other and not their colonization. It is an initiation of dialogue by re-spacing oneself and creating conditions for conversational inclusion of the other. It is a gesture of welcoming all foreigners, aliens, strangers literally on their own terms.

The all-inclusive multiplicity of languages employed by the Spirit in sharing the Good News about 'the mighty deeds of God' (v. 11) on behalf of all humanity brings together two significant dimensions of the divine hospitality. On the one hand, it demonstrates a differentiation among the ethnic groups within the multitude and pays attention to the unique singularities present within such diversity. On the other hand, the multiplicity of languages also expresses an affirmation of each separate ethnic identity and establishes the equality of each one before and in the presence of the Creator. Therefore, the self-expression of God's Word in all ethnic tongues

---

[36] Jacques Derrida, *Of Hospitality* (trans. Rachel Bowlby; Stanford, California: Stanford University Press, 2000), p. 91.

[37] Derrida, *Of Hospitality*, pp. 87, 89.

could also be viewed as their consecration. The Word fills the words of the nations with the story of God. The languages of the people become the vocal embodiment of God's active, creative presence. The Word translates itself into all languages while sustaining their unique distinctions. The invitation to the people to embrace a common spiritual genesis and destiny does not eliminate but sustains ethnic diversity. The divine Word reminds us (in the words of Desmond Tutu) that among humanity 'God has no enemies, only family.'[38]

On the day of Pentecost, the diverse multitude within the empire hears the Word of God, each in their own tongue. The hearers are aware of the transitionality of empires, of their sudden rise and fall, and of their succession by other empires competing for time and space in the global history. Among the hearers are those who themselves have become displaced and dislocated as a result of the rise and fall of empires. They have become strangers in new lands, refugees and exiles under the commodifying rule of the empire. As the Spirit brings the Word of God to them in the form and sound of their mother tongue, the one non-transitional and immutable eternal reality that 'will never pass away' (Mt. 24.35) visits them in their mutability and displacement. As it indwells the mother tongue—the single ethnic identity dimension that accompanies the listener in their journey from the cradle to the grave—the Word of God welcomes them as a motherland in which they can find rest from their wandering and uncertainty of belonging. God becomes their eternal home, an act consistent with Who He is in His self-giving from before the foundations of the world (1 Pet. 1.20).

Xenolalia and *Glossolalia* as the First Audible Sign of our Eschatological Destiny

The *xenolalic* translatability of languages at the event of Pentecost points to the eschatological destiny of humanity as being called to one human community in the household of God. All of us are His offspring (Acts 17.28) sharing a common origin and purpose. 'God in the Spirit is God existing in community'[39] and the event of Pen-

---

[38] Desmond Tutu, *God Has a Dream: A Vision of Hope for Our Time* (New York: Doubleday, 2004), p. 47.

[39] Peter Hodgson, *Winds of the Spirit: A Constructive Christian Theology* (Louisville, KY: Westminster/John Knox Press, 1994), p. 296.

tecost as the authentic work of the Spirit is expressed in His building the bonds of the charismatic *koinonia* and renewing the communal covenant within the spiritual context of God's salvific covenant. The Spirit empowers humanity to recover the speech of the other across lines of alienation and mutual exclusion into a 'covenantal conversation that fosters the root form of human relatedness: communion'.[40] His therapeutic presence deconstructs stereotypes and walls of divisions across gender, class, ethnicity, and language, divides and ministers healing and wholeness to individuals and communities. Therefore, Pentecost could be viewed as a redemptive eschatological recovery of Eden[41] where the community of the Trinity is once again the community of humanity and the rest of creation; where humanity is restored into harmony with one another and God in a radical communal unity of diversity as the Spirit makes all things new.

In view of this conclusion, we can discuss the significance of the *glossolalic* translatability as the converging of the tongues of heaven and earth. Illuminated by the vision of the final eschatological unity of all existence in Christ, the charismatic practice of *glossolalia* (and interpretation), may be viewed as a foretaste of the ultimate destiny of heaven and earth as being called together into one holy *koinonia*. It points to the teleological joining of the terrestrial and celestial in Christ and, therefore, in His Church as the new redeemed community of the Spirit. The charismatic gift unites the material and spiritual dimensions of existence—the visible and the invisible reality. It manifests the Church as the new creation in which heaven and earth are reunited in the life of the Triune God. Therefore, the Spirit-baptized Church becomes the embodied experience of heaven on earth—heaven transforming and transfiguring the earth into the Kingdom of God.

The Kingdom, as the sovereign rule of God, summons the hosts of heaven and earth in the unity of the Spirit within the liturgy of the Church. Thus, in her worship and work (*leitourgia*) the Church becomes the future of the world, as well as the spiritual location where the once invisible celestial realm is made present, transparent,

---

[40] Eleasar S. Fernandez, 'From Babel to Pentecost: Finding a Home in the Belly of Empire,' *Semeia* 90-91 (Spring-Summer 2002), pp. 29-51 [41].

[41] Vigen Guroian, 'Fruits of Pentecost: The Christian Gardener,' *The Christian Century*, 113.21 (July 3, 1996), pp. 684-86.

and visible. *Glossolalia* is an audible sign of this eschatological un-folding within the Body of Christ—the mutual indwelling of heaven and earth as the foretaste of their ultimate Christic destiny.

The liturgy of the Church celebrates this union as its very es-sence and self-expression. The liturgical worship of the community of faith is not only a portal to heaven but a merging of the celestial and earthly celebration of God's presence. There is one altar, one sacrifice, one presence, and all the invisible host of heaven joins the redeemed humanity around that altar—the table of the Lord. We worship surrounded by 'the great cloud of witnesses' (Heb. 12.1), our spiritual eyes open to the nearness of the angels and the saints from all generations standing with us around the throne of God Who meets us in the familiar face of Christ—the incarnated eternal Word, the Lamb of God, the *Pantokrator* of all (Rev. 1.8).

Therefore, both *xenolalia* and *glossolalia* have a sacramental func-tion in the life of the charismatic community,[42] articulating the mys-tery of the union of the redeemed creation with its Creator and experiencing the in-breaking of the eschatological fullness of Christ in His Body. It is an experience of the presence and self-sharing of God in His Spirit that welcomes us in the life of the Trinity and makes us an extension of His life on earth.

Speaking in Tongues as Liturgical *Askesis*

In embracing the language of the other, the speaker surrenders to the movement of the Spirit who shapes the oneness of the Body in its Christ-likeness. The translatability of languages has already pointed to this sacramental oneness—the unity of heaven and earth and all humanity in Christ as the *omega* of all existence (Rev. 1.8).

---

[42] Frank Macchia's work on speaking in tongues as a sacrament offers impor-tant insights into the liturgical practice of the charismatic gift. See his essay 'Tongues as a Sign: Towards a Sacramental Understanding of Tongues,' *Pneuma* 15.1 (Spring 1993), pp. 61-76. As Kenneth Archer has stated, the sacraments 'are prophetic narrative signs involving words and deeds through which the commu-nity can experience the redemptive living presence of God in Christ through the Holy Spirit.' ('Nourishment for Our Journey: The Pentecostal *Via Salutis* and Sacramental Ordinances', *Journal of Pentecostal Theology* 13.1 (2004), pp. 79-96 [p. 86]. Archer's definition clearly applies to both *xenolalia* and *glossolalia* as discussed in the present essay.

The initial surrender of our tongue to the language of the other (both xenolalic and glossolalic) is an expression of embracing this call to oneness in Christ as our personal and communal destiny. Therefore, the continual practice of speaking in tongues by the believer could be viewed as an act of *praktikê* (ascetic struggle) within the context of liturgy. These are acts of fasting from oneself on behalf of the other in sacramental gestures of proclaiming the will of God as one's freely chosen destiny—the redemptive joining of all creation in the One Christ until He is 'all in all' (Eph. 1.23). This proclamation is consistent with the understanding of theology 'as internal vision, which requires personal, ascetic effort'. It requires not only an individual, but also a communal effort, 'an effort made within the community of saints.'[43] This is the eschatological vision of the Cosmic Christ, which becomes a 'Christoforming'[44] force in the life of the faith community. This ascetic effort asserts that 'He must increase', but we 'must decrease' (Jn 3.30) so that the reality of the Kingdom may become the reality of our life in the Spirit-formed *koinonia* with God and neighbor.

As Margaret Pfeil asserts, *paraktikê* takes place

as the Christian worshiper's graced and free response to God's gratuitous love celebrated in Christian liturgy. First, liturgical asceticism springs from and seeks to nourish the life of the Christian worshiping community, and second, it implies an eschatological horizon in which the ultimate *telos* of *askesis* consists in the fullness of life in God.[45]

Speaking in tongues is, therefore, also a prophetic assertion of the inevitability of God's future and its *parousia* in the community of faith. It is an evidence of the coming of God as the Holy Spirit takes residence in the Body of Christ and articulates through its voice the presence of the Kingdom on earth.

---

[43] John Meyendorff, 'Doing Theology in an Eastern Orthodox Perspective', in Daniel B. Clendenin (ed.), *Eastern Orthodox Theology: A Contemporary Reader* (Grand Rapids, MI: Baker Books, 1995), p. 87.

[44] The term is used by Frank Macchia in *Baptized in the Spirit*, p. 106.

[45] Margaret R. Pfeil, 'Liturgy and Ethics: The Liturgical Asceticism of Energy Conservation', pp. 127-28.

The sacramental life of the Church in its liturgical expression has been described in terms of 'eschatological symbolism'.[46] As Alexander Schmemann points out, in the early Christian community the 'eschatological' meaning was defined as the belief that

> the coming of Christ, His life, His death and resurrection from the dead, His ascension to heaven and the sending by Him, on the day of Pentecost, of the Holy Spirit, have brought about the Lord's Day; the *Yom Yahweh* announced by the prophets has inaugurated the new *aeon* of the Kingdom of God.[47]

In its union with Christ, as His Body anointed with the Holy Spirit, the Church already indwells this new *aeon* and manifests it on earth as the embodied future. Therefore, the sacramental eschatological symbolism has as essential particularity 'the fact that in it the very distinction between the sign and the signified is simply ignored'. In it 'the sign and that which it signifies are one and the same thing'.[48] In a way, 'the liturgy happens to us', since the liturgical entrance is 'the church's entrance to heaven'.[49] Because we are *in* Christ, we are one with Him in the unfolding of the *eschaton* in the present, which transforms the sacramental life of the Church into a realized eschatology. As the Church walks through the present as a prophetic unfolding of its eschatological destiny, the sacraments articulate the three continual movements in her liturgical life: her ascent to heaven—to the table of the Lord and His sustaining loving presence, her descend to earth carrying in her midst the reality of heaven so that there may be heaven on earth that welcomes all humanity in the embrace of God, and finally her going out into the world to proclaim the Gospel and share the reality of the Kingdom—of redemption, healing and restoration, until it covers the earth as the waters of the sea (Hab. 2.14).

As Frank Macchia points out, through the agency of the Holy Spirit 'we participate in that which signifies the sanctification of creation to become the very dwelling place of God through the

---

[46] Alexander Schmemann, *Liturgy and Tradition* (ed. Thomas Fish; Crestwood, NY: St. Vladimir's Seminary Press, 1990), p. 125.

[47] Schmemann, *Liturgy and Tradition*, p. 125.

[48] Schmemann, *Liturgy and Tradition*, p. 127.

[49] Schmemann, *Liturgy and Tradition*, p. 127.

crucifixion and resurrection of the Spirit Baptizer.'[50] Therefore the sacramental practice of *xenolalia* and *glossolalia* mediates to us the power of the invisible grace that transforms us into a visible extension of Christ on earth, makes us co-sharers in the life of God and through it in one another as the Body of Christ.

Conclusion: The Prophesying Community of Faith as an Embodiment of the Future of the World

The Pentecost vision of the prophesying community of faith (Acts 2.17-18) articulates the radical hospitality of God to humanity and the rest of creation. It is a vision of the future of the world as God's future. He invites and empowers humanity to speak forth its reality and content. The voices of the Spirit-saturated believers shape and form God's future for humanity by calling it forth in prophetic utterance. The speakers and the Word become one incarnated creative force. This is a striking vision of the democratization of society, one in which radical emancipation and inclusivity permeate all socio-economic strata. Sons and daughters, old and young, bound slaves and free persons join their voices in speaking forth the just future of God. They all participate in the envisioning, articulation, and realization of that future. In a self-consistent act of hospitality, God grants them ownership of His future where He is all in all. In the Spirit, they extend the hospitality of God to the other and the different (to the class-opponent, to the demographically opposite) by embracing them as a part of their own destiny. Because the Spirit mandates the Body with the ministry of reconciliation (2 Cor. 5.18-19), the future becomes impossible without the voice of the other, even without the enemy.[51] Therefore, global democracy becomes an outcome of divine hospitality taking residence in a Spirit-infused humanity.

This vision of radical divine hospitality is further extended to the rest of creation, welcomed by the self-pouring of God upon all flesh in the embrace of the Redeeming Trinity. The Pentecost re-

---

[50] Macchia, *Baptized in the Spirit*, p. 253.

[51] In his book, *No Future without Forgiveness* (New York: Doubleday, 1999), pp. 257-63, Desmond Tutu offers a reflection out of the African context of tribal conflicts, genocide, and apartheid. He points to the impossibility of societal future apart from forgiveness to the ones identified as enemies.

vealing of the sons and daughters of God, long-anticipated by the groaning creation (Rom. 8.20-23) declares the inevitability of God's redistributive justice. This justice that brings comprehensive healing and restoration starts with the Body of Christ as the embodiment of the Kingdom reality on earth, and is extended in and through it to the rest of the terrestrial realm.

The event of Pentecost, therefore, stages the Church in the power of the Spirit as the embodiment of the very future of the world. Through the agency of the Holy Spirit, Christ becomes incarnated in the community of faith and the Church becomes His living extension here and now. Her voice proclaims the redemptive presence of God in Christ on behalf of humanity and her work as the work of God in this world manifests the inbreaking of His Kingdom in the present age as a foretaste of the age to come.

In a Christ-like manner, the Church is anointed and empowered by the Spirit to share herself with the world—offering her life as a sacrament mediating God's presence and grace to all of creation. Therefore, the Pentecost community as the Body of the risen Christ continues His ministry of hospitality to a starved and destitute humanity. Under the messianic anointing of the Spirit, the community of Christ is empowered daily to follow the Lord who gives His broken body so that others may live. Through the incarnational agency of the Spirit, the Pentecost community becomes an extension of this Messianic self-giving and lays down its bruised and broken Body as a table where the nations can come and feast freely. After they have tasted the Lord, nothing else may satisfy their hunger. From the beginning, 'it was God's intention to bring all things in heaven and on earth to a unity in Christ, and each of us participates in this great movement.'[52] This process of transformation of all reality has its ultimate goal in Christ, the 'omega' of all existence. The process is one of 'the 'Christification' of the whole cosmos.'[53] Beyond the historical horizon stands the cosmic Christ.

This future is not a matter of speculation. It is incarnated by the Spirit in the Pentecost community—in that community's identifica-

---

[52] Desmond Tutu, *No Future without Forgiveness*, p. 265.

[53] Jürgen Moltmann, *Jesus Christ for Today's World* (Minneapolis: Fortress Press, 1994), p. 101. Moltmann picks up the idea of cosmic evolving towards Christ from Teillhard de Chardin's 'Christ the Evolver' in *Christianity and Evolution* (trans. R. Hugue: London: Collins, 1971).

tion with Christ as the *telos* of all creation. Therefore, the community of Pentecost enters the present from the future of the world as the realization of its social destiny. The Spirit-filled ecclesia sees in her rear-view mirror the Spirit-Baptizer Who has sent her into the world to continue His mission and ministry of reconciliation. She walks in the Spirit as the bridge on which heaven arrives daily on earth and the future of God's Kingdom permeates the present with hopeful grace transfiguring it into the likeness of the life of God. The good news of this advent of the Kingdom is her very message and content and as the Church is transfigured into her message, she becomes a living gospel for a needy world.

PART FIVE

THE PENTECOSTAL CHURCH AS HEALING COMMUNITY

8

THE PENTECOSTAL HEALING COMMUNITY

KIMBERLY E. ALEXANDER*

Kenneth E.M. Spooner, missionary to South Africa, wrote to the readers of the *Pentecostal Holiness Advocate* in 1920:

> My dear wife who has been very sick unto death is much better. Truly it pays to serve Jesus and be true to His teaching. Our dear people whom we have taught the truth of divine healing, gathered around her last Sunday, August 21st, and they took hold upon God for her in prayer, and I can tell you that never were more earnest prayers heard for the healing of any one as were heard on Sunday for her.[1]

There is little room for discussion, either at the popular or academic level, as to whether or not healing is a prominent feature of the Pentecostal Church. Popular depictions of Pentecostals most often portray worship services where prayer for the sick is being conducted. News stories about Pentecostalism are likely to focus on healing evangelists or deliverance ministries. Academic studies about the explosion of Pentecostalism around the world point to the place of healing ministries in the growth of the movement. Allan Anderson contends, 'The main attraction of Pentecostalism in the Majority World is still the emphasis on healing and deliverance from evil. Preaching a message that promises solutions for present

---

* Kimberly E. Alexander (PhD, Open University, St Johns College Nottingham) is Associate Professor of Historical Theology and Assistant Dean for Academics and Assessment at the Pentecostal Theological Seminary in Cleveland, TN, USA.

[1] *Pentecostal Holiness Advocate* 5.25 (October 20, 1921), p. 6.

felt needs, the "full gospel" of Pentecostal preachers is readily accepted."[2]

A recent survey by the Pew Research Center found that 'at least half of pentecostals [in seven out of ten countries surveyed] say that the church services they attend frequently include people practicing the gifts of the Holy Spirit, such as speaking in tongues, prophesying or praying for miraculous healing.'[3] Further, the study indicates that the large majority of Pentecostals report a personal experience or witness of divine healing of illness or injury.[4] In all 10 countries surveyed, large majorities of Pentecostals (ranging from 56% in South Korea to 87% in Kenya) say that they have personally experienced or witnessed the divine healing of an illness or injury.

While the statistics have been analyzed and the history documented, to date little has been written about the Pentecostal theology of healing and certainly very little has been written about Pentecostal ecclesiology through the lens of healing theology. This would seem to be a promising avenue of study given the prominence of healing in both the doctrine and practice of Pentecostal communities.

This study will pursue this end, first articulating the distinction between the two models of healing theology and practice found within classical Pentecostalism and then positing an ecclesiology, informed by the testimonies and experiences of healing of those within the Wesleyan-Pentecostal communities of faith.

Jesus is Healer—2 Models

Following their mothers and fathers in the 19th century Healing Movement, many of the earliest faith statements of various churches, missions, and denominations included a tenet expressing

---

[2] Allan Anderson, *An Introduction to Pentecostalism* (Cambridge: Cambridge University Press, 2004), p. 234.

[3] This survey by Pew looked at Pentecostals in the following countries: United States, Brazil, Chile, Guatemala, Kenya, Nigeria, South Africa, India, the Philippines, and South Korea (http://pewresearch.org/pubs/254/pentecostal-power).

[4] (http://pewresearch.org/pubs/254/pentecostal-power).

'Divine Healing is provided in the atonement'.[5] Continuing in this trajectory, many Pentecostal and many Charismatic groups today articulate a belief about healing that links it to the atoning work of Christ, situating it in the theological category of soteriology.[6]

Research shows that even with the seeming comparability of these early statements, testimonies of healing experience, reports of healing practice, and even further exposition of healing theology by early Pentecostals reveal two distinct ways of viewing the beneficial work of Jesus the Healer. This distinction rather easily falls along the soteriological lines drawn during the sanctification controversy of 1910-11.[7] Wesleyan-Pentecostals tend to view healing as a sign of the in-breaking of the already-not yet Kingdom. For those who altered their view and incorporated the Finished Work view of the work of Christ, healing in the present was a sign of a work already accomplished.

In the Wesleyan-Pentecostal model of healing, just as Jesus identified the hallmarks of his Kingdom in his preaching in Luke 4, the believer, as s/he preaches, is 'followed by' signs which not only

---

[5] The earliest statement of faith for the Church of God (Cleveland, TN) listed 'teaching that is being made prominent' and included the following statement: 'Divine healing provided for all in the atonement.' ('Teaching', *Echoes From the General Assembly Held January 9-14, 1912* [Cleveland, TN, 1912], p. 31.) The tenet adopted by the General Council of the Assemblies of God states: 'Deliverance from sickness is provided for in the atonement, and is the privilege of all believers.' ('Statement of Fundamental Truths', *Combined Minutes of the General Council of the Assemblies of God in the United States of America, Canada and Foreign Lands, 1914-1917* [St. Louis, MO: Gospel Publishing House, n.d.], p. 15.)

[6] See the International Pentecostal Holiness Church 'Articles of Faith' which articulates the classical Pentecostal position 'We believe in divine healing as in the atonement.' ('Articles of Faith' http://arc.iphc.org/theology/artfaith.html). The Foursquare Church maintains a statement of faith that equates Jesus' present activity of healing the physical body with the healing of the soul and spirit. ('Doctrine', http://www.foursquare.org/landing_pages/4,3.html). Bethany World Prayer Center, a charismatic mega-church in Baton Rouge, LA states: 'We affirm that the "stripes" placed upon Jesus Christ at his crucifixion provide physical healing to all who will believe and receive.' (http://south.bethany.com/content/what_we_believe)

[7] William Durham (1873-1912), a prominent Pentecostal pastor in Chicago, in 1910 modified his theology, accommodating it to his Baptist roots. This new Pentecostal soteriology disclaimed sanctification as a second definite work of grace, seeing justification and sanctification as occurring at the moment of conversion. He based his theology on what he termed the Finished Work of Christ on the cross. This move, in effect, collapsed the three stages into two by combining initial conversion and sanctification into one work.

point to but *are* the Kingdom which is to come.[8] If they believed that the Church lived in that tension between the ages, the tension of the *already-not yet*, and the believer and or church obeyed by going and preaching, then they held that, in the Age of the Spirit, the Kingdom of God would break in with miraculous speech and phenomena which could only be a part of another world. Just as speaking in tongues was thought to signify that the immanent-transcendent God had filled the human vessel, the healing of the sick signified that the Spirit of Life had broken into the cursed and fallen world.

This thought is nowhere better expressed than in the writings of Hattie M. Barth, a writer and educator from the Pentecostal community centered in Atlanta, Georgia out of which *The Bridegroom's Messenger* was published from 1907. Barth, in a polemic against a cessationist view of spiritual gifts and against those who would see the manifestation of these gifts, including gifts of healing, as belonging solely to 'the next dispensation' proposes a third view:

> The ages overlap like links in a chain. From the time of Pentecost till now there have been some living by faith a few thousands, or hundreds of years ahead. Pentecost itself really belongs to the next dispensation. The prophecy in Joel 2.28, 'I will pour out My Spirit upon all flesh,' only began to be fulfilled on the day of Pentecost (Acts 2.17), the complete fulfillment, as the context shows, is in the next dispensation.[9]

The manifestation of spiritual gifts and presence of 'signs following believers' is a 'foretaste of that coming age'. She explains,

> Are we to cast out devils in His name? Satan will be bound the thousand years. Are we to drink deadly poison without hurt? Thorns, weeds, poisonous plants shall no more infest the ground. Are we to take up serpents? The suckling child shall play

---

[8] Their reading of the so-called longer ending of Mark heavily influenced this view. See Kimberly Ervin Alexander, *Pentecostal Healing: Models of Theology and Practice* (Blandford Forum, Dorset, UK: Deo, 2006) and Kimberly Ervin Alexander and John Christopher Thomas, '"And the Signs Are Following": Mark 16.9-20— A Journey Into Pentecostal Hermeneutics', *Journal of Pentecostal Theology* 11.2 (April 2003), pp. 147-70.

[9] Hattie M. Barth, 'Things of the Kingdom', *The Bridegroom's Messenger* 2.34 (March 15, 1909), p. 4.

on the hole of the asp and the weaned child shall put his hand on the cockatrice den. Are we to heal the sick? When Jesus comes, 'The inhabitant shall not say, 'I am sick.' Are we to overcome this age, all sin, sickness, death, and be caught up to meet him in the air without dying? He must reign, till he hath put all enemies under His feet. The last enemy that shall be destroyed is death. Do we begin now to speak with other tongues of men and of angels, and have gifts of interpretation? The time is coming when that old curse given at Babel shall be lifted, and the inhabitants of the earth shall be no more divided, but shall have knowledge of His power, and be one people with God. Do we have knowledge of His power and taste of the glories of the age to come? 'The earth shall be filled with the knowledge of the glory of the Lord, as the waters cover the sea.'[10]

All healings, then, like all gifts of grace, were to be viewed as foretastes, or as an earnest, of the resurrection. According to Romans 8, the Spirit quickens the mortal body and gives life as a foretaste of the life in the age to come, the age of cosmic redemption or future glory. Just as the Spirit raised Jesus from the dead, so the Spirit raises, or deifies, our mortal bodies. Wesleyan-Pentecostals understood that they were presently participating in the resurrection; they were living in the age of the Spirit.[11] Healing and restoration to health, while still wrapped in mortality, was viewed as a sign of the time when mortality will put on immortality.

For those Pentecostals subscribing to William H. Durham's Finished Work theology, though the doctrinal tenet was the same, the revision of soteriology necessarily called for a new understanding of the effects of the Fall and also its remedy in the atoning work of Christ.

Finished Work Pentecostal theology viewed the Genesis account of the Fall as focusing on the sentence that had been delivered. Death, rather than being understood therapeutically, was understood positionally. Now, the human creature stood in a position of

---

[10] Barth, 'Things of the Kingdom', p. 4.

[11] The early twentieth century revival had been anticipated as a new outpouring of the Spirit. William Arthur's *The Tongue of Fire,* published in 1856, predicted an infusion of 'Pentecostal power' in order that a worldwide revival could occur, ushering in the Millennium.

guilt and condemnation. As a result of this transgression and its accompanying sentence of death, sickness had also entered the world. Sickness, like sin, is a state in which the human now found himself/herself. The need was for a judicial act resulting in reversal of the sentence.

The action called for in the view of these Pentecostals was one of atonement. The atonement that was needed on this view was a definitive, punctiliar action. Because the problem was understood *primarily* in this way, the soteriology was pushed into an extreme Christocentrism, focusing on the event of the cross. This decisive action by Jesus was viewed as perfect, in the sense of complete and final. It was a *finished* work. Jesus was seen as a substitute for condemned humanity, paying the penalty price for redemption. This was a once and for all act which had eternal effect. In Durham's view, the resurrection had no apparent salvific effect. It was proof of 'His mighty power' and gave 'assurance to all men that He was His Son'. Additionally, it might be said that the life of Jesus leading up to the cross event had no particular salvific value in the view of Finished Work Pentecostal theology. It was the obedient act of Christ on the cross that was all-significant. He was made sin for the sinner, took the sinner's place and paid the full penalty.

By Durham's own admission, this was primarily a 'judicial' or forensic view of atonement. With the juridical action of Christ in atonement, and satisfaction of God the Judge having been made, merit was made available to humanity. This atonement was 'Perfect and Eternal'.

This substitutionary act of Christ was appropriated by faith and belief on the name of Jesus. In so doing, the Finished Work Pentecostals held that the believer is identifying with Christ, seeing themselves dead in Christ, crucified with Him, and quickened to newness of life. It was through that one act that the sinner is made righteous. Both justification and sanctification were states of righteousness or merit obtained through faith. As one reckoned himself/herself dead in Christ, s/he was in a state of justification and sanctification, pardoned and cleansed, outwardly and inwardly. Unlike others in the Reformed camp, Durham and his followers apparently did not want to maintain a doctrine of 'Perseverance of the Saints'. However, Finished Work theology did emphasize abiding, or continuing, in the Finished Work. They talked about 'growing in grace', but clearly this was understood as a growing awareness of what it meant to identify with Christ. There was no need for a further definitive experience to deal with any remaining sin. Durham wrote, 'So we being dead, and raised from the dead in Christ, one time, are supposed to live unto God in the Spirit; and in His goodness He bestows the Spirit upon us to walk in.'[12]

The atonement, then, was complete and was an act performed to deal with what was lost in the Fall. One of the effects of the Fall, that the Finished Work of Calvary was capable of dealing with, was the loss of the state of health. While Durham said little about healing in relation to his Finished Work view, it is clear that his followers, and even some of his predecessors who were already proposing a Finished Work theology[13] linked their understanding of 'healing provided for all in the atonement' to a Finished Work soteriology. The same faith claims made about justification and sanctification were made about healing. One simply reckoned it done. Indeed, healing was accomplished at the cross. It, too, was merit added to the account of the believer. As one identified with Jesus, counting on his finished work, one simply resisted the 'temptation' toward illness, denying the symptoms.

Finished Work Pentecostals recognized that the Spirit who quickened Jesus and raised him from the dead was also the Spirit who gave life to the mortality of the believer. The interpretation of the Rom. 8.11 passage emphasized more the present implications of the passage than its future ones. This was brought on by an exchange of old mortality for new creation and accomplished through baptism in the Spirit. This baptism in the Spirit, the new revelation that had come since the 1906 revival, was actually the 'seal of the finished salvation in Jesus Christ'. Baptism in the Spirit was a kind of affirmation of a work already completed. These Pentecostals did allow that the experience was the time when the Spirit 'took up His abode within' and is an 'indwelling presence'; Durham testified that the Spirit in the believer, 'teaches us all things, bringing to our remembrance the words of Jesus, bears His fruits in our lives, imparts

---

[12] William Durham, 'The Gospel of Light', *Pentecostal Testimony* 2.1 (January 1912), p. 9.

[13] Carrie Judd (Montgomery), for instance, had espoused this soteriology as early as January 1882. See Carrie Judd, 'The Finished Work of Calvary', *Triumphs of Faith* 2.1 (Jan. 1882).

His gifts unto us, searches and reveals the deep things of God, and guides us into all truth.'[14] It was talked about as an anointing for service that gives power. Though in this discussion the experience *could* be interpreted as being transformative or definitive, they still maintained that the experience looked back to the Finished Work. Most of the reflection on this experience seemed to focus on the manifestations at the time of the event and conclude that this was an enabling event. As a result, the new life or creation was manifested in the life of the believer as Divine Health, literally Jesus' health. As Jesus was understood to be sitting on the throne, in a resurrected body, the Spirit-filled believer could have this very resurrection life while still in this world. One was able to maintain this state as long as one had faith.

Logically, signs of the Spirit, or signs following believers were interpreted by these Pentecostals as signs, or demonstrations, of a work already done. Whether the demonstration was of speaking in tongues, healing, or exorcism of a demon, it pointed back to the time when the work of Christ was accomplished. That event and the seating of Christ by the right hand of the Father had been evidenced on the day of Pentecost, as the Spirit was poured out on believers and was now being evidenced in the same way. The sign was anticipated as the sick person was prayed for. *Sign* seems to be a way of understanding proof or confirmation. While it was lack of belief to wait for assurance before testifying of experience, one should expect the sign to follow.

Implications for Pentecostal Ecclesiology

It should be expected that there is a correlation between a community's soteriology and its ecclesiology. This is especially evident in the early Pentecostal movement, especially in the first couple of decades of the movement. Wesleyan-Pentecostals, like their antecedents in the Wesleyan Methodist and Holiness movements, tended toward a more centralized form of government and an appreciation for the accompanying accountability offered by such a governmental structure. Finished Work Pentecostals, primarily coming from

---

[14] William Durham, 'Personal Testimony of Pastor Durham', *Pentecostal Testimony* 2.3 (n.d.), p. 4.

Baptistic backgrounds, tended toward congregational forms of government. In a related way, their respective soteriologies, and thereby healing theologies, tend, in the former toward communal reflection and practice or in the latter, toward individualistic theology and practice. Obviously, with each group, there is much overlap and respect for spiritual authority. However, obtaining healing was discussed in each camp in decidedly different ways. In the extreme, one was either a part of a healing community, calling for the elders to anoint with oil, or one reckoned the work already done, as an act of the individual will, possibly calling for the elders out of obedience and to confirm the work already accomplished.

Given the individualistic impulse of Finished Work Pentecostalism, it would seem more beneficial to focus on the Wesleyan-Pentecostal stream of the movement when attempting to forge a study of how healing theology informs Pentecostal ecclesiology. While the level of critical reflection on ecclesiology in early Pentecostalism continues to be debated,[15] the numerous healing (and other) testimonies generating out of the Spirit-filled communities of faith provide a glimpse into not only how healing functioned in these communities but also into how the communities themselves functioned. In other words, by examining testimonies of healing, one gains insight into the Pentecostal Church as a healing community.

The Healing Home Model

Like their antecedents in the 19th Century Healing Movement, Wesleyan-Pentecostals saw the ministry of healing as an extension of the practice of care for those inside and outside the community of faith. In fact, healing was often a doorway *into* the community of faith. In the previous century, because the healing ministry was not a regular part of the life of the churches, adherents of the doctrine of divine healing began opening their homes to those who were sick. By the end of the century it was estimated that about thirty of these 'healing homes' operated in North America and many others were in operation throughout Europe.

---

[15] See Dale M. Coulter, 'The Development of Ecclesiology in the Church of God (Cleveland, TN): A Forgotten Contribution', *Pneuma* 29.1 (2007), pp. 59-85 and Veli-Matti Kärkkäinen, *An Introduction to Ecclesiology: Ecumenical, Historical and Global Perspectives* (Downers Grove, IL: InterVarsity Press, 2002), p. 73.

Built on the model developed by Dorothea Trudel and Samuel Zeller at Mannedorf in Switzerland and Johann Blumhardt in Bad Boll, Germany healing homes were built on the idea that Jas 5.14 was prescriptive. Here a sick, weak, or sinful person could confess his/her sin, call for elders to anoint her/him with oil and come to the point of being able to pray the prayer of faith. The healing of the soul was primary. Here, one could find wholeness and holiness.

These homes were what William E. Boardman called a 'nursery of faith'. Boardman's home, 'Bethshan' [House of Rest], in London was a place where those seeking to know Christ as ' "healer in spirit, soul and body" could withdraw from the ordinary environment of daily life and concentrate upon communion with God.' The home aimed at bringing people to faith by teaching the Biblical truth regarding holiness and healing. One resident wrote, 'in most cases [of healing] time is needful in order to learn what God's Word promises, and rightly to understand what the cause and purpose of the disease really are, and which the conditions and what [is] the meaning of healing. The stay in such a Home, with all its surroundings, helps to make this matter plain, and to strengthen faith.'[16] It was at Bethshan that Andrew Murray both came to believe in the doctrine of divine healing and experienced it.

In the healing home model, adherents found a way to provide nurture that included both physical and spiritual care. It was a place where one was formed in the faith. Pentecostals, in the next century, seemed to revision this model in the life of the Church. Rather than nurture and formation taking place outside of the Church, in a separate facility, this ministry took place within the walls, whether literal or figurative, of the Pentecostal Church or community.

In a way reminiscent of Christians in the early centuries of the Church,[17] Pentecostals both prayed for and attended to the needs of the sick, often in contrast to those in society. During the 1918 influenza epidemic, Pentecostals struggled with the meaning of the onslaught of disease and death while caring for those in their community who were stricken. Wesleyan-Pentecostals understood the epi-

---

[16] Paul Gale Chappell, 'The Divine Healing Movement in America' (PhD diss. Drew University, 1983), pp. 204-205.

[17] See Amanda Porterfield, *Healing in the History of Christianity* (NY: Oxford, 2005), pp. 43-65.

demic as a test of fidelity to Jesus the Healer. It was referred to as a 'judgment'[18] and a furnace of 'seven-fold heat' sent from God.[19] Through this trial and testing, the Pentecostal Church would learn to be dependent upon Jesus and would 'learn righteousness', as did Israel as they waited for the Exodus.[20] The Church became an even more pronounced healing community during this grim period in its history. Tomlinson writes, 'During the time the Influenza epidemic has been raging our home has been a veritable hospital excepting the use of medicine, having cared for twelve or more cases.... Out of the twelve or more cases only one had to be taken away in a casket.'[21] Not only did they pray for the sick, but the homes of the Pentecostal saints became infirmaries, reminiscent of the nineteenth-century healing homes. Here the sick received physical, emotional, and spiritual care. Pentecostals became caregivers, going into the quarantined homes, providing the needed services as well as offering prayer for the sick. Because this group believed that the Pentecostals would not be exempt from this horrible test, it stood to reason that they would see the need to provide care for the tested. During this period of extreme testing, the Church and ministry carried out its healing vocation in most obvious ways, reflecting its belief that the Church was missionary fellowship.[22]

A Communal Responsibility

In the following account of a Sunday morning service at a Church of God congregation in Cleveland, Tennessee, A.J. Tomlinson, pastor, describes a time of prayer for the sick through the medium of the anointed handkerchief:

> We pray for the sick every day, but on Sunday about 12:30 we have special prayer and every Sunday we have from twenty to forty handkerchiefs to pray over besides quite a number of re-

---

[18] See A.J. Tomlinson, 'The Last Days "Perilous Times" Have Come Upon the World', *Church of God Evangel* 10.2 (January 11, 1919), p. 1 and *Pentecostal Holiness Advocate* 2.33-34 (Dec 19-26, 1918), p. 16.

[19] Mattie Lemons, 'We Walk by Faith' reprinted in *Church of God Evangel* 10.2 (Jan 11, 1919), p. 1.

[20] Tomlinson, 'The Last Days "Perilous Times" Have Come Upon the World', p. 1.

[21] *Church of God Evangel* 12.1 (Jan 4, 1919), p. 2.

[22] For an extended analysis of Pentecostals and the 1918 Influenza Epidemic see Alexander, *Pentecostal Healing*, pp. 215-24.

quests. When this time comes we spread the handkerchiefs out on the altar and the saints gather around and the prayers are offered up in the earnestness of our souls. We are often reminded of the experience of the apostles when the sick folks were brought in on couches and beds and placed in the streets with a hope that even a shadow of Peter might fall upon them. We think of every handkerchief representing a sick person, and when we have forty or fifty handkerchiefs we think of being in the midst of that many sick folks. And oh, how the saints pray![23]

This quote gives insight not only into the sacramental nature of healing in the Pentecostal community but also into how the community viewed its responsibility toward the sick, even those not in their immediate presence. In this case, the Pentecostal Church carries on the ministry of the apostles by praying over the dozens of handkerchiefs, representing dozens of sick individuals. Clearly they saw it as their role and responsibility. The saints envisioning themselves as Peter and the other apostles evidence the real possibility of these people being healed.

Numerous reports from these early revival centers attest to the corporate nature of the healing ministry. A.J. Tomlinson's explanation of the healing mandate includes the following: 'We do not consider that men who are ordained as ministers are the only ones to pray, but anybody can pray. And often a few of the members pray for the sick and anoint them with oil and the sick are healed just as well as when the ministers pray.'[24] As evidence of this understanding within the Church of God, the *COGE* cites reports where prayer for the sick and anointing with oil is undertaken by evangelists,[25] 'saints',[26] 'sisters',[27] 'brothers',[28] and children.[29] Nettie Eckert's testimony in *The Bridegroom's Messenger* describes being prayed for and anointed with oil by the members of her church and by her

---

[23] *Church of God Evangel* 13.23 (June 10, 1922), p. 1. Tomlinson here describes what happens to the handkerchiefs sent by readers into the office of *The Church of God Evangel*.

[24] *Church of God Evangel* 13.23 (June 10, 1922), p. 1.

[25] *Church of God Evangel* 7.21 (May 20, 1916), p. 2.

[26] *Church of God Evangel* 9.44 (Nov. 2, 1918), p. 2.

[27] *Church of God Evangel* 12.27 (July 2, 1921), p. 2.

[28] *Church of God Evangel* 8.42 (Oct. 27, 1917), p. 2.

[29] *Church of God Evangel* 9.44 (Nov. 2, 1918), p. 3.

husband.[30] Otha M. Kelly, of the Church of God in Christ, attributed his healing of severe appendicitis to the prayer of the saints.[31] The *Pentecostal Holiness Advocate* published a report of a child who had been severely burned. The response of the parents was to call 'for the saints to come and pray for him' with the result that the child was healed of the burns and able to attend church the next evening.[32]

These reports and testimonies indicate that a Pentecostal ecclesiology must take seriously the communal aspects of the healing ministry. The practices associated with healing the sick are indicative of a robust Pentecostal theology that includes both the priesthood and prophethood of believers. Though clergy-laity distinctions do exist within Pentecostal communities, there is an explicit leveling of the ministerial function where these Spirit-empowered ministries are concerned.

The Healing Vocation

From its onset, the Pentecostal community did understand that certain women and men were charged with the vocation of care and leadership of the community as well as for the evangelism of the lost. Included in this ministry was prayer for the sick. At the Azusa St. Mission, this ministry was reportedly now more effective with the added benefit of Spirit baptism. One man described this empowerment in praying for the sick: he could 'accomplish a hundred times as much in a day and much more easily than formerly. It is simply letting the Holy Ghost do the work.'[33]

Likewise in the Church of God, women and men were charged with a ministerial vocation that included the ministry of healing. The preaching role was understood to include the ministry of prayer for the sick: 'He who does not firmly believe that God heals the sick in answer to prayer, is not fully qualified for the Lord's work.'[34] It was the duty of a Pentecostal minister, especially one in

---

[30] Nettie Eckert, 'A Testimony of Healing, Healing in the Atonement' in *The Bridegroom's Messenger* 3.50 (Nov. 15, 1909), p. 1.

[31] Otha M. Kelly, *Profile of A Churchman* (Jamaica, NY: K&C, 1976), pp. 51-53.

[32] *Pentecostal Holiness Advocate* 1.17 (Aug. 23, 1917), p. 8.

[33] *The Apostolic Faith* 1.8 (May 1907), p. 3.

[34] B.H. Doss, 'Healing Faith in the Church', *Church of God Evangel* 12.26 (June 25, 1921), p. 3.

the Church of God, to be 'subject to a call from any member of his congregation at any time, and it is his duty to respond. James says he is to take with him, his oil vial, faith in God and common sense.'[35] J.C. Bower exhorted:

> If we want the power to heal the sick in Jesus' name like the Apostles, let us leave our homes if necessary, sacrifice our lives, like they did, obey the orders of our Captain, which is Jesus Christ, and believe like Peter did, when he and John commanded the lame man who was born lame, to rise up an walk.[36]

An even more pronounced view of the authority and responsibility of the Pentecostal minister was articulated by Elder Charles H. Mason of the Church of God in Christ who held that with ordination as a minister of the Gospel came power. He contended that it was to the empowered disciples in the book of Acts that the 'sick and the afflicted' came to be healed.[37] Bishop Mason described the Pentecostal vocation in a 'psalm' given by the Spirit:

> Tell men how to come out of shame.
> Tell men how to be watchful.
> Tell men how to be strong;
> Tell men how to be brotherly
> Tell men how to be healed.
> Tell me, Jesus' wonder is able to keep.
> Put in me more love for men.
> Tell them the blood of Jesus will keep them.
> The Lord delivers men.[38]

Beyond the proclamation and practice of healing, the Pentecostal ministerial vocation was also one that required living with fidelity to the theology. During a doctrinal upheaval in the Pentecostal Holi-

---

[35] Doss, 'Healing Faith in the Church', *Church of God Evangel* 12.26 (June 25, 1921), p. 3.

[36] J.C. Bower, 'Birchwood, Tenn.', *Church of God Evangel* 10.6 (Feb 8, 1919), p. 2.

[37] Elsie W. Mason, *The Man, Charles Harrison Mason (1866-1961)* (No publisher, location or date. Reprinted by Bass, Wayne M. and W.L. Porter; Memphis, TN: Pioneer Series Publication, 1979), p. 25.

[38] Elnora L. Lee, *A Life Fully Dedicated to God* (No publisher or location, copyright applied for 1967), p. 87.

ness Church, centering on the doctrine of healing in the atonement, F.M. Britton exhorted:

> We preachers are to be an example to the flock, and if we will preach the full gospel, and live it and demonstrate it by having God to work with us and confirm His Word with signs following, there is bound to be others that will follow and seek and enjoy the blessings of the gospel. Somehow the straighter I preach and live and hold up Jesus as the all sufficient remedy for sin and sickness, the more calls I get.[39]

In addition, the ministry of healing was understood to be a vital part of the missionary vocation and endeavor. A letter from missionary to South Africa, John G. Lake, written to a Reverend Bryant of Zion, Illinois, and reprinted in January 1909 issue of *The Bridegroom's Messenger* reveals Lake's unique perspective on praying for the sick. He reports that ninety-two percent of those prayed for in each meeting were healed and seventy-five percent of those healings were instantaneous. Lake writes,

> We do not preach Divine Healing. It is not worthwhile. We say to the sick people, 'Come up on the platform and get it.' Brother, one man healed in the sight of your audience beats all the sermons that ever you preached in convincing proof in power of the gospel of the Son of God, and the reality of the power of the blood of Jesus Christ.[40]

It is clear that there was a well-defined understanding of the role of the ministry in the life of the Church. Instructions given to ministry include not only what should be preached and practiced but also how a minister should live.

The Sacramental Healing Community

Even a superficial reading of early Pentecostal literature reveals that this was a community where participation in the life of the Church involved more than a cognitive assent or merely a passive attendance. In reading, one is aware that Pentecostalism was marked by a variety of sights, sounds, and sensations. These were part and parcel of the Pentecostal experience and ethos. Indeed, one of the hall-

---

[39] *Pentecostal Holiness Advocate* 4.41 (Jan 3, 1921), p. 12.

[40] *The Bridegroom's Messenger* 2.29 (January 1, 1909), p. 4.

marks of Pentecostalism, from a doctrinal and experiential perspective, was its almost universal insistence on the experience of speaking in tongues as the 'Bible sign' that one had been baptized in the Holy Spirit. From an outsider's perspective, there were numerous observable 'signs' that one was in a Pentecostal worship service. As stated earlier, for the insider, the appearance of the sign of tongues and other signs following believers was indicative of a legitimate Pentecostal revival. One early Pentecostal minister, J.E. Sawders, called the signs of Mark 16, 'The Pentecostal Standard'.[41]

It seems that Pentecostals understood 'signs' in the Johannine sense. As John Christopher Thomas has surmised, 'In the first part of the Gospel [of John], the Book of Signs, Jesus interacts with the public at large and many of *his miraculous actions serve as signs, which point beyond themselves to one or more aspects of his identity.*' [italics mine][42] For the Pentecostal community, the signs of speaking in tongues, healing miracles, and others pointed beyond themselves to Jesus. A miracle of healing was a sign that Jesus is Healer. This understanding was reminiscent of Wesley's view of signs. Henry H. Knight discusses Ole E. Borgen's assessment of Wesley and the sacraments and concludes, 'Sign and grace are not the same, but neither are they separable; grace gives life to the sign, while the sign points to Christ as the source of grace.'[43]

It was in this atmosphere of signs that could be witnessed by the eye or ear that a kind of sacramentalism developed in Pentecostalism. In addition to the 'Bible sign' of speaking in tongues, and the other signs that were to follow believers, Pentecostals were quite comfortable with utilizing other materials and means as signs of the work of the Spirit or as channels of the Spirit's work. The most common practices for those ministering healing, for instance, involved using material means to convey a spiritual gift. The two most often employed methods were those specifically linked to the healing ministry in the New Testament: imposition of hands and anointing with oil. In both cases, it was said that these actions were

---

[41] *The Bridegroom's Messenger* 1.4 (December 15, 1907), p. 4.

[42] John Christopher Thomas, *He Loved Them Until the End: The Farewell Materials in the Gospel according to John* (Pune, India: Fountain Press, 2003), p. 18.

[43] Henry H. Knight, III, *The Presence of God in the Christian Life: John Wesley and the Means of Grace* (Metuchen, NJ: Scarecrow Press, 1992), p. 131.

'undertaken in obedience to the Word'. Clearly, these were actions understood to be instituted and practiced by Jesus and the Apostles.

There is little discussion of the significance of anointing with oil in early Pentecostal literature though there are numerous references to the practice. G.F. Taylor offers a brief explanation in *The Pentecostal Holiness Advocate*. Taylor compares the use of oil in anointing the sick, as well as the imposition of hands, to the waters of the Jordan River in the healing of Naaman's leprosy: it may be considered a 'foolish thing'.[44]

The next most prevalent means of healing is the imposition of hands. Elders, ministers or saints may have been called upon to lay hands on a sick person. James F. Epps describes two such instances involving a 'Sister Wood', who had been healed of a serious stomach obstruction. Later she laid hands on her daughter, who was healed instantly. Along with 'Sister Plummer' she also laid hands on Epps. He writes, 'When they laid their hands on me the healing virtue was felt, and my lungs felt as though they had been made over new, and since that time I have felt like a new man.' He also recounts he and his wife laying hands on their sick young daughter in the night.[45] The sacramental interpretation of this practice is evident in the account. There is a direct connection between the imposition of hands and the perceived reception of 'healing virtue', sensed or felt by the sick person.

Sacramental practices associated with healing were not limited to these two more traditional methods, however. As early as the Azusa St. revival, Pentecostals, following the example of Acts 19.12, anointed handkerchiefs with oil. These objects were taken to or mailed to the sick who were not present in the revival services. The following account from *The Apostolic Faith* is revealing:

> I feel led by the Holy Spirit to testify to the glory of God what He has done for me and my wife. The Lord has wonderfully healed me from catarrh of nine years standing. Glory! glory!

---

[44] *Pentecostal Holiness Advocate* 4.11 (Jul 15, 1920), p. 9. Apparently, Taylor is here countering the argument that Naaman's use of extraordinary means and the use of olive oil for anointing purposes warrant the use of medicine. H.C. Webb also refers to the argument that the anointing in James 5 is 'skillful use of medicine' in *Pentecostal Holiness Advocate* 2.43 (Feb 27, 1919), p. 6. See also *Pentecostal Holiness Advocate* 4.8 (Jun 24, 1920), p. 9.

[45] *Pentecostal Holiness Advocate* 2.5 (May 30, 1918), p. 12.

> Glory! glory be to my dear Redeemer's name! Soon as I received the handkerchief, or as soon as I opened the letter, such power went through my whole being as I have never felt before and I praise Him, I feel the healing balm just now go through soul and body. Glory to King Jesus, the Great Physician of soul and body.[46]

In this letter, a Canadian reader testifies that through the medium of the handkerchief he experienced a healing that was accompanied by a reception of power that could be sensed or felt throughout his body and soul. Clearly there is an understanding that the presence of God (the Holy Spirit) is manifested through this common material item in this and numerous other testimonies related to these 'anointed handkerchiefs'.[47]

Another less common, though early, understanding of healing in Pentecostalism is associated with the reception of healing while partaking of the Lord's Supper. In the fourth issue of *The Apostolic Faith*, Seymour likens the sacrifice of Christ to the Passover lamb, which was eaten by the Israelites as they left Egypt, giving them 'strength and health' for the journey. Following the analogy, he concludes that the body of the Lord is taken for health, one part of the 'two-fold salvation' remembered in observance of the meal. One who does not honor this 'two-fold salvation' is not properly discerning the body of Christ, a reference to 1 Cor. 11.29.[48]

Though it is nowhere articulated, early Pentecostals certainly moved beyond a Zwinglian or merely symbolic view of ordinances. While they may have been hesitant to use the language of *sacrament*, it seems that there was an inherent *sacramentalism* in the ethos of Pentecostalism. As heirs to Wesley's soteriology and, in some respects, Wesleyan ecclesiology, Pentecostals understood that *grace* or the presence of God was offered in situations of worship within the community.

---

[46] *Apostolic Faith* 1.9 (Jun-Sep, 1907), p. 3.

[47] See *The Bridegroom's Messenger* 2.31 (Feb 1, 1909), p. 3; *Church of God Evangel* 11.17 (Apr 24, 1920), p. 2; 13.40 (Oct 7, 1922), p. 2; 13.42 (Dec 21, 1922); 14.2 (Jan 13, 1923), p. 4; *The Whole Truth* 4.4, p. 4. *Pentecostal Holiness Advocate* 4.10 (Jul 8, 1920), p. 14; 4.34 (Dec 23, 1920), p. 12; 5.10 (Jul 20, 1922), p. 2; 5.49 (Apr 6, 1922), p. 14.

[48] *Apostolic Faith* 1.4 (Dec 1906), p. 2.

Knight describes Wesley's view of the Christian life as participatory and as progressive, but he emphasizes that for Wesley the Christian life is not a simple *ordo salutis* pursued individualistically and in just any contexts. As Knight points out, for Wesley it is not enough to talk about progress or growth in grace, but one must also talk about *how* this growth occurs. For those in the Methodist movement, the *how* was well defined and structured. Knight writes,

> The term for these contexts is the means of grace. By 'means of grace' Wesley meant much more than the two Protestant sacraments ... the means of grace include a whole range of activities associated with public worship, personal devotion, and Christian community and discipleship ... the means of grace form an interrelated context within which the Christian life is lived and through which relationships with God and one's neighbor are maintained.... Means of grace are means through which persons experience and respond to the loving presence of God.[49]

This 'loving presence of God', transforming grace, for healing or for other forms of spiritual nourishment, was available to all who participate and the *sign* of that grace was most often a common element, such as human touch, oil, or the bread of the Lord's Supper, or even more extraordinary elements such as an anointed handkerchief.

Given the prominence of James 5 in early Pentecostal literature and its use in the life of the community, it seems safe to say that anointing with oil serves as the quintessential sign of healing. In harmony with a Wesleyan sacramental view, the oil used in the healing ritual is viewed as a sign of the *real presence* or dynamic presence of God. It is a *sacred sign*.[50] Anointing with oil may be thought of as analogous to the Lord's Supper observance as Wesley understood it. Knight interprets Wesley's view: 'God's power may "more or less" manifest itself in each eucharist celebration, but God is always present, and the Lord's Supper is always a means of grace. The degree of efficacy depends on God, but the lack of efficacy is not due to the absence of God but to the absence of faith.'[51] While Pentecos-

---

[49] Knight, *The Presence of God in the Christian Life*, p. 2.

[50] See Knight's discussion of the Lord's Supper, *The Presence of God in the Christian Life*, pp. 130-48.

[51] Knight, *The Presence of God in the Christian Life*, p. 135.

tals would generally caution that the oil is symbolic of the Holy Spirit and that healing power is not the oil itself, they would see, and demonstrate, an understanding that 'something happens' when this ritual is observed. This sacramental anointing signified the work of the Holy Spirit in the gift of healing. It was the Spirit who continued and made effective the work of Jesus, including His atonement; therefore this action dramatizes something occurring in the spiritual realm.

In keeping with this understanding, Pentecostals would also emphasize the necessity of faith, specifically 'the prayer of faith' according to James 5. Any and everyone in the Pentecostal community could pray the prayer of faith. Prayer for the sick, like all prayer in the Wesleyan-Pentecostal community, involved active seeking and pursuit of God and His answer. The individual believer or corporate body could be urged by the Spirit to 'pray through' with regard to this special need. The prayer was thought to be going somewhere and pushing or pressing through what may have prevented the needed transformation; it was viewed as movement toward God, anticipating an in-breaking of the Spirit and a gift of His grace. In this way, this prayer of faith is a means of grace. It involves a specific discipline or action, undertaken in the context of the community, anticipating a work of transforming grace.

As stated above, the full community could be involved in the ministry of healing. Regardless of age, gender or ethnicity, any or all members of the church could pray the prayer of faith. In a very real sense, the ministry of healing expresses the communal nature of Pentecostalism, particularly Wesleyan-Pentecostalism, more vividly than any other of the movement's many ministries. Here, the needs of the one are brought before the community. The sick person, sometimes visibly so, is as much a part of the community as the well ones. The effects of the Fall are dramatically depicted in the life affected by the curse. Brokenness collides with the eschatological hope of healing in the Redeemed (and Healed) Community. As the sick one is anointed with a tangible substance of oil and touched by human hands, the presence of God, the Holy Spirit, is just as real. The prayers of the community accompany the other signs and further signs are anticipated—signs of the in-breaking of the Kingdom of God, signs of the gracious presence of God, signs that one day all will be healed.

The Ministry of Healing in Postmodernity: Recovery and Expansion

In his work, *Postmodern Pilgrims: First Century Passion for the Twenty-First Century World,* Leonard Sweet, a Wesleyan, describes postmodern culture as EPIC: experiential, participatory, image-driven, and connected. He laments, 'In the midst of one of the greatest transitions in history—from modern to postmodern—Christian churches are owned lock, stock, and barrel by modernity. They have clung to modern modes of thought and action, their ways of embodying and enacting the Christian tradition frozen in patterns of high modernity.'[52] He continues, 'Western Christianity went to sleep in a modern world governed by the gods of reason and observation. It is awakening to a postmodern world open to revelation and hungry for experience.'[53]

Given Pentecostalism's penchant for sight and sound, its insistence on transformative experience and participation in the life of God and the community, it seems that the Pentecostal ministry of healing would find a much more comfortable home in the 21st century than it did in the 20th. Already 'in place' are many of the elements of Sweet's EPIC Church. The challenge for the Pentecostal Church will not be to create new methodologies but rather to *recover* the authenticity of the Pentecostal communal experience, necessarily moving away from healing crusade and mega-church models and to more relationally-oriented communities of faith. Pentecostal healing ministry must recover the healing home model ensuring that the sick are included in the life of the community as they pursue healing and are ministered to by the community. A recovery of a Wesleyan-Pentecostal model of healing theology would push Pentecostals back to a more communal approach and away from individualistic appropriation.

Further, Pentecostals must once again fully embrace a gospel of transformation, shedding Saul's armour of Fundamentalist Evangelicalism: fine armour, but armour that is ill-fitting. They must also recover an understanding of their identity as the people of God not tied to any nationalist ideology. No political system must be allowed

---

[52] Leonard Sweet, *Postmodern Pilgrims: First Century Passion for the 21st Century World* (Nashville, TN: Broadman & Holman Publishers, 2000), p. 28.

[53] Sweet, *Postmodern Pilgrims*, p. 29.

to overwhelm or dilute the message of Kingdom: Healing is provided *for all*.

Beyond this recovery, Pentecostals must endeavor to *expand* their view of the saving-healing work of Jesus the healer to include more holistic understandings. The healing ministry of Jesus is not separate from the work of social justice; it was and is, in fact, part and parcel of it. Jesus touched the outcasts and healed them, thus fulfilling his mother, Mary's, prophecy that her son would exalt those of low degree. For Pentecostals to minister healing effectively in the 21st century, they must embrace a ministry of healing that addresses all areas effected by sin and the Fall: the healing of the earth, the healing of divisions of race and gender, the oppression of the weak by the strong, the exploitation of the poor by the rich. Empowered by the Spirit, Pentecostals must bring healing to every area made sick by structural sin.

Finally, the Pentecostal movement must recognize that from its inception it has been a contextual movement and must be open to further contextualization; that is, its theology and practice have adapted to various cultures in which it takes root. Though the movement grew as a result of the catalyst of the Azusa St. revival occurring in a primarily African-American urban church, its basic tenets and practices have been retained but transformed as it has moved from urban centers to rural areas, from culture to culture. Even at the beginning, the commitment to the freedom of the Spirit and the sense that 'God was doing a new thing' led the leadership and adherents to be open to new practices and even doctrinal revision.[54] The ministry of healing is a case in point. While they were committed to what they believed was a biblical standard or prescription (as in James 5) and to what was modeled in the gospels and Acts, there was contextualization. For example, there are no testimonies of early Pentecostals actually *taking cloths from* the bodies of ministers to the sick, a literal interpretation of Acts 19.12. Instead, handkerchiefs and later 'prayer cloths' were *brought to* the minister and congregation to be anointed with oil. There are even examples of neckties and 'suits of underwear' being anointed and taken to the sick person and Pentecostal periodicals being placed on

---

[54] Grant Wacker has noted that Pentecostals were both primitivistic and pragmatic. See Grant Wacker, *Heaven Below: Early Pentecostals and American Culture* (Cambridge, MA: Harvard University Press, 2001).

the sick person as the saints prayed.[55] The interpretation of Mk 16.18-20 and practices associated with that text have been contextualized throughout the United States. Oral Roberts made adaptations to his own interpretation of it and those interpretations follow the trajectory of his own ministry. The early Roberts understood that the sign of healing was given in his right hand (the point of contact).[56] Later, the point of contact, shifted to the responsibility of the sick person as s/he touched the television screen, as Roberts' ministry moved to the medium of television and even later to the joining of the hands of the healing minister coupled with the hands of medical science at the City of Faith.[57] Additionally, a note from the editor of a revision of Roberts' *Best Loved Tent Sermons* explains that at a later stage in Roberts' ministry he was shown the power of the 'Word of Faith' methodology in the ministry of healing, a method that allowed him to reach even more sick persons.[58] Another example of contextualization of this text is found in the some Appalachian expressions of Pentecostalism. Research has shown that the literal interpretation of Mk 16.18, that believers should 'take up serpents', and the practice of snake-handling, is found only in the Southeastern United States, an area where poisonous vipers are commonplace.[59]

For the ministry of healing to be effective in the 21st century, the cultural group must contextualize it so that there is ownership where it is practiced. For instance, in some Native American Pentecostal churches the biblical injunction to anoint with oil has been

---

[55] Alexander, *Pentecostal Healing*, pp. 111, 174.

[56] Oral Roberts, *The Fourth Man*, Revised Edition (Tulsa, OK: Oral Roberts, 1960), p. 27; *idem, Your Healing Problems and How to Solve Them* (Tulsa, OK: Oral Roberts, 1966), pp. 60-61; *idem, If You Need Healing Do These Things* (no place: Oral Roberts, 4th ed. 1969), p. 11-14, 39; *idem, How to Find Your Point of Contact With God* (Tulsa, OK: Oral Roberts, Rev. Ed. 1966), p. 11.

[57] Oral Roberts. *How To Get Through Your Struggles (or You Can Walk On the Stormy Waters of Your Life)* (Tulsa, OK: Oral Roberts Evangelistic Association, Inc., 1977), pp. 271-73.

[58] Oral Roberts, *Best Loved Tent Sermons* (Tulsa, OK: Oral Roberts, 1983), pp. 54-55.

[59] J.A. Kelhoffer, *Miracle and Mission: The Authentication of Missionaries and Their Message in the Longer Ending of Mark* (WUNT 112; Tübingen: Mohr Siebeck, 2000). For a more thorough study of the serpent-handling in Pentecostalism see Ralph W. Hood and W. Paul Williamson, *Them That Believe: The Power and Meaning of the Christian Serpent-Handling Tradition* (Berkeley: University of California Press, 2008).

replaced with the ancient practice of smudging, in which sage is burned and the smoke resulting from the burning of the sage and the oil therein is waved over the sick person. The justification offered by Cheryl Bear-Barnetson, a First Nations and Foursquare Church of Canada denominational leader, is that olive oil is native to the Mediterranean region while sage is native to most Native American contexts.[60]

As Pentecostals engage the *missio Dei* they do so in community, with sacramental signs, and with 'signs following', revealing to all the Creator Spirit, already at work in the earth, healing the pains of the past and moving us toward the Day when all will be healed.

---

[60] See Jack L. 'Corky' Alexander, 'Inter-Tribal Pentecost: Praxis Transformation in Native American Worship' (Fuller Theological Seminary, DMiss dissertation, 2010).

9

PENTECOSTAL HEALING COMMUNITIES

OPOKU ONYINAH[*]

Introduction

Christian churches have been playing a significant role in the provision of health and healing. They are doing this through a variety of spiritual approaches to healing and also the provision of conventional health care. Where does this stem from? Divine healing has been one of the pillars of the fivefold gospel. The first pillar of the fivefold gospel is the gospel of regeneration. The rebirth is a prerequisite to salvation (Jn 3.3). As such, the gospel of regeneration can be called the gospel of salvation. In order for people to be free from the curse of sin, the final judgement, and the authority of Satan, they must first receive salvation. Through an act of rebellion by one man, Adam, all people were destined to be born sinners (Rom. 5.16), and unable to reach the glory of God through their own means (Rom. 3.23).

Those who have been reborn must be baptised and filled with the Holy Spirit. When Christians are filled with the Holy Spirit, they become filled with power and are able to witness effectively. Furthermore, since the Spirit of God is Holy, a Christian filled with the Holy Spirit can shed off the authority of sin and curses and live in holiness.

Once a person enters the kingdom of God and is filled with the Holy Spirit, then healing becomes his/her portion. Thus the Chris-

---

[*] Opoku Onyinah (PhD, University of Birmingham) is an Apostle of the Church of Pentecost in Accra, Ghana.

tian understanding of healing is related to his/her understanding of salvation. There is also the expectation of the children of God to possess the full blessing of God, including healing and prosperity. This state has been described as *shalom* by a group which studied healing by the World Council of Churches and DIFAEM, 'Shalom can be described as an ultimate state of reconciled and healed relationships between creation and God, between humanity and God, between humanity and creation, and between humans as individuals and as groups or societies. Every single act of healing is a sign of the realisation of shalom'.[1] The ultimate condition of the Christian where the full blessing of Christ will be consummated is after the second advent of Christ. However, before this period, the Christian is still expected to experience physical healing of the body.

It is in light of this that Pentecostal Christian healing communities become important. Christian churches seek to provide healing through prayer, the laying on of hands, and anointing with oil. In addition to this, other churches get involved in the provision of conventional health care. This essay is concerned about the role Christian churches play as healing communities, using African traditional and Pentecostal healing communities as examples.

HEALING OF JESUS AND THE EARLY CHURCH

The healing ministry of the Church takes its cue from the healing ministry of the Lord Jesus. The disobedience of the covenanted people, Israel, sent them to captivity. The prophets spoke of the restoration of Israel and the establishment of the kingdom of God, where God would continue to live with his people. This was to begin with the coming of the Servant of the Lord, the Messiah. Outstanding miracles of healing, unprecedented throughout the Old Testament, were expected with the eschaton (Isa. 35.4-6; 42.6-9; and 61.1).[2]

---

[1] WCC and DIFAEM, A contribution towards the Christian healing ministry compiled by a study group on mission and healing from the World Council of Churches (WCC), Geneva, Switzerland, and the German Institute for Medical Mission (DIFAEM), Tübingen, Germany, http://www.difaem.de (2010).

[2] Opoku Onyinah, 'Faith, Healing and Mission: Perspective from the Bible', in J. Kwabena Asamoah-Gyadu (ed.) *Christianity, Missions, Ecumenism in Ghana: Essays in Honour of Robert K. Aboagye-Mensah.* (Accra: Asempa Publishers, 2009), pp. 213-23.

Jesus the Messiah came into the world to offer salvation— restoring relationship between God and humanity—and to witness through his life, deeds, and words that show the ways in which God cares for humanity and his entire creation. Jesus affirms this at the beginning of his early ministry. He proclaims the eschatological jubilee by announcing liberty from bondage to sin, Satan, and sickness (Lk. 4.18-19). The healings and casting out of demons were visible signs that the kingdom of God was at hand (Mk 1.15, Mt. 12.28). Thus, Jesus comes alongside human beings, and through his healing ministry cares particularly for those whose dignity was not respected in his day. This is an indication that Jesus' healing ministry had a far greater aim than simply curing the physical or mental diseases of certain individuals. The restoring of people's relationship with God was an essential part of his healing ministry. Many of the diseases Jesus healed were those that were infectious or that demanded that the sufferer be ostracised from society. For instance, people who were lepers, insane, or women suffering from hemorrhage were excluded from the secular or religious community. The healing of such people, however, led to their reinstatement within the community, and with God.

Healing was not only a central feature of Jesus' ministry but also something in which he wanted his disciples to participate. Among other things, he called the disciples and charged them to preach about the kingdom of God, have authority over unclean spirits, heal the sick, and cleanse the lepers (Mt. 10.1-7; Lk. 10.1-16). As the commission was put into effect during the life of Jesus, so also did the ministry of the disciples demonstrate after the resurrection that they obeyed his command to proclaim the kingdom by preaching and healing. For example, Philip was found in Samaria preaching the good news of the kingdom of God and healing all manner of diseases (Acts 8.1-12). Healing also characterised the ministry of Peter (Acts 3.1-10; 9.32-35; 9.36-43) and Paul (Acts 14.8-10; 16.16-18; 20.7-12; 28.1-10). The book of Acts indicates that the power of the risen Christ was always experienced, when the kingdom of God was preached or when they came together. Morris Maddocks rightly observes that 'This gave them a deep commitment to each other, in Pauline language, to fellow members of the body, as well as to its Head.... The power to heal and all the other gifts were given, as far as they were concerned, to build up the body, to help *all* toward that maturity in Christ....'[3]

The apostle Paul described the Christian community as one body (1 Cor. 12.12-31). It then follows that if one member of the body is sick, the whole body suffers. Therefore James directs sick members of the community to call for the elders, who would pray for them and anoint them with oil (Jas 5.13-16). Thus, it is made clear that the sick are and remain essential parts of the community.

The early church took Jesus' healing ministry seriously, and Christianity presented itself to the Mediterranean societies of the time as a healing community. The final chapter of Mark's gospel, which was probably added in the second century CE, reflects this. Many writings of the early church fathers also affirm the centrality of the Church as a healing community, and proclaim Christ as the healer of the world. Maddocks therefore summarizes the characteristic of the early church to include 'obedience, the expectancy, the corporate experience, the attractive joy, and the positive zeal'.[4]

However, the Western churches often eschew the whole topic of spiritual powers through the influence of the Enlightenment. Christian theology and the way the clergy were trained did not only ignore the topic but often also helped demythologise even the biblical concept of demons and spirits. As a result, within the churches and with regard to medical science, churches became increasingly indifferent to the thought that a wholistic healing ministry should be an integral part of their being.[5]

---

[3] Morris Maddocks, *The Christian Healing Ministry* (London: SPCK, 1995), pp. 85-86.

[4] Maddocks, *The Christian Healing Ministry*, p. 87.

[5] Peter Bartmann, Beate Jakob, Ulrich Laepple, Dietrich Werner, 'Health, Healing and Spirituality: The Future of the Church's Ministry of Healing'. A German position paper offering ecumenical, diaconal, and missiological perspectives on a holistic understanding of Christian witness for healing in western societies, at the German Institute for Medical Mission (DIFAEM), Tübingen, available, www.mission 2005.org.

Contributions from African Worldviews and Healing Communities

The Akan Cultural Perspective

The traditional healing community forms the basis for African Pentecostal beliefs and practices. Although the traditional healing practices differ from one nation to the other, there are some similarities among them.

Formerly in many African societies, every adult was expected to know the available herbs used for certain common ailments such as headache, stomach-ache, rheumatism, waist pain, and piles. If anyone felt ill, he/she would try one or another of these remedies. If this failed, a close relative would call in a 'traditional healer'.

For example, among the Akans of Ghana, three types of healers treated diseases. The first was the general practitioner who had knowledge of many plants, their roots, and leaves, and the diseases they might be expected to cure.[6] The second type of healer also had expert knowledge of herbs, but in addition, he possessed powerful charms or secret of divination, or he knew how to deal with witchcraft attack. The third type of healer was the priest or priestess. There were two types of these priests: the priest of the tutelar gods and the priest of the anti-witchcraft shines. These were the specialists in the diagnoses of spiritual diseases.

The first task of the priest was to find out the causes of the disease. This was done through the priest's ability to divine or consult the deities. There were various ways of doing this to find out whether the disease was caused by the person's own sin, an offense he/she had committed against the ancestors, gods, or an attack by spiritual forces, such as witches and sorcerers. Thus, the diagnosis of the priest was to search for the psychological or supernatural cause of the disease. The supernatural cause of a disease could be attributed to many issues such as a punishment from the Supreme Being or an offended god whose sanctions had been broken, the casting of spell by a witch or an enemy, the judicial punitive actions of ancestors, or the effect of an ancestral curse in the family. Nor-

---

[6] K.A. Busia, *The Challenge of Africa* (New York: Frederick A. Praeger, 1962), p. 13.

mally, it was perceived that if it was of a natural cause, the administration of the herbs would have cured the person.

Once the diagnosis was done, the priest would request the family to present a person from among themselves who would 'stand behind' the patient, that is, the one who would support the patient. On receipt of the nomination, the priest would discuss with the nominee the nature of disease, the cause, and treatment needed for the patient. If the supporter agreed then he/she would request the relative to appoint another person who would nurse and attend to the patient at the shrine. After this, the priest would administer herbs and if needed the pacification of the gods to cleanse the community. A patient could spend about two months at a shrine until he/she was cured. The payment of the fee was the responsibility of the family.

There have been some reports that the treatment of the traditional priests, both tutelar and anti-witchcraft shrine, could cure or heal some diseases. For example, Margaret Field, an English ethnopsychiatrist, in the mid-twentieth century, remarked about the traditional priest's ability to cure diseases. She affirms:

> Personally I am convinced that a good witch-doctor can recognise a witch when he sees one and that he can tell when an illness is an ordinary one or brought about by witchcraft. Translated into European idiom, he can tell when a person is a compulsive neurotic and when an illness is a functional or hysterical one. *And he can and does cure* (italic mine).[7]

Here, Field was quite convinced that traditional priests could cure some diseases. The curing of such diseases was regarded as taking place through the supernatural power of the deities working through the medication of the priests. Thus healing here is both medical, as evidenced by the application of the herbs, and magico-religious, as implied in the ritual and the process of divinatory-consultation.

---

[7] Margaret J. Field, *Religion and Medicine of the Ga People* (London: Oxford University Press, 1937), p. 160. It is worth noting that Field uses the term witch-doctor in 1937, but writing in 1960, when she had better understood the Ghanaian situation, she adopted the Akan term *okomfo* (priest). For example, see *Search for Security: An Ethno-Psychiatric Study of Rural Ghana* (London: Faber and Faber, 1960), p. 67.

This concept of the Akan culture demonstrates that the African worldview has consequences for diagnosis and treatment. A disease may include a spiritual element, which may affect the whole community. The treatment of the sick person involves the whole community or the family. It needs the attention of the spiritual person to handle. The healing of a person may restore the broken relationships in the ethnic and family communities. Thus the aspects of social peace, restoring broken relationships, and love within the family community are crucial to understanding and overcoming illness in the African setting.

Apparently there are many points of contact between the African worldview and that of New Testament and ancient times. This type of community traditional healing becomes a base for some forms of Christian healings in sub-Saharan Africa.

The African Initiated Churches

The early African Initiated Churches' (AICs) way of healing followed the traditional way.[8] From that backdrop, Harold Turner postulates that in the whole continent of Africa, 'they range from churches almost indistinguishable from the most westernized products of Christian missions, to cults that are a revival of traditional pagan religions with no more than a few Christian glosses.' Here it is apparent that Turner was finding it difficult to distinguish between the culture and traditional religion, an exercise that is still difficult to differentiate, since the culture is closely linked with the religion. Nevertheless, the traditional healing practice is a good way of linking Africans to Christian healing practices.

A good deal of discussion has been devoted to the causes of the proliferation of these churches in Africa, specifically, sub-Sahara.[9]

---

[8] Harold W. Turner, 'The Significance of African Prophet Movements', *Hibbert Journal* 61.242 (1963), p. 2 (copy at Harold Turner Collection numbered as 1-8).

[9] For example, see Emmanuel Kenneth Browne, 'A Study of Spiritual Churches in Ghana with Particular Reference to Developments in Axim', PhD Thesis, University of Exeter (1983), pp. 65-90, Turner, 'The Significance of African Prophet Movements.', pp. 112-16; Lamin Sanneh, *Translating the Message: The Missionary Impact on Culture* (New York: Orbis Books, 1989), pp. 180-209; John S. Mbiti, *Bible and Theology in African Christianity* (Nairobi: Oxford University Press, 1986), pp. 28-31; Allan H. Anderson, 'A Failure in Love?' Western Missions and the Emergence of African Initiated Churches in the Twentieth Century', *Missiology: An International Review* 29.3 (2001), pp. 276-86.

They all seem to center around the eight causative factors discussed by Barrett. These are historical, political, economical, sociological, ethnic, non-religious, religious, and theological.[10] A careful examination of their activities, however, reveals that the churches' claim to solve problems and heal various diseases is the main attraction. For example, it can be deduced from Baëta's work that 'prophetism'[11] is the dominant causative factor;[12] and if pressed hard, it can be recognised that the divinatory-consultation aspect of 'prophetism' is the major attraction of these churches. The purpose of divinatory-consultation is to find out the cause of problems and disease and solve them. Healing and exorcism are central in their activities.

The methods used in healing and exorcism differ from one church to another. However, there are some commonalities. Almost all of them have healing camps (also called gardens or centres). Healing and deliverance usually take place on Friday, at the camp or chapel, while the people are fasting. Prayers are said to command spirits behind disease to leave. Turner notices that in Africa the majority of people use aids such as olive oil, crosses, incense, ritualistic bath, water, and florida water,[13] but without any indigenous herbs.[14] In Ghana, however, others use these aids in addition to the native herbs or western medicine.[15]

The approach of these churches demonstrates a blend of Christian faith and traditional practices. The camps and their use of special days follow that of the traditional day of consultation of the

---

[10] David B. Barrett, *Schism and Renewal in Africa* (Nairobi: Oxford University Press, 1968), pp. 92-99. Cf. Browne, 'A Study of Spiritual Churches in Ghana', pp. 70-104; Turner, 'African Prophet Movements', p. 6.

[11] Baëta's description of prophetism, brings this point out, especially considering his strong emphasis that 'prophetism appears to me to be a perennial phenomenon of African life'. Christian G.K. Baëta, *Prophetism in Ghana: A Study of Spiritual Churches* (London: SCM Press Ltd, 1962), pp. 6-7.

[12] Baëta, *Prophetism in Ghana*, pp. 3-4.

[13] This was some sort of perfume which came from the US. It was believed to have some curative powers.

[14] Harold W. Turner, *Religious Innovation in Africa: Collected Essays on New Religious Movements* (Boston: G.K. Halls, 1979), p. 167; cf. Kofi Asare Opoku, 'Letters to a Spiritual Father', *Research Review* 7.1 (1970), p. 1532; Robert W. Wyllie, 'Perceptions of the Spiritist Churches: A Survey of Methodists and Roman Catholics in Winneba, Ghana', *Journal of African Religion* 15.2 (1985), pp. 157, 142-67.

[15] Baëta, *Prophetism in Ghana*, p. 91, Cf. Asamoah-Gyadu, 'Renewal Within African Christianity', p. 101.

gods. Fasting, prayer, and commands appear to be a reinterpretation of Jesus' dealing with the demoniacs in the gospels (e.g. Mt. 17.21, KJV).

The strength of this sort of prayer is the concern of the church community, coming together to pray for people who are sick. The observation of Sundkler about the Zulu is relevant here. He states, 'the most pressing need was the promise of health and abundant life through methods he could understand.'[16] The ritualistic healing of these churches enhanced by the giving of aids certainly strengthen the personality-spirit of those who are fearful of spiritual forces such as witchcraft and demons, so that they can face life with little fear. In many cases, people claim they are healed following such prayers. It was therefore not a surprise that when the Government of Ghana, for example, found it necessary to keep the anti-witchcraft shrines within limits, their activities resurfaced within the African Initiated Churches whose methods could be understood. Against this background, a number of scholars, including Turner, Peel, and Baëta, have acknowledged the contributions that the AICs have made to African Christianity.[17]

African Pentecostal/Charismatic Healing Communities

The next healing community to be considered is the role played by Pentecostals and Charismatics. For Pentecostals, just like the African Initiated Churches, healing and reconciliation are part of their tradition and necessarily part of the normal worship service. The service is cooperative and participatory, which involves body-mind relationship. It is believed that this time of corporate worship brings blessing of healing, freedom in one's spirit, and forms the basis of peace and reconciliation within one's self as well as unity among Christians. The opportunity to speak aloud or quietly, individually or collectively with the hope that God will answer them, as individuals, is itself therapeutic. It enriches their spiritual lives in order for them to be able to face practical life situations with fortitude and hope.

---

[16] Bengt G. Sundkler, *Bantu Prophets in South Africa* (2nd ed.; Oxford: Oxford University Press, 1961), p. 236.

[17] J.D.Y. Peel *Aladura: A Religious Movement Among the Yoruba* (London: Oxford University Press, 1968); Baëta, *Prophetism in Ghana*.

Another trend that sequentially follows the healing practices of the Pentecostal/Charismatic community is the emergence of prayer/healing groups and prayer camps/centres.[18] Adubofour, a Ghanaian theologian, sees the prayer warrior movements as a Pentecostal holiness movement, which seeks to recover and apply the power of the gospel of Christ in terms meaningful to the African.[19] Both the Pentecostal prayer group and prayer centre seek to help people receive their healing and needs in the Lord. The main difference, however, is that while the Pentecostal healing prayer services may be held once or twice a week, the focus of the prayer centres is prayer for healing at all their meetings, which can be held once a week to every day in a week.

Prayer camps are grouped into two, residential and non-residential. On the one hand, the prayer camps are similar to the shrines of the traditional gods. On the other hand, they are similar to divine healing practices of special healing homes, which developed in the mid-nineteenth century in Europe and America by ministers, such as Edward Irving in the UK (1830), Johann Blumhardt in Germany (1843), Dorothea Trudel in Switzerland (1851), Otto Stockmayer in Switzerland (1867), and the following from the USA: Charles Cullis (1880s), Adoniram Gordon (1882), Alexander Dowie (1888-1907), and Charles Parham (1898-1900).[20] All types of diseases and problems, such as headaches, stomach-aches, epilepsy, convulsions, asthma, impotency, diabetes, high blood pressure, and mental disorders are brought to such prayer centres for healing.

---

[18] A prayer camp/centre is a place where a person goes with a problem to fast and pray with the aim of meeting God in a special way to answer his/her request. Both terms, camps and centres, are used interchangeably.

[19] Samuel Adubofour, 'Evangelical Para-Church Movement in Ghanaian Christianity: 1950 to Early 1990s', PhD thesis, University of Edinburgh (1994), pp. 244-61.

[20] For the development of healing movements and approaches to healing in Pentecostalism, see Paul Chappell, 'Healing Movements', in Stanley Burgess and Gary B. McGee (eds.), *Dictionary of Pentecostal and Charismatic Movements* (Grand Rapid: Regency Reference Library, 1988), pp. 353-74; D. William Faupel, *The Everlasting Gospel: The Significance of Eschatology in The Development of Pentecostal Thought* (JPTSup 10; Sheffield: Sheffield Academic Press, 1996), pp. 115-86; Donald W. Dayton, *Theological Roots of Pentecostalism* (Grand Rapids: Zondervan, 1987), pp. 115-41; Morton Kelsey, *Healing Christianity: A Case Study* (Minneapolis: Augsburg, 3rd edn, 1995), pp. 188-92.

The services at the prayer centres are similar to a Pentecostal type of healing prayer meeting. The emphasis at the Prayer centres is the special attention given to those who are sick. In addition, opportunity is given to those who want to confess their sins to do so. Furthermore, some leaders use questionnaires for interviews, which make the approach similar to that of professional psychoanalysts who allow the patients to talk freely about personal experience, in order to extract information from them. Through these means people are able to receive their healing after prayers are said for them.

Generally, when the family is considered, the healing amongst Pentecostals/Charismatics is similar to those in the shrine. Nevertheless, it differs from those at both the shrines, where physical effigies represent the gods which are consulted, and at the AICs, where water, crosses, and crucifixes are used. It must, however, be said that the concretisation of prayer languages and gestures is strong among the Pentecostal community. In addition, recently the Charismatic community has renewed the use of oil for the sick, and in some cases the oil is mystified to the point of being advocated to be used in farms, on market products, and in rooms to ward off evil. This brings into focus Schomburg-Scherff's observation about the power of images. Besides his recognition that specific images are stronger in certain cultures than others, he also feels that some 'conceptions and actions ... seem to transcend historical, geographical, social, and cultural boundaries.'[21] That is, for him, no matter how some people try to convince others that images are misconceptions, they will continue to have a strong impact on religion.[22] The impact that this concretisation has on the psyche of the people is significant.

---

[21] Sylvia M. Schomburg-Scherff, 'The Power of Images: New Approaches to the Anthropological Study of Images', *Anthropos* 95 (2000), p. 195. For the role that images play in Religion and Media in Ghana see Birgit Meyer, 'Money, Power and Morality in Popular Ghanaian Cinema', *Paper Presented to the Consultation, Religion and Media* Accra, May 21-27, 2000.

[22] See Kelleher who explores some of the biological, social, cultural, and spiritual dimensions of a liturgical body in action. Margaret Mary Kelleher, 'The Liturgical Body: Symbol and Ritual', in Bruce T. Morrill (ed.), *Bodies of Worship: Exploration in Theory and Practice* (Collegeville: The Liturgical Press, 1999), pp. 51-66.

The Challenge of African Concepts

A major challenge to the African healing communities is that which happens to be their strength—African Religiosity. The discussion so far reveals that the African concept of family and belief in the supernatural help the sick and the needy in times of trouble, yet the current beliefs of the causation of diseases are mainly of supernatural origin.[23] The result is that when there are complex medical challenges people fail to patronise the services at the health centres against the background of supernatural origin.

Thus, while in African churches the contemporary concept of healing is still strongly based on the African worldview, in the Western churches, the Enlightenment and advances in medicine have led to a separation of medicine from religion and the supernatural. Currently, however, a paradigm shift is taking place in Western culture as a result of postmodernity—which is challenging the rationalistic worldview and theology. It is against this background that this paper proposes the following.

Christian Healing Communities: The Way Forward

A Balanced Understanding of Healing

Understanding of healing must correspond with an anthropology that is rooted in the biblical-theological tradition of the Church, which sees a human being as a multidimensional unity. Body, soul, and spirit are not separate entities but are interrelated and interdependent. Therefore, health has physical, psychological, and spiritual dimensions. The individual person is part of a community and society and, therefore, health also has social and political dimensions. Insights from persons with disability reveal that healing refers to

---

[23] Birgit Meyer, *Translating the Devil: Religion and Modernity Among the Ewe in Ghana* (Edinburgh: Edinburgh University Press, 1999), pp. 146-216; Jane Parish, 'The Dynamics of Witchcraft and Indigenous Shrines Among the Akan', *Africa* 69.3 (1999), pp. 427-47; Paul Gifford, *African Christianity: Its Public Role* (London: Hurst & Company, 1998), pp. 97-98. This belief is also held through the whole continent of Africa and elsewhere, see Isaac Zokoue, 'The Crises of Maturity in Africa', *Evangelical Review of Theology* 20.4 (1996), pp. 362-64; Allen Anderson, *Zion and Pentecost: The Spirituality and Experience of Pentecostal and Zionist/Apostolic Churches in South Africa* (Pretoria: Unisa Press, 2000), pp. 264-75; David Burnett, *World of Spirits: A Christian Perspective on Traditional and Folk Religions* (Grenville Place: Monarch Books, 2000), pp. 122-56.

experiences such as actions, attitudes, words, and processes which reflect something of God's empowering, renewing, reconciling, and liberating power that is working to reverse the negation of God's good creation.[24]

Such a comprehensive understanding of healing challenges any understanding of health as something that is simply about having a strong and functional body, and enjoying mental well-being. Rather, it leads us to an understanding that people with chronic physical or mental sickness, and who cope with their ailments and live in harmonious relationships with their fellow human beings and with God, may be healthier than those who are physically and mentally healthy but have little awareness of, for example, the meaning of their lives.

The task of the Church, therefore, is to attempt to make it clear that healing needs to be understood and approached in a multidimensional way as described, such as social, economical, cultural, and spiritual.

Healing Congregations

Christians need to understand that the local congregation or Christian community is the primary agent for healing. This is based on a comprehensive understanding of health, suffering, sickness, and healing, as issues that should concern the entire community collectively.

The Church needs to give enough room for healing in its liturgy. The congregation is entrusted with sanctified means of healing by its ministry of the word of God, prayer with and for the sick. These mean their inclusion in the healing process is a special and unique feature of healing communities. They include worship, the communion, praying for the sick, confession and forgiveness, the laying-on of hands, anointing with oil, and the use of charismatic spiritual gifts. Time therefore needs to be allocated in our services to pray for those who are sick.

Creating safe spaces for people to testify or tell their stories within church communities is a first step through which congrega-

---

[24] Samuel Kabue, 'Addressing Disability in a Healing and Reconciling Community' in *Come Holy Spirit Heal and Reconcile: Report of the WCC Conference on World Mission and Evangelism*, Athens, Greece in May 2005 (Geneva: WCC Publications, 2008), pp. 172-78.

tions can become healing communities. Healing is fostered where churches relate to daily life and where people feel safe to share their stories and testimonies. Broken, rejected, and suffering people need places where they can be comfortable in sharing their pain in an atmosphere of openness and acceptance. The local church can offer such a forum.

The New Testament practice of laying on of hands has been an act that has brought blessings to some sick people. In healing situations, many people have the desire to be touched. The laying on of hands becomes an act of sympathy and compassion, which also becomes an opportunity for God's power to be manifested. Through the laying on of hands many people have claimed to have felt some physical manifestation such as shaking, heat, laughing, or crying, which lead to healing.[25]

Recently Keith Warrington has reiterated the significance of the anointing with oil in healing. The significance, he concludes, 'is therefore primarily symbolic, reminding sufferers that they can feel secure in the presence of friends who care and a God who restores'.[26] Oil therefore can be used in this sense, not however to be mystified in its usage so as to take people's attention off Christ.

Those endowed with the gifts of healing within a given community must be encouraged to use them. Those with these gifts must not only be given deliberate encouragement, spiritual nurture, education, and enrichment, but also a proper ministry of pastoral accompaniment and ecclesial oversight.

Contribution of Tangible and Intangible Assets to the Church

The Church may also contribute to health systems tangible assets, including the creation and support of health-related jobs, clinics and mission hospitals, as well as groups visiting sick congregation members, and the provision of counseling services, care groups, and health programmes. Serving by showing love, giving comfort, caring, simply being with somebody, and by offering practical assistance may lead to healing.

The intangible assets of a religious community are also essential contributions to healing. These include trust, prayer, love, compas-

---

[25] Keith Warrington, 'Healing and Exorcism: The Path to Wholeness' in Keith Warrington (ed.), *Pentecostal Perspectives* (Carlisle: Paternoster, 1998), p 161.

[26] Warrington, 'Healing and Exorcism', p 159.

sion, reconciliation, encouragement, and the giving of hope and a meaning to life.

In addition, the Church can be a place of teaching, learning, and promoting health related issues. These include Bible study on health, healing, and wholeness, facilitating the self-discovery of causes of ill health, and learning to take personal responsibility for one's own health. Through playing such roles the Church assumes the role of a healing community.

Congregations can take part in positive steps towards healing, reconciliation, and peace. The African traditional concepts of sickness and healing support the view that disharmony in relationships between individuals and families or society leads to alienation and brokenness, and physical disease. Similarly, modern sciences have increasingly acknowledged the importance of harmonious relationships with oneself, and that having a social network might protect people from physical and mental diseases. That may, consequently, help people overcome disease or cope with chronic sickness. Local congregations can initiate such activities, which can eventually lead to healing.

CONCLUSION

This paper has shown that healing has been one of the pillars of the fivefold gospel. However, although Jesus carried out healing in his earthly ministry and the early church was obedient to the commission of Jesus, due to the influence of the Enlightenment, the Church has experienced a decline in its healing ministry.

Citing the traditional concept of healing in the African culture and the churches in Africa, the Christian world has been challenged to reconsider its role as a healing community.

In order to play its proper role as a healing community, churches have been charged to reconsider their Christian understanding of what constitutes healing and what promotes health. Realising that the local congregation or Christian community could be the primary agent for healing, congregations have been asked to give healing a place in their liturgies, noting that prayer, laying on of hands, and anointing with oil could be practised.

The Church has been asked to contribute to health by way of both tangible assets and intangible assets. Such assets, it is suggested, could include the creation and support of health-related jobs, visiting sick members, and showing love and compassion. As Jesus associated with the marginalized, the downtrodden, and the imperfect, so also the Church has been called to be a community of 'wounded healers' where care needs to be paramount.

It is considered that since God is sovereign whether healing takes place through prayers, caring, or medicine, God must be seen to be at work in all healing processes.

PART SIX

THE PENTECOSTAL CHURCH AS ESCHATOLOGICAL COMMUNITY

10

ASCENSION—PENTECOST—ESCHATON: A THEOLOGICAL FRAMEWORK FOR PENTECOSTAL ECCLESIOLOGY

PETER ALTHOUSE*

From the beginning, Pentecostals proclaimed that Jesus Christ saves, sanctifies, heals, baptizes in the Holy Spirit, and is coming in glory to fulfill his kingly reign. Presupposed but seldom articulated is the role that the ecclesial community plays as the eschatological fellowship of faith in the outworking of God's mission to the world. The inauguration of the Church at Pentecost and its growth through the activity of the Spirit as accounted in the Acts of the Apostles and continuing throughout history, looks in anticipation to its eschatological fulfillment in the age to come.

The gift of the Spirit promised in the ascension of Christ and fulfilled in the Spirit's descent, inaugurated the Church as the people of God under the eschatological reign of the Lord Jesus Christ (Acts 2.2-4).[1] The tension between ascension and Pentecost as found in Luke-Acts is a tension between the absence and the presence of God in the world that highlights the intersection of not only Christology, eschatology, and ecclesiology in the Lukan narrative,[2] but pneumatology and Trinitarian theology as well. The prom-

---

* Peter Althouse (PhD, Saint Michael's College, University of Toronto) is Associate Professor of Theology at Southeastern University, Lakeland, FL, USA.

[1] All scripture references will be from the New International Version unless otherwise stated.

[2] Douglas Farrow, *Ascension and Ecclesia: On the Significance of the Doctrine of the Ascension for Ecclesiology and Christian Cosmology* (Grand Rapids: Eerdmans, 1999), p. 16, n. 6.

ise of the Spirit at Christ's ascension, who will 'clothe with power from on high' (Lk. 24.49; Acts 1.8) and who will baptize with the Holy Spirit (Acts 1.5), is fulfilled at Pentecost by and with the Spirit (Acts 2.4). The promise that Jesus 'will come back in the same way you have seen him go into heaven' (Acts 1.11b) is the hope of the fulfillment of Christ's future parousia. It is partially fulfilled in Pentecost as the 'last days' in which the Spirit of God is being poured out on the people participating in and witnessing the event and its growth into the known world, as Luke describes in Acts. It will also be poured out in the future as a sign that the day of the Lord has come (Acts 2.17-21). Images of 'violent wind' and 'tongues of fire' witnessed at the inauguration of the Church on the day of Pentecost signify the renewal of the covenant in which the election of God spans back to the patriarchs, the nations, and as far back as creation itself. The implication of Luke-Acts is that covenant law is renewed in that the fire which alights on them harkens back to the giving of the Mosaic law (e.g. burning bush; fire in exodus journey). The nations are involved in this renewed work of God for the tongues spoken through the Spirit's filling are heard by the 'Parthians, Medes and Elamites; residents of Mesopotamia, Judea and Cappadocia, Pontus and Asia, Phrygia and Pamphylia, Egypt and the parts of Libya near Cyrene; visitors from Rome (both Jews and converts to Judaism); Cretans and Arabs' (Acts 2.9-11). Indeed, the nations have now been grafted into God's covenant with Israel, so that they too in all their diversity are to be included as the people of God. Creation itself is the focus of hope for its eschatological renewal in that the Spirit depicted as a 'violent wind came from heaven and filled the whole house', alludes to the creation narrative of Genesis when the Spirit of God (wind) broods over the waters (Gen. 1.2).

Unfortunately, the depth of meaning of Luke-Acts is overlooked by a shallow reading of the text, which truncates the giving of the Spirit to an experience of 'baptism in the Spirit' and the 'initial evidence of speaking in tongues'. Without diminishing Pentecostal distinctives, I shall argue that a fuller reading of the text and of the entire biblical canon generally envisions a theologically robust ecclesiology within the framework of an inaugural or proleptic eschatology following the threefold pattern of ascension—Pentecost—eschaton: The Church as the body of the crucified and risen Christ is the eschatological community, who by the promise of the Spirit given at Pentecost lives in the tension of the already and not yet of the eschaton. I shall also advocate a holistic eschatology that includes the movement of a pilgrim people in concrete history who are drawn by Christ through the Spirit into the coming kingdom, the calling to diverse nations to participate in God's new work and a robust cosmology that advocates nothing less than the renewal of creation. In both cases, the Church is called to give witness to and participate in the sovereign activity of God in which Christ by the Spirit is already establishing in the present his kingdom reign as an anticipatory foretaste of what is to come. My purpose here is to propose a preliminary framework by which an eschatologically nuanced Pentecostal ecclesiology can be constructed.

The Current Status of Pentecostal Ecclesiology

Although Pentecostalism is now over a century old, its theology of the Church is sorely underdeveloped. In practice, Pentecostal churches eclectically borrow from other theological traditions and apply their practices in pragmatic and technical ways, but with little understanding of their philosophical and theological implications. As a result, Pentecostal churches today appear to sustain and advocate social ideologies of consumer capitalism and market place values, borrowing heavily from corporate business practices to govern the Church. Michael Horton's scathing criticism of Pentecostal and evangelical ecclesiologies focuses on their accommodation to individualistic choices in the religious marketplace. 'The nihilistic *eros* of the consumer society, which seems to have drawn much of American Christianity into its wake, creates a desire that can never be satisfied. Ads and shop windows offer us a perpetual stream of icons promising to fulfill our ambitions to have the life that they represent: a fully realized eschatology'.[3] At least in North America, one is left to wonder what is unique about the Pentecostal Church, and thus it too is succumbing to the accommodation process that has influenced most denominations in the Western world. Although sectors of Pentecostalism are at risk in relation to consumer culture,

---

[3] Michael S. Horton, *People and Place: A Covenant Ecclesiology* (London: Westminster John Knox, 2008), p. 56, cf. pp. 176-81.

the state of the Pentecostal Church may not be quite as grim as Horton asserts. In their advocacy for a missional ecclesiology, Michael Frost and Alan Hirsch insist that 'for a brief time some forms of Pentecostalism came closer than the rest of the church' in meeting the experiential and social needs of the lost in the postmodern world.[4] However, Horton is likewise askance of discussions in evangelicalism regarding missional ecclesiology.

Theological scholarship that attempts to voice the distinctiveness of Pentecostalism and provide a theological foundation on which to construct its ecclesiology is starting to emerge. Miroslav Volf's excellent work in *After Our Likeness*[5] places Roman Catholic, Eastern Orthodox, and Free Church ecclesiologies into ecumenical dialogue in order to construct a theology of the local church, but Pentecostal churches are given scant reference except as one of the many evangelical-type churches. Simon Chan's *Spiritual Theology*[6] and *Liturgical Theology*[7] advocate an ontology of the Church in which worship shapes the spiritual disciplines. Veli-Matti Kärkkäinen's *Introduction to Ecclesiology*[8] and *Toward a Pneumatological Theology*[9] places Pentecostal ecclesiology defined as a fellowship in the power of the Holy Spirit in ecumenical context. Frank Macchia's *Baptized in the Spirit*[10] is a constructive work around the Pentecostal distinctive of Spirit baptism and valuable in its clarion call for the reintegration of Christology and pneumatology around the Pentecost event, so that the Church is not only inaugurated around the Spirit's outpouring but continues to receive the Spirit in baptism, understood not as two separate acts of grace (i.e. initiation and empowerment), but as one

---

[4] Michael Frost and Alan Hirsch, *The Shaping of Things to Come: Innovation and Mission for the 21ˢᵗ-Century Church* (Peabody, MA: Hendrickson, 2003), p. 6.

[5] Miroslav Volf, *After Our Likeness: The Church as the Image of the Trinity* (Grand Rapids: Eerdmans, 1998).

[6] Simon Chan, *Spiritual Theology: A Systematic Study of the Christian Life* (Downers Grove, IL: InterVarsity Press, 1998), especially chapter 5.

[7] Simon Chan, *Liturgical Theology: The Church as Worshiping Community* (Downers Grove, IL: InterVarsity Press, 2006).

[8] Veli-Matti Kärkkäinen, *An Introduction to Ecclesiology: Ecumenical, Historical & Global Perspectives* (Downers Grove, IL: InterVarsity Press, 2002).

[9] Veli-Matti Kärkkäinen, *Toward a Pneumatological Theology: Pentecostal and Ecumenical Perspectives on Ecclesiology, Soteriology, and Theology of Mission* (ed. Amos Yong; Lanham: University of America, 2002).

[10] Frank D. Macchia, *Baptized in the Spirit: A Global Pentecostal Theology* (Grand Rapids: Zondervan, 2006).

sustained activity of the Spirit. Shane Clifton's *Pentecostal Churches in Transition*[11] is a description of the contextual changes of the Pentecostal churches in Australia, but more of a sociological assessment from below than an ecclesiological theology proper.

Yet when turning to the broader Christian tradition and the vast array of ecclesiological options one barely sees the Pentecostal Church anywhere, except perhaps as 'straw man'. A perusal of Avery Dulles' *Models of the Church*, for instance, develops a useful taxonomy of Roman Catholic and conciliar Protestantism, but one is disappointed in that none of the models fits easily the Pentecostal Church. Although there are some affinities if one merges the Word and Servant models, even this amalgam does not really speak to a Pentecostal ecclesial context. The question then is, how does one start to develop a Pentecostal ecclesiology that incorporates that which Pentecostals hold dear to their understanding of the Church without displacing its theological contributions in adopting other theologies of the Church? I would suggest that the place to begin is the Pentecost narrative of Luke-Acts, in the fulfillment of the descending Spirit promised by the ascending Christ.

The Eschatological Significance of the Ascension

In *Ascension and Ecclesia*, Douglas Farrow argues that Christ's ascension is critical to an ecclesiology that grapples with the tension of divine absence and presence. Although the tendency in theology is either to ignore the ascension, or to subsume it under a theology of resurrection,[12] Farrow insists that it is an important eschatological account of the climax of the history of Jesus. The ascension is the hermeneutical key connecting the story of Jesus' vindication and exaltation as the messianic hope for Israel to the new history of God's people, who have received and are formed by the Spirit. The ascension does not abandon eschatology to the ongoing process of history, but 'brings history into the *service* of eschatology'. No longer is the end of history (apocalyptic) the guarantee of the

---

[11] Shane Clifton, *Pentecostal Churches in Transition: Analysing the Developing Ecclesiology of the Assemblies of God in Australia* (Global Pentecostal and Charismatic Studies, 3; Leiden: Brill, 2009).

[12] For instance, Pheme Perkins, *Resurrection: New Testament Witness and Contemporary Reflection* (New York: Doubleday, 1984) as a case in point.

claims made by or about Jesus, but the ascension guarantees that these are already in history. 'The ascension (not the resurrection or parousia) thus becomes the climax of Jesus' history and *the* eschatological event fulfilling all the prophetic hopes of Israel. And thus eschatologicalizes what is left in history by setting it within the tension of his departure and still impending return.'[13] Conflating the resurrection and ascension 'puts in jeopardy the continuity between our present world and the higher places of the new order established by God in Christ. For in that conflation the ascension, insofar as it can still be distinguished from the resurrection, is regarded as an event with no *historical* component, separating it from the Old Testament expectation'.[14] Without the ascension, argues Farrow, the resurrection takes on a docetic interpretation, an otherworldly eschatology in which our hope is merely a spiritual 'going to heaven' and the parousia is seen merely as the 'end of the world'. No longer is there discontinuity between Jesus' messianic history and world history and consequently the eschatological goal of history is human ascension.[15] In the ancient world, human ascension was interpreted along the dualistic lines of Plato as an overrealized eschatology and in the patristic and medieval world as the mystical ascent of the mind.[16] In the modern world, human ascension is interpreted according to Cartesian dualism in which the subjectivity of human experience is displaced from bodily experience. The ascension of Christ, however, eschews the anthropological priority of the mind by pointing to a real history between the resurrection and the ascension in which Jesus walked among his disciples.

New Testament scholar N.T. Wright likewise argues that the role of the ascension in Luke-Acts provides a holistic account that insists that Jesus is indeed alive in 'new bodily life' and not merely visionary or inner experiences as modern scholars of religion want to insist.[17] Yet the ascension was not understood by the ancient world as some place called heaven that is above the earth. 'Heaven' and 'earth' are interlocking universes existing simultaneously, not a dif-

---

[13] Farrow, *Ascension and Ecclesia*, pp. 16-17.

[14] Farrow, *Ascension and Ecclesia*, p. 28.

[15] Farrow, *Ascension and Ecclesia*, p. 29.

[16] Horton, *People*, p. 7

[17] N.T. Wright, *The Resurrection of the Son of God* (Minneapolis, MN: Fortress Press, 2003), p. 653.

ferent place in time and space in the beyond.[18] 'They are two different dimensions of God's good creation.... First, heaven relates to earth tangentially so that the one who is in heaven can be present simultaneously anywhere and everywhere on earth: the ascension therefore means that Jesus is available, accessible, without people having to travel to a particular spot on the earth to find him. Second, heaven is, as it were, the control room for earth.... "All authority is given to me", said Jesus at the end of Matthew's gospel, "in heaven and on earth"'.[19] In other words, heaven and earth inhabit each other simultaneously, and not as Rudolph Bultmann asserted as an ancient mythology above and below that needs to be demythologized. However, in contradiction to Farrow, Wright argues that it is inaccurate to suppose that Luke's emphasis on the physicality of the risen and ascended Jesus was to combat docetic tendencies. Nevertheless, the primary purpose of the resurrection and ascension is to accent both the physicality of Jesus' risen body and what it means for a holistic view of the world and Israel. The type of spiritual experiences these followers of Jesus had from Easter to the ascension is discontinuous and qualitatively different however from the experiences of the Church afterward.[20]

Michael Horton builds on Farrow's ecclesiology to develop a covenantal view of the Church interpreted through the lens of Reformed theology. I find his work both promising in helping Pentecostals develop a doctrine of the Church that looks to Pentecost as an integrating theme, but irritating in his antagonism to Christian experience and Pentecostal spirituality. Nevertheless, in an earlier work Horton argues against a Platonic or mystical reading that dichotomizes the eternal soul seeking its form and the bodily or material world of appearance. Biblical eschatology contrasts 'this age' under the darkness of sin brought on by human rebellion, whose only remedy is the cross, and the 'age to come' which is divine vindication through redemptive history.[21] The theology of the cross points to an eschatology that advocates 'neither escaping nature nor

---

[18] Wright, *Resurrection*, p. 655.

[19] N.T. Wright, *Surprised by Hope: Rethinking Heaven, the Resurrection, and the Mission of the Church* (New York: HarperOne, 2008), p. 111.

[20] Wright, *Resurrection*, pp. 658-59.

[21] Michael S. Horton, *Covenant and Eschatology: The Divine Drama* (Louisville: Westminster John Knox Press, 2002), especially chapter 1.

conquering nature, but leading the chorus of nature groaning for the consummation. It begins not from an ontological-cosmological dualism, but an ethical-eschatological one; not from spirit vs. nature, or from any intrinsic fallenness or 'thrownness' of human existence, but from the corruption of nature by human rejection of God's reign'.[22]

The ascension is the culmination of the cross and resists all attempts to 'idealize' reality or give priority to mystical assent.

> [T]he 'earthiness of redeemed creation in the consummation depends entirely on whether the ascension was a historical, bodily, and pneumatologically constituted event. If Jesus is the firstfruits, a docetic ascension requires a docetic consummation. At the same time, the ascension cannot be reduced to history; it reveals the power of the new, eschatological life, not simply packing up where left off in his historical existence.[23]

Jesus is the firstfruits of creation and his ascension incorporates history so that this age of sin and death is not jettisoned for some otherworldly beyond. The Church looks to its headship in the resurrected and ascended Christ and lives in tension between 'this age' and 'the age to come' in which Jesus is neither fully absent or fully presence.[24]

The Eschatological Significance of Pentecost

The ascension of Christ, which resists all attempts to define the resurrection as merely a spiritual process coinciding with death and the ascent of the mind or spirit into the heavens or as an escape of the Church from this world in a dispensational rapture, is only one side of the story pointing to the promised continuation of the ministry of Christ in the world despite his absence. The promise of the Comforter to come is fulfilled on the day of Pentecost, when the Spirit's filling of the hearers of the gospel begin to form and shape an apostolic people. The promise is partially realized at Pentecost in that the covenantal renewal of the people of God, in whom the

---

[22] Horton, *Covenant*, p. 42.

[23] Horton, *People*, p. 4.

[24] Horton, *People*, p. 4.

nations of the world now have redemptive hope, also hints at the renewal of creation itself. The images of Pentecost harken back to the Spirit's descent as the wind of creation when the Spirit (as wind) broods over the waters (Gen. 1.2). The pillar and cloud that guides the Israelites through the desert to the Promised Land leads the people of God to their Sabbath Rest (Exodus 19). The descent of the Spirit is depicted in a cloud of winged creatures (Isa. 63.11-14; Hag. 2.5) and wind (Ps. 104.1-3). The fire of Pentecost is suggestive of the giving of law at Sinai, starting with Moses and the bushing bush that is not consumed (Exod. 3.2-3), and the fire of Yahweh that consumes Elijah's sacrifice, judging, and calling a sinful nation back to God (1 Kgs 18.36-39). The Spirit of Pentecost is the same Spirit who creates and renews all things, providing space for a covenantal community to inhabit the covenant of creation, who at times descends in judgment to right that which has been corrupted.[25]

At Pentecost, and throughout the narrative of Luke-Acts, creation and new creation are interdependent with the goal of creation being its consummation in the Sabbath Rest, a goal that includes creation that will finally become what it was intended to be, and a creaturely people who will truly be the image and likeness of God. The covenantal renewal occurring at Pentecost is the beginning of God's intent for creation and creature. 'The Creator Spirit is, even in the very beginning, a divine witness to the goal of creation: the consummation. Thwarted by Adam in the first creation, this goal is finally achieved by the last Adam in the new creation. No wonder, then, that the outpouring of the Spirit is identified with the 'last days' and the age to come. Already in creation, therefore, we need the Spirit of promise: the one who propels creation towards the goal, which is nothing less than the consummation at the end of the trial'.[26]

---

[25] Horton, *People*, p. 14; cf. Michael Wilkinson and Peter Althouse, 'Like a Mighty Rushing Wind: Innovation and the Transnational Character of Pentecostalism', in *Winds from the North: Canadian Contributions to the Pentecostal Movement* (Religion in the Americas Series, 10; Leiden: Brill, 2010), pp. 3-5; Alasdair I.C. Heron, *The Holy Spirit: The Holy Spirit in the Bible, and History of Christian Thought, and Recent Theology* (Philadelphia: The Westminster Press, 1983), especially chapter 1 and 3.

[26] Horton, *People*, p. 15.

The Church is part of God's plan for the eschatological renewal and transformation of creation in which the Church commits itself to the world as part of its mission, not that it can accomplish this transformation, but that it has been called to participate in it. Present renewal and future transformation are in and through Christ by his Spirit who draws the Church and with it creation into its eschatological time. The Bible 'claims to show us the shape, the structure, the origin, and the goal not merely of human history, but of cosmic history. It does not accept a view of nature as simply the arena upon which the drama of human history is played out. Much less does it seek the secret of the individual's true being within the self—a self for which the public history of the world can have no ultimate significance. Rather it sees the history of the nations and the history of nature within the large framework of God's history—carrying forward to its completion of the gracious purpose that has its source in the love of the Father for the Son in the unity of the Spirit'.[27] Because it is Christ who unfolds his kingdom reign in time, the Church is always anchored in the cross as the criterion for all activity. In other words, while the activity of the people of God under the lordship of Christ is the liberative hope of the world, it is not liberation from below by human activity seeking a progressively better world, but God's liberative reign that graces human activity and draws it into the activity of the kingdom. Because the cross is the discerning criteria for all engagement inside and outside the Church, there is no place for triumphalism as already having achieved God's kingdom.[28] The Church stands in profound ambiguity to the light of the risen Lord, representing the kingdom as a foretaste of Christ's full presence by his Spirit, but realizes his absence in the creaturely brokenness of a people who await the judgment of sin and the fullness of redemption.

Implied in the Pentecost narrative is God's mission to include the nations and the Church's responsibility to the nations. The outpouring of the Spirit is symbolized as diverse tongues in which people from many nations hear and understand, though some wonder if the speakers are in fact drunk. Together the descent of the

---

[27] Lesslie Newbigin, *The Open Secret: An Introduction to the Theology of Mission*, rev. ed. (Grand Rapids: Eerdmans, 1995), pp. 30-31.

[28] Farrow, *Ascension and Ecclesia*, pp. 72-73.

Spirit and the inauguration of the Church bring hope to the nations and all their cultural and linguistic distinctiveness in that they too will be included in God's eschatological mission. Frank Macchia argues that this event represents a catholicity in the Church that respects the diversity of nations,[29] and while I would agree I would suggest that the narrative indicates that the language of God's kingdom includes the nations as corporate entities in all their social, political, and economic realities, but where the nations are broken by corruption the kingdom of God provides a just reign that also respects the diversity of nations.

Lesslie Newbigin advocates a missional approach that begins with the scandal of particularity in national Israel's calling and her Messiah Jesus Christ, and through him the universal call to all nations corporately. Newbigin argues 'The Bible, then, is covered with God's purpose of blessing for all the nations. It is concerned with the completion of God's purpose in the creation of the world and of men in the world. It is not—to put it crudely—concerned with offering a way of escape for the redeemed soul out of history, but with the action of God to bring history to its true end'.[30] The implication is that the Church through which the mission of God is revealed includes compassion, justice, and reconciliation, seeking to bring ultimate transformation. 'The concern of those who see mission primarily in terms of action for God's justice is embodied mainly in programs carried out on a supra-congregational level by boards and committees, whether denominational or ecumenical. The concern of those who see mission primarily in terms of personal conversion is expressed mainly at the local or congregational life. The effect is that each is robbed of its character by its separating from the other. Christian programs for justice and compassion are severed from their proper roots in the liturgical and sacramental life of the congregation, and so lose their character as signs of the presence of Christ'.[31]

Social justice and peace-making for the nations are anticipatory signs for ultimate reconciliation to come in the eschaton. Although

---

[29] Frank D. Macchia, 'The Tongues of Pentecost: A Pentecostal Perspective on the Promise and Challenge of Pentecostal/Roman Catholic Dialogue', *Journal of Ecumenical Studies* 35.1 (Winter 1998), pp. 1-18.

[30] Newbigin, *The Open Secret*, pp. 33-34.

[31] Newbigin, *The Open Secret*, pp. 10-11.

not speaking specifically about the Church proper, Miroslav Volf's work in *Exclusion and Embrace* places reconciliation now in the context of ultimate reconciliation in the future kingdom, in which the elimination of oppression and the embrace of cultural and national otherness expresses God's ultimate justice for the world. 'It is God and the new world that God is creating, a world in which people from every nation and every tribe, with their cultural goods, will gather around the triune God, a world in which every tear will be wiped away and "pain will be no more" (Revelation 21:3)'.[32] A theological reading of Acts 2, however, does not suggest uniformity or a form of hegemony, but that 'when the Spirit comes, all understand each other, not because one language is restored or a new all-encompassing meta-language is designed, but because each hears his or her own language spoken. Pentecost overcomes the "confusion" ... but it does so not by reverting to the unity of cultural uniformity, but by advocating toward the harmony of cultural diversity'.[33] Liberation is the first step to overcoming oppression committed by and upon the nations, but in itself a problematic approach because the liberated oppressed eventually become the perpetuators of oppression. Reconciliation among the nations, however, is the ultimate goal of justice and peace-making because it sees reconciliation as the ultimate significance of the eschatological reign that includes the nations (Rev. 15.4; 22.2). The Church is the locale where national reconciliation has begun, a focus of its mission in seeking peace as a foretaste of God's shalom.

The Church cannot be severed from its head: the Lordship of Jesus Christ who has ascended to sit in judgment at the right hand of the Father and reigns from the throne over the Church and the nations of the world. The promise of being 'clothed with power from on high' is not a reference to some raw, ubiquitous supernatural power in the Church (as is often naively assumed by Pentecostals), but nothing less than being clothed by the Spirit of Christ himself. '[T]he Spirit who clothed Christ in our flesh and in consummated glory now clothes us with Christ' so that we are now 'partakers of the divine nature which is nothing less than the re-

---

[32] Miroslav Volf, *Exclusion and Embrace: A Theological Exploration of Identity, Otherness, and Reconciliation* (Nashville: Abingdon Press, 1996), pp. 50-51.

[33] Volf, *Exclusion and Embrace*, p. 228.

newal of the *imago dei*.[34] Roger Stronstad has noted this connection between the charismatic Spirit who endows Christ and his mission, and the transfer of this Spirit to the now charismatically endowed people of God at Pentecost.[35] The people of God are empowered to go out and preach, teach, and do those things that Jesus preached, taught, and did, because the Spirit that enabled him now enables the Church. Yet the victory of the Spirit in mediating Christ to the nations is also part of the unfolding story, the kingdom of God growing is history displacing the oppressive powers of nations, which need Christ's liberative reign; the Church gives witness to and acts to see God's reign come to fruition.

The Eschatological Significance of Ascension and Pentecost in the Pauline Corpus

The ascension—Pentecost—eschaton vector of the Church is noted in the Pauline corpus[36] and other New Testament writings. Paul clearly distinguishes the ascension from the resurrection, usually with variations of the phrase: 'at the right hand of God' (1 Cor. 15.24; Rom. 8.34; Eph. 1.20, 2.6; Col. 3.1), though the two are integrally connected. Both Mt. 22.44 and the longer version of Mk 16.19 make reference to the ascension as do Heb. 1.13, 10.12, 1 Pet. 3.22 and Rev. 3.21.[37] Moreover, the Christological pattern of descent-ascent in Philippians and the ecclesiological priority of Christ's enthronement as head of the Church and cosmos in Ephesians highlight the importance of the ascension. Since Christ is at the right hand of God and head of the Church, the Church is a prophetic sign of the divine reordering of the world around the enthroned Christ and anticipation of the divine reordering of the cosmic order.[38]

The celebration of Pentecost, which is fifty days after Passover in the Jewish calendar and follows the agricultural pattern of Pales-

---

[34] Horton, *People*, p. 15.

[35] Roger Stronstad, *The Charismatic Theology of St. Luke* (Peabody, MA: Hendrickson, 1984), p. 49.

[36] I am aware that the Pauline authorship of some of these texts is disputed. Nevertheless for the sake of simplicity I will refer to them as Pauline.

[37] Wright, *Surprised*, pp. 109, 305 nn. 1, 2.

[38] Farrow, *Ascension*, pp. 31-33.

tine, was an early harvest known as firstfruits. Also called Feast of Weeks, Feast of Harvest, and Firstfruits, Pentecost marked the end of the grain harvest (cf. Exod. 23.16, 34.22; Lev. 23.15-22; Num. 28.26-31; Deut. 16.9-12).[39] Paul alludes to Pentecost in his discussion of firstfruits, which connects Christ's resurrection to our future hope of resurrection. Paul makes a case for the future resurrection of all believers and the future hope for creation in identifying Christ's resurrection as the 'firstfruits' that is mediated by the Spirit: 'But Christ has indeed been raised from the dead, the firstfruits of those who have fallen asleep' (1 Cor. 15.20). The resurrection of Christ takes on eschatological significance making it more than just a historical, past event that must be celebrated in remembrance because Christ has commanded it (i.e. ordinance), but also provides the basis for the future hope of our redemption and that of the entire creation mediated through God's covenantal reign (sacramental). The Spirit of Pentecost is the guarantee of the eschatological consummation of that which has begun in Christ. 'Jesus Christ is the first fruits of our own complete redemption (Rom. 8:23). What we now savor of the Spirit's gracious activity is only a foretaste of the feast we will relish on that day.... As such, the present gift of the Holy Spirit is the guarantee that God will complete what he has begun. According to Rom 5.1-5, the hope of sharing God's glory survives because of the Holy Spirit. Precisely because God's love is already powerfully present and active in his Spirit, there is hope for something more, namely, the fulfillment of salvation, the completion and perfection of God's redemptive activity'.[40] Thus Gordon Fee argues the Spirit is the promise of the final consummation of the future kingdom, which for Paul is based in his encounter with the risen Christ and the gift of the eschatological Spirit. Believers live in the last days in the sense that they have already been raised with Christ in new birth, which guarantees the not yet of bodily resurrection in the eschaton, and that the tension between promise

---

[39] Horton, *People*, p. 17.

[40] T. David Beck, *The Holy Spirit and the Renewal of All Things: Pneumatology in Paul and Jürgen Moltmann* (Princeton Theological Monograph Series; Eugene, OR: Pickwick, 2007), p. 33.

and fulfillment is realized only through the outpouring of the eschatological Spirit.[41]

Paul uses a number of pneumatological metaphors to accent the promise of Christ's resurrection as the foundation of Christian hope, that in the future parousia believers too will be raised: firstfruits, down payment, and seal. The metaphor of firstfruits is used in relation to both Christ and the Spirit and has obvious connections to Luke's Pentecost narrative. Within the framework of a proleptic eschatology, Christ's resurrection is the first occurrence which anticipates and is the guarantee of the resurrection that is to come in the eschaton (1 Cor. 15.20, 23). It also connotes that while Christ is the first (Rom. 8.23), his resurrection is mediated to us in the present 'as both evidence and guarantee that the future is now and yet to be'.[42] However, firstfruits also connote a number of meanings: 1) that the initial harvest implies a completed harvest to come and therefore a temporal process spanning the seasons of time; 2) although the firstfruits is the first of the crop the full harvest to follow is of like kind, implying that our 'spiritual, bodily resurrection' will be of like kind as Christ's bodily resurrection, and because Christ has ascended and now sits at the right hand of the Father our resurrection is unequivocally a bodily resurrection; 3) Paul uses the metaphor in regards to both Christ and the Spirit, for both persons of the Trinity are eschatologically active 'between the times'. Christ's resurrection is the firstfruits because he has been raised from the dead and because he has been raised so will we. Yet the Spirit is the firstfruits because we experience the energies of the resurrection from his future reign breaking into the present shaping the fellowship of believers; and 4) firstfruits expresses the proleptic tension between the present victory of the Spirit who is forming the people of God and the future victory through which the Spirit is inviting God's people to turn their attention outward into the world and creation. Although the world is currently under the corruption of sin and darkness, the eschatological Spirit mediates Christ's reign bringing anticipatory hope for redemption for all

---

[41] Gordon D. Fee, *God's Empowering Presence: The Holy Spirit in the Letters of Paul* (Peabody, MA: Hendrickson, 1994), pp. 805-806.

[42] Fee, *God's Empowering Presence*, p. 807.

creation. Consequently, individual believers,[43] the community of believers who constitute the Church and the whole of creation 'groan' for the redemption that is yet to come. Yet our groaning is not alone for the Spirit intercedes with and for us with 'sighs too deep for words. '[S]ince the Spirit groans in us and with us, and we groan along with creation, the Spirit must also groan along with all creation'.[44]

Down payment (2 Cor. 1.21-22; 5.5; Eph. 1.4) is also a metaphor that conveys a sense of eschatological tension in that we have an installment guaranteeing our part in God's inheritance. Here the Spirit is the down payment for our inheritance, who is both the fulfillment of the promise, but as fulfilled promise is the guarantee of our future inheritance.[45] (Note the connection to Luke's account of the promise of and giving of the Spirit at Pentecost, but also the eschatological expectation of the final fulfillment in the future.) Down payment is a business term in which a first installment secures the purchase of property or service that will be fully paid sometime in the future, a pledge of full payment that will come to complete the transaction. However, the first installment is possible only by the Spirit. In fact 2 Cor. 1.22 implies more than that it is a down payment *of* the Spirit, but that the Spirit *is* the down payment. 'It is not an installment of some of the Spirit's gifts to be followed by the future by the full measure of gifts; rather, the installment is the Spirit himself'.[46] There are no further giftings of the Spirit to come because the Spirit has already been given *in toto*, but there are increased measures of the Spirit already having been given. Similar to firstfruits, the metaphor of down payment is connected to our groaning (2 Cor. 5.4), but not in the platonic sense that the soul groans to be freed from bodily existence, but in the Pauline sense that our spirit groans with God's Spirit for new bodily existence freed from corruption.[47]

---

[43] I use individual in the sense of personhood contingent on God and not in the modernist non-contingent, non-communal sense. Although overstated, see David F. Wells, *No Place for Truth: Or Whatever Happened to Evangelical Theology* (Grand Rapids: Eerdmans, 1993), pp. 144-49.

[44] Beck, *Holy Spirit*, pp. 34-38, quotes from p. 38.

[45] Fee, *Empowering Presence*, pp. 806-807.

[46] Beck, *Holy Spirit*, p. 39.

[47] Beck, *Holy Spirit*, pp. 39-40.

The third metaphor is seal (2 Cor. 1.21-22; Eph. 1.13; 4.30), which is a wax stamp that seals a document and signifies the ownership and authority of the one who sets the seal. The metaphor was also used to describe the branding of animals or slaves to identify their ownership, and later to brand soldiers to mark them as the emperor's men. The term has Hebrew relevance in that during the Exodus (and the celebration of Passover) the Israelites marked their doorposts with blood as a sign for the angel of death to pass over their firstborn sons (Exod. 12.15). Often the marking signifies that God's people will be spared judgment but that the unrighteous are marked for wrath (4 Ez. 6.5; Ps. of Sol. 15.6-10).[48] Seal does not imply eschatological significance in itself, but the way Paul uses it does. Normally not understood pneumatologically by scholars, Gordon Fee highlights its pneumatological sense. The seal is the Spirit who marks believers as God's people, both now and in the future. God seals those who are elected and called with the Spirit, sealing them for the day of redemption (Eph. 4.30).[49] 2 Corinthians 1.21-22 ties down payment and seal together through the giving of the Spirit: Christ 'has anointed us, by putting his seal on us and giving us his Spirit in our hearts as a first installment'. 'Therefore, both Paul and the author of Ephesians appear to understand the Holy Spirit to be a seal that marks us for redemption and the down payment toward that redemption—two closely related eschatological notions'.[50]

The point is that for Paul these three metaphors and the ascension language of being 'at the right hand of God' have obvious eschatological overtones, as long as the eschatological is understood in a proleptic sense, but also meshes with the ascension—Pentecost—Eschaton vector, which, I shall now attempt to argue, situates the Church as the people of God and body of Christ under its ascended Lord as an anticipatory community of peoples on an eschatological journey to their heavenly home—the New Heaven and the New Earth.

---

[48] Beck, *Holy Spirit*, pp. 41-42.

[49] Fee, *Empowering Presence*, pp. 807-808.

[50] Beck, *Holy Spirit*, p. 43.

Ecclesial Implications of the Ascension—Pentecost—Eschaton Vector

A growing consensus has started to emerge in theology that biblical eschatology is proleptic in that what God has begun in Christ through the cross and resurrection will find its completion in the eschatological future. Defined in terms of the already-not yet (proleptic), promise-fulfillment (covenantal) or inauguration-completion (inaugural), the tension between the now and the not yet cannot be resolved in favor of the now as with realized, existential or mystical eschatologies, nor can it be resolved in favor of the future as with through-going, futurist or dispensational fundamentalist eschatologies, but that in the eschatological tension God is drawing the Church, the world and the whole of creation into its eschatological goal: the glorification of God when God will be 'all in all' (1 Cor. 15.28). The Church is not the beneficiary of the kingdom per se, but is the bearer of the kingdom in that the people of God are shaped into a fellowship of believers under the headship of Jesus Christ, and by the power of the Holy Spirit carry the good news into the world in both proclamation and action.[51] Indeed this binary tension can be seen in Jürgen Moltmann's theology of hope in that the eschatological *novum* of the coming of God has transformative and therefore revolutionary power in the present world, calling the Church to liberative acts in overcoming oppression.[52] In *The Church and the Power of the Spirit*, Moltmann writes, 'As the eschatological future the kingdom has become the power that determines the present. The future has already begun'.[53] Likewise N.T. Wright argues: 'You should press for some form of inaugural eschatology. You should insist that the new life of the Spirit, in obedience to the lordship of Jesus Christ, should produce radical transformation of behavior in the present life, *anticipating* the life to come even though we know we shall never be complete and whole until then'.[54]

---

[51] George R. Hunsberger, *Bearing the Witness of the Spirit: Lesslie Newbigin's Theology of Cultural Plurality* (Grand Rapids: Eerdmans, 1998), pp. 96-104.

[52] Jürgen Moltmann, *Theology of Hope: On the Ground and the Implications of a Christian Eschatology* (tran. James W. Leitch; London: SCM Press, 1967), p. 16.

[53] Jürgen Moltmann, *Church in the Power of the Spirit: A Contribution to Messianic Ecclesiology* (London: SCM Press, 1977), p. 192.

[54] Wright, *Surprised*, p. 221.

The Church then is situated within this inaugural tension in that it is called and put into service by and for Christ Jesus and his reign, but the Church cannot see itself as the realization of the totality of the eschatological future in the present except as partial. The Church is not equated with kingdom reign, but 'as a messianic community is both spawned by the reign of God and directed toward it.... The Church always stands in a position of dependence on and humble service to the divine reign.... But at the same time we must say with equal force that the reign of God must not be divorced from the Church. The Church is constituted by those who are eating and receiving the reign of God'.[55] Or as Donald Bloesch argues, 'The church is an anticipatory sign of the kingdom that is coming, but it is something more—the springboard and vanguard of this kingdom.... The kingdom creates the church just as the church prepares the way for the kingdom'.[56]

As good as these descriptions are, and I have no problem with an inaugural approach that holds the tension between the now and not yet, the Spirit who in the event of Pentecost mediates the absence of the risen Christ and his future reign in the present through anticipatory hope, comes across as an afterthought. Kärkkäinen suggests that the pneumatological field is expanded when the Spirit's relation to eschatology is strengthened because through the Spirit, creation finds its consummation in the new creation. Jesus Christ as the Word is the content the kingdom expressed through mediation of the Spirit. Kärkkäinen insists that 'Pneumatology and eschatology belong together because the eschatological consummation itself is ascribed to the Spirit, who as the end-time gift already given governs the historical present of believers. Consequently then, eschatology does not merely have to do with the future consummation; it is also at work in the present by the Spirit'.[57]

Karl Barth's modified version of inaugural eschatology attempts to integrate the pneumatological implications of Pentecost in his doctrine of the Church. His sustained focus on the revelation of Jesus Christ as the Word made flesh weaves through his entire theo-

---

[55] Darrell L. Guder, *Missional Church: A Vision for the Sending of the Church in North America* (Grand Rapids: Eerdmans, 1998), pp. 98-99.

[56] Donald G. Bloesch, *The Church: Sacraments, Worship, Ministry, Mission* (Christian Foundations; Downers Grove, IL: InterVarsity Press, 2002), p. 76.

[57] Kärkkäinen, *Toward a Pneumatological Theology*, pp. 223.

logical project. However, toward the end of *Church Dogmatics* Barth starts to think about the Spirit and wonders if the Spirit can be integrated into all of theology in a way similar to the revelation of the Word made flesh.[58] In volume IV Barth includes the event of Pentecost in the eschatological landscape to argue that Christ's parousia follows a threefold pattern of Easter—Pentecost—Future Parousia. Indeed, all three events are defined by Barth as the simultaneous inbreaking parousia of Christ, even though in time they appear chronological. The death and resurrection at Easter and Christ's giving of the Spirit at Pentecost provides the hope for future fulfillment. The outpouring of the Spirit of Pentecost creates hopeful expectation in God's people, which according to Barth 'still takes place in Christians up to our own day, in virtue of the gift and in the doing of the work of the Holy Spirit.... Without reference to Easter and Pentecost, it is impossible to give an answer, at least in the New Testament sense, to the question of the possibility of the turning which took place for and in the New Testament community from the past history of Jesus Christ and the coming of God's kingdom to their future'.[59] In *Church Dogmatics* IV/3 Barth writes that 'the return of Jesus Christ in the Easter event is not yet as such His return in the Holy Ghost and certainly not His return at the end of days. Similarly His return in the Easter event and at the end of days cannot be dissolved into His return in the Holy Ghost, not the Easter event and the outpouring of the Holy Spirit into His last coming'.[60] Thus Barth integrates the outpouring of the Spirit at Pentecost into his eschatology, as the means by which the Church now has hope for Christ's final self-revelation at the end of days.

At this point I would like to suggest a modification of Barth's threefold parousia to include the ascension as the promise of Pentecost. At issue is the Spirit's mediation of the absence of Christ's presence in the world. Easter is constituted by the death (absence) and resurrection (presence) of Christ in the world and Pentecost is the fulfillment of the promise of the ascension in which the presence of the absent Christ is mediated by the outpouring of the

---

[58] Philip J. Rosato, *The Spirit as Lord: The Pneumatology of Karth Barth* (Edinburgh: T & T Clark, 1981).

[59] Karl Barth, *The Christian Life: Church Dogmatics IV,4 Lecture Fragments* (trans. Geoffrey W. Bromiley; Grand Rapids: Eerdmans, 1981), p. 256.

[60] Barth, CD IV/3, p. 294.

Spirit. In the eschaton, absence and presence merge so that the Church and all creation are taken up into God while simultaneously God descends to indwell creation, so that 'God will be all and all'. The modified vector is Easter—Ascension/Pentecost—Eschaton. The Church is inaugurated in the event of Pentecost but looks back to the work of Christ in his death and resurrection which makes new life possible, in hopeful anticipation of the eschatological coming partially breaking into the present. The eschatological inbreaking creates signs and foretastes of the kingdom calling the Church to participate in God's reign, not to establish the divine reign by human effort but in humble and joyful service in gratitude for the good things of God.

The Sacrament of the Eucharist as Eschatological Sign
Before concluding, let me comment briefly on the role of the sacraments in mediating the presence of God and the kingdom reign to the Church for the world. I am deliberate in my use of the word sacrament rather than ordinance, because the Eucharistic celebration and rite of water baptism are more than just remembrance of what Christ has done (though the sacraments include remembrance), or a rite that Christ has ordained (though they are divinely ordained): Sacraments are anticipatory signs of the eschatological presence of Christ coming into the world.

Acts 2.41-42 clearly indicates that those who received the word (KJV)[61] were baptized after which they continued in the 'apostles' teaching and fellowshipped', and by 'breaking bread and prayer'. The immediate result of the event of Pentecost was Eucharistic celebration. Jesus Christ is representative of the Father and the sacrament of God in the world, but Kärkkäinen is right to insist that the Eucharist is also a sacrament of the Spirit. After the 'outpouring of the Spirit' and 'a mighty manifestation of the Spirit's power with accompanying signs and wonders, following the scriptural exposition of Peter, the new converts with the apostles celebrated the meal. Rather than limiting themselves to an occasional sharing of the meal, they started church life with the daily breaking of bread.'[62]

---

[61] Theologically, 'word' (KJV, ASV) rather than 'message' (NIV) is a better rendering in that it connects to the Word preached, the Spirit's enlivening of the Word in the hearts of the hearers of the Word.

[62] Kärkkäinen, *Toward a Pneumatological Theology*, p. 141.

The breaking of bread formed the unity by which the Church lived, despite the real problems of disunity both in the apostolic church and today, though full unity will come only in the eschatological dawn. Yet the Eucharist is eschatological not only because it is the eschatological Spirit who establishes Christian fellowship in the present as a sign and promise of divine fellowship in the eschaton, but because it represents the kingdom in the present, '"Come Lord Jesus" (*maranatha*, 1 Cor. 16:22) not only requests the eschatological coming of the Lord, but also calls for his coming for table fellowship in anticipation of the coming Kingdom.'[63]

Therefore the Eucharistic sacrament (as with all sacraments) has both a backward-looking remembrance (*anamnesis*) for what Christ has done through the cross, resurrection, and giving of the Spirit who is poured out at Pentecost, but also a forward-looking anticipation of the eschatological banquet when God's people will share in full unity and God's full eschatological reign when Christ by the Spirit will hand over the keys of the kingdom to the Father and God will be 'all in all'. The shared meal is not merely like-minded individuals coming together as an association of believers, but a corporate act of 'God's eschatological kingdom community—when faithful to God's calling—seeks to break down divisions between rival groups, including Jews and Greeks, males and females, slaves and free, through reenactment of the scriptures through such practices as table fellowship. The Lord's Supper summons people from various demographics [to which I would add cultures, ethnicities and languages] to sit down together, calling for the eradication of barriers of hostility between various groups within the Church.'[64] Through the unity of the Eucharist, the Church thereby models the kingdom to the world as a sign of the unity that is to come in all creation. However, this is no mere human effort of remembering and anticipating, but Jesus Christ through the outpouring of the Spirit enables remembering and anticipation, mediating God's presence through the Eucharistic meal. In other words, the unity that comes through the sacrament of the fellowship meal is an act of divine grace, God's activity and presence that comes to the people

---

[63] Kärkkäinen, *Toward a Pneumatological Theology*, pp. 139-40.

[64] Brad Harper and Paul Louis Metzger, *Exploring Ecclesiology: An Evangelical and Ecumenical Introduction* (Grand Rapids: Brazos Press, 2009), p. 132.

of God gathered together around the Eucharist, and through the Church is witnessed by and in the world, as God seeks to establish the eschatological kingdom.

Conclusion

I have attempted to outline a framework upon which a Pentecostal ecclesiology can be constituted, one that takes seriously the Spirit's mediation of Christ and his eschatological reign. Important is the Lucan account of the promise of the ascension and its fulfillment in the descent of the Spirit at Pentecost, through which the firstfruits of Christ's resurrection and the giving of the Spirit is the pledge that will find its fulfillment in the eschatological transformation of the new creation as the kingdom of God. The Church then is made the sign, foretaste, and instrument of Christ's eschatological reign by the mediation of the Spirit, but an instrument not of our own doing but of God's gracious activity through us. The sacraments (re)present God's presence in commemoration of Christ's paschal work and resurrection, but also as signs of the eschatological kingdom mediated to the present. We work for the kingdom, not as God's instrument (though God will make use of us), but as God's vessel in which all human activity is our humble service and gracious response to God's calling and God's work in and through the Church. To construct a Pentecostal ecclesiology that is Pentecostal in identity one must take account of Pentecost as the juncture through which the Spirit begins to mediate Christ to and through his Church into the world.

11

THE CHURCH OF THE LATTER RAIN:
THE CHURCH AND ESCHATOLOGY IN
PENTECOSTAL PERSPECTIVE

FRANK D. MACCHIA[*]

The relationship between the Church and eschatology seems obvious to us now. In fact, the corresponding coupling of the Church and the Kingdom of God is so common today that the mere mention of it seems almost cliché. This state of affairs is due to the fact that there has been a revival of interest in eschatology in the modern era, first in terms of its centrality to the message of the New Testament, but also in terms of its essential role in the life of faith. As Jürgen Moltmann has shown, eschatology can no longer be confined to the end of a doctrinal treatise, functioning merely to conclude a dogmatic system under the title of 'end times'. As a living hope for the coming Kingdom of God, eschatology pervades all aspects of Christian life and thought. It provides all other doctrinal discussions with their dynamism, hope, and critical realism. It is now nearly impossible to discuss the Church without framing that discussion within the Kingdom of God and the hope that leads us to yearn for its victory in the world.

Pentecostals have always felt very much at home in this discussion. Their hope for Christ's coming was nourished by the former and latter rains of the Holy Spirit. One Pentecostal pioneer wrote, '[Christ] gave the former rain moderately at Pentecost and he is go-

---
[*] Frank D. Macchia (DTheol, University of Basel) is Professor of Theology at Vanguard University, Costa Mesa, CA, USA.

ing to send upon us in these last days ... the latter rain.'[1] This statement concerning the former and latter rain of the Spirit indicates that the Church in Pentecostal preaching is the Church of the Spirit's outpouring on all flesh, which means that it is the Church dedicated to the eschatological fulfillment of God's Kingdom or reign on earth. There has thus always existed in Pentecostal thought a close relationship between the Church and eschatology or the reality of the Kingdom of God. This relationship between the Church and eschatology is also suggested by the final element of the distinctively Pentecostal fivefold Gospel of Jesus as Savior, Spirit Baptizer, Sanctifier, Healer, and Coming King. I think the fivefold gospel has by now become fairly well established within the scholarship (ever since the publication of Donald W. Dayton's *Theological Roots of Pentecostalism*)[2] as a helpful structure for characterizing the major points of Pentecostal theology globally. Jesus as the coming King is, of course, the final element of that structure, a point highlighted by David William Faupel and Steven J. Land.[3] Though in my book, *Baptized in the Spirit*,[4] I qualified the place given to eschatology in Pentecostal scholarship, I also noted that the attention given to it has been illuminating. It becomes clear in relation to the Church, for example, that Pentecostals typically viewed themselves as a missionary fellowship living from the outpouring of the Holy Spirit and anticipating the ultimate fulfillment of the divine goals for history.

More particularly for this study, I want to discuss three major points of emphasis concerning the relationship of the Church to the Kingdom of God that I have gained from the Pentecostal Movement. The first is the attention paid to Pentecost. Specifically, I refer here to the reality of Christ's act of bestowing the Holy Spirit on behalf of the heavenly Father (Acts 2.33). This point of

---

[1] Author unknown, No title, *Apostolic Faith* (Los Angeles) 1.1 (September 1906), p. 2.

[2] Donald W. Dayton, *Theological Roots of Pentecostalism* (Grand Rapids: Zondervan, 1988).

[3] See David William Faupel, *The Everlasting Gospel: The Significance of Eschatology in the Development of Pentecostal Thought* (JPTSup 10; Sheffield: Sheffield Academic Press, 1996), and Steven J. Land, *Pentecostal Spirituality: A Passion for the Kingdom* (JPTSup 1; Sheffield: Sheffield Academic Press, 1993).

[4] Frank D. Macchia, *Baptized in the Spirit: A Global Pentecostal Theology* (Grand Rapids: Zondervan, 2006).

emphasis represents for me the *dogmatic foundations* of the relationship between the Church and the Kingdom of God. The second is
the *critical relationship* between the Church and the Kingdom, a relationship that creates the condition for revival, or for repentance and
renewal. The third is the *positive correlation* between the Church and
the Kingdom of God in the powerful witness of the Church to the
reign of God among us and before us. Both the critical and positive
aspects of the relationship between the Church and the Kingdom
represent two sides of a dynamic *dialectic* between the Church and
the Kingdom. We will begin with dogmatic foundations and then
explore the two sides of the dynamic dialectic between the Church
and the Kingdom (critical and positive). My goal is to bring to the
surface issues that relate to the nature and purpose of the Church
in the light of our eschatological hope.

Dogmatic Foundations

The relationship of the Church to the Kingdom has dogmatic
foundations in the impartation of the Spirit, or in Christ as the one
who bestows the Spirit on all flesh in fulfillment of the will of the
heavenly Father for creation. The Church finds its eschatological
direction and fulfillment in this dogmatic framework of God's self-
impartation through the bestowal of the Spirit. As Ralph Del Colle
wrote, 'The church exists in the outpouring of the Holy Spirit.'[5]
The church is thus constituted by the baptism in the Holy Spirit,
which grants the church the down payment of the future inheritance of redemption (Eph. 1.13-14). I understand Spirit baptism
here as an eschatological reality and, therefore, as complex, illuminating in some sense all aspects of the Spirit's work in establishing
God's reign or Kingdom in the world. Not coincidentally, both
John the Baptist's and Jesus' teachings on Spirit baptism has the
Kingdom of God as its theological context (Mt. 3.1-2, 13-16; Acts
1.3-8). Paul as well defines the Kingdom of God as righteousness,
peace, and joy in the Holy Spirit (Rom. 14.17). Indeed, all four
Gospels and Acts, the narrative foundation of the New Testament

---

[5] Ralph Del Colle, 'The Outpouring of the Holy Spirit: Implications for the
Church and Ecumenism', in D. Donnelly, A. Denaux, J. Farnerée (eds.), *The Holy
Spirit, the Church, and Christian Unity. Proceedings of the Consultation held at Monastery of
Bose, Italy, 14-20, October, 2002* (Leuven: Leuven U. Press, 2005), p. 249.

canon, introduce Jesus as the Spirit Baptizer in the context of the coming reign of God. Oscar Cullmann argued that John baptized by having candidates enter the water and kneel before him to have water poured over them. [6] John and Jesus then used this baptism as a root metaphor for describing God's eschatological goals for creation within the outpouring of the Spirit. As a pneumatological reality, this Kingdom is not a place or the sum total of human moral strivings but is rather the dynamic presence of the Spirit through Christ to set the captives free and to involve them in God's liberating reign in the world: 'If I drive out demons by the Spirit of God, then the Kingdom of God has come upon you' (Mt. 12.28).

The implication is that Spirit baptism is a root metaphor of the eschatological outpouring of the Spirit on all flesh (and the fulfillment of all things in realizing their God-given *telos* of becoming God's dwelling place; see Gen. 2.7). The life and mission of the Church is constituted by this divine outpouring of the Spirit. Insightful here is Robert Jenson's remark that the Spirit's work in raising the crucified Christ could have ended the age and fully established God's reign in the creation, but then the eschatological call of Israel to be a light and a blessing to the nations would have gone unfulfilled. The eschatological outpouring of the Spirit creates space for the fulfillment of this eschatological calling which in turn determines the essence and goal of the Church. The Church is created by the Spirit (and founded by Christ) to fulfill this eschatological calling.[7] The creation of the Church, the eschatological outpouring of the Spirit on all flesh, and the delay of the *Parousia* in the patience of God become in my view integral components of the eschatological baptism of all flesh in the Spirit.

Eschatology thus qualifies the life and ministry of the Church precisely because the Church is constituted by the Spirit and directed by the eschatological calling of Israel to bless the nations. The Church does not administer Spirit baptism, Spirit baptism administers the Church. Moreover, the Church is not founded by Christ and the apostles and then granted the Holy Spirit as an added bonus or supplemental gift. The Church is rather constituted by the

---

[6] Oscar Cullmann, *Baptism in the New Testament* (London: SCM, 1950), p. 62.

[7] Robert Jenson, *Systematic Theology, Vol. 2: The Works of God* (NY: Oxford University Press, 1999), pp. 171-72.

outpouring and presence of the Spirit. As the dwelling place of the Spirit, the Church is eschatological through and through. The Church is humbled in service to the Spirit's realization of Kingdom goals for creation. There is in the light of Spirit baptism a necessarily intimate relationship between the Church and the Kingdom of God.

When I speak of Spirit baptism, I am not limiting myself to a post-conversion experience of Spirit filling. Most Pentecostals have indeed focused their understanding of Spirit baptism in this experience of filling. But one thing the recent attention paid to eschatology among Pentecostal scholars did was to show that Spirit baptism has eschatological breadth. The experience of Spirit filling is rooted in God's self-impartation through the Spirit to the Church and has its ultimate horizon in the resurrection of the dead and the new creation. Spirit filling here and now 'releases' the Spirit in life with fresh power, the power of divine love. For the one who believes in Jesus, 'streams of living water will flow from within him' (Jn 7.38). This eschatological breadth to the impartation of the Spirit is not meant to eclipse our focus on the experience here-and-now of Spirit filling, but it does help us to see that Spirit baptism in the New Testament is a broadly eschatological reality.

The dogmatic foundations of the relation between the Church and eschatology are not limited to pneumatology. In speaking of the Church and the Kingdom we cannot neglect Christ as the coming King of the Kingdom. As Gregory of Nyssa noted, Christ is the King and the Spirit is the Kingdom. After all, the fivefold Gospel has Christ as its focal point and the Spirit as its substance. Christ as the Son of the heavenly Father was the unique *bearer* of the Spirit. Unique to the message of the New Testament, however, is the insight that Christ would also *impart* the Spirit (e.g. Acts 2.33) in order to inaugurate the Kingdom of God. Christ did this not only at Pentecost as an isolated event but also through his life, death, and resurrection. As the man of the Spirit, Christ descended on the cross into the abyss of godless flesh in order that through his resurrection all flesh might be taken up into the realm of the Spirit.[8] Pentecost thus flows out from Jesus' life, death, and resurrection as the

---

[8] I develop this in my recent, *Justified in the Spirit: Creation, Redemption, and the Triune God* (Grand Rapids: Eerdmans, 2010).

man of the Spirit. In imparting the Spirit to constitute the Church, Jesus was also imparting his crucified and risen life and all that this implies for the Church's character, life, and mission. The Church's charismatic structure and core practices involving sacraments, proclamation, and discipleship were also bequeathed to the Church. By imparting the Spirit from his crucified and risen life, Christ was leading the Church towards eschatological fulfillment in him.

Ultimately, however, we cannot forget the role of the heavenly Father in establishing the Church as an eschatological fellowship. Paul prayed 'before the Father, from whom his whole family in heaven and on earth derives its name' (Eph. 3.15-16). Being named by the heavenly Father, the Church has its eschatological purpose in the fulfillment of the Father's will for the earth. In imparting the eschatological Spirit through the Son, the Father opened the love that he shared with the Son to a much larger circle. The Spirit as the bond of love between the Father and the Son opens this communion to the Church and, through the Church, to the world. The Church is on a missionary journey towards an ever-more powerful expression of the Father's love for the world.

Let us explore in the light of these dogmatic foundations the relationship of Church and eschatology more precisely in the light of the dynamic dialectic in both its critical and positive dimensions.

The Critical Relationship of Church and Kingdom

The Church in the light of eschatology implies a critical dialectic between the Church and the Kingdom of God. To understand this dialectic, I will begin with Alfred Loisy's well-known statement that Jesus proclaimed the Kingdom of God but what we got was the Church.[9] There is truth to this statement. Jesus' proclamation (as John the Baptist's before him) announced the coming reign or Kingdom of God in the world (Lk. 16.16). There was a fervent hope for a mighty outpouring of the Holy Spirit that will bring the reign of God to the earth and with it both cleansing and the liberty of life lived under the peace and justice of God's holy law. Why was the fulfillment of the Kingdom delayed and the reality of the

---

[9] A. Loisy, *L'evangile et l'église* (Paris: A. Picard, 1902), p. 111; quoted in Hans Küng, *The Church* (New York: Sheed and Ward, 1967), p. 43.

Church created in its place? Does the Church represent a weak and inadequate substitute for what the prophets and Christ yearned for prior to the resurrection and ascension of Christ? Is Loisy right? Did we end up with something far less than what we had hoped for?[10]

As we noted, the Church was founded as the agent of the Spirit to witness to and bless the nations. Yet, there is no question but that the Church presently and on the way towards this goal falls short of the reality for which prophets and sages had yearned. The relationship between the Church and eschatology implies recognition of the weakness or fallen-ness of the Church. Kingdom theology has thus justifiably been used throughout the history of the Church as a source of criticism of the Church, and the Church must be humble enough to receive it. True revival depends on this humility and the repentance that it occasions. St. Augustine's near identification of the Kingdom of God with the Church led to numerous abuses throughout the middle ages, especially in the context of the Constantinian wedding of church and state. An imperial church cannot serve as an effective witness to the liberating reign of God in the world! There can be no identification of the Church with the Kingdom of God, no simple identification of the Church with either Christ (as the King of the Kingdom) or the Spirit (as the substance of the Kingdom). The Spirit constitutes the Church but the Church is also a historical reality deeply rooted in the fallenness of the human condition. The Church is not the *Christus prolongatus* (prolongation of Christ) in the world, at least not without serious qualification. And, as Hans Küng wrote, 'a church that identifies itself with the Spirit has no need to listen, to believe, to obey.'[11]

The Kingdom of God thus transcends the Church and constantly calls it to repentance and renewal. There is a critical dialectic between the Kingdom and the Church that cannot be resolved this side of eternity and by any other power than the power of the Kingdom itself. In the words of Jan Milić Lochman, the Spirit is **the great** *dialectician* in the area of ecclesiology, showing the Church where it falls short of the Kingdom of God and calling the Church

---

[10] I do not want to say that Loisy meant his statement to be taken in such a negative light, though it has been quoted in this way by everyone since the time that he first wrote it.

[11] Küng, *The Church*, p. 175.

to greater identification with Christ and his Kingdom in the world.[12] In the context of eschatology, this dialectic is dynamic and changing, moving the Church through ever-more-meaningful realizations of God's reign in its life and mission. As Wolfhart Pannenberg has noted, the apocalyptic nature of the eschatology of the Scriptures helps to preserve the critical function of eschatology in relation to the Church.[13] Though the eschatology of the Scriptures also has a prophetic dimension that involves signs of the justice and mercy of the Kingdom in the world, the apocalyptic nature of biblical eschatology prevents us from merely identifying such signs with the reality of the Kingdom itself.

Yet, the dialectic in the light of such signs of the Kingdom not only implies a critical distance between the Kingdom and the Church but also a positive correlation (a 'yes' as well as a 'no'). Pentecostals not only seek revival as occasions of repentance and renewal, they also seek greater empowerment by which they can represent a valuable sign and instrument of God's coming reign. The positive correlation between the Church and the Kingdom will be discussed next.

The Positive Correlation of Church and Kingdom

The challenge of the Kingdom in relation to the Church also implies a blessing. The Church is indwelt, sanctified, and empowered by the Spirit in order to function as a sign and instrument of the Kingdom of God in the world. The Church is the field of God (1 Cor. 3.9), the body of Christ (1 Cor. 12.27), and the temple of the Spirit (1 Cor. 3.16). Each of these metaphors implies an eschatological dimension. The Church is meant to be the first fruits of a greater harvest, the body that will one day be conformed perfectly to the risen body of Jesus, and the temple that will one day represent the perfectly sanctified dwelling place of God's holy presence. We are a people who are meant to signify in our common life an array of eschatological gifts revolving around God's self-

---

[12] Jan Milič Lochman, 'Kirche', in Fritz Büri, Heinrich Ott, and Jan Milič Lochman (eds.), *Dogmatik im Dialogue* (Gütersloh: Gütersloher Verlagshaus Gerd Mohn, 1973), I, p. 135.

[13] W. Pannenberg, 'Constructive and Critical Functions of Christian Eschatology', *Harvard Theological Review* 77 (1984), pp. 119-39.

impartation as Father, Son, and Holy Spirit. The Church gives forth this witness by what it does in service to Christ in the world but also by what it is in the richness of its life or *koinonia* in the Spirit. Jesus prayed that the Church be one in its devotion to God, to one another, and to the world that God loves 'so that the world may believe that you have sent me' (Jn 17.21). This unity will only be realized at the end before the throne of grace, after the Spirit has been poured out on all flesh. Repenting of the scandal of our divisions, we make every effort to realize as much of this now as we can.

The Church of the outpoured Spirit is the Church that gives forth signs of the coming Kingdom. More specifically, the outpoured Spirit incorporates the Church into Christ, launches the Church into God's mission for the world, and opens the Church to the ultimate horizon of new creation. Even the structures and ministries that characterize the Church are creations of the Holy Spirit and thus serve the *koinonia* and mission of the Spirit. Hans Küng was right: the offices of the Church are to be understood as specific components of the Church's *charismatic structure*. Küng notes that fear of spiritual enthusiasm caused the Church to begin with the ordained office when defining ministry and only then to understand the *charismata* as a separate and subordinate category. Küng wishes to start instead with the *charismata* of the Spirit and to define the ordained ministry of oversight as a unique expression of the Church's charismatic structure.[14] This move grants the Spirit's universal witness to the Kingdom dawning in our midst priority in our definition of the Church. As a body flourishing with spiritual gifts, the Church's mission in the world is ultimately to take humanity into the divine *koinonia*, thus facilitating the reign of life and its victory over sin and death in creation. These gifts are 'powers of the age to come' (Heb. 6.5) encroaching on present realities and establishing a beach head in this present world for the coming Kingdom.

Of course, the Spirit not only constitutes the Church but the life of the Church grants an ever-more-expansive and diverse shape to the life of the Spirit in the world. As Simon Chan has shown, the

---

[14] Küng, *The Church*, pp. 184-85.

Spirit freely becomes at Pentecost the ecclesial Spirit.[15] The *koinonia* of the Spirit shapes and constitutes the life of the Church and the life of the Church expands and diversifies the eschatological shape of this *koinonia* by incorporating the many (the Church) into the reality of God's presence inaugurated by the one (Christ). As an eschatological reality, Spirit baptism throughout the expanding life of the Church becomes an ever more diverse and interactive dynamic. 'Be filled with the Spirit', Paul wrote, and then added, 'Speak to one another with psalms, hymns and spiritual songs. Sing and make music in your heart to the Lord' (Eph. 5.18-19). Within this increasingly diverse and interactive body, barriers are broken down between people. The Church as an eschatological body becomes a reconciled and reconciling people. Speaking in tongues as an eschatological language signifies this increasingly-expansive reality of the Church under the reign of the Kingdom of God in the world.

At the heart of the Church's many ministries is the preaching of the Word of God. All believers bear the Word of God (Eph. 4.15). Those who exercise the ministry of oversight, however, have the special responsibility of calling the congregation to the unfinished business of their devotion to the Word of God. The Scriptures are not simply a list of infallible propositions but are rather a living witness that calls the Church to the unfinished business of its devotion to the Kingdom of God in the world. Bearing the Word of God is thus a pneumatological and an eschatological act. Indeed, as Jesus said, 'until heaven and earth disappear, not the smallest letter, not the least stroke of a pen, will by any means disappear from the Law until everything is accomplished' (Mt. 5.17). The Scriptures point the Church to God's unfinished business in the world, or to the fulfillment of God's promises in the world and to the Church's role in this unfolding drama. In bearing the Word of God we are carried on the winds of the Spirit towards the fulfillment of the Kingdom of God on earth.

The Church's celebration of the sacraments also signifies the reality of the coming Kingdom. Baptism confirms a dying to the world and a rising to Christ. This rising is a rising to Christ as the Savior, Spirit Baptizer, Sanctifier, Healer, and Coming King. We rise

---

[15] Simon Chan, 'Mother Church: Toward a Pentecostal Ecclesiology', *Pneuma* 22 (Fall, 2000), pp. 177-208.

to the reality of the Kingdom of God dawning in the world and to our lives in service to this reality. The sacred supper in a similar vein anticipates the messianic feast and the renewal of the earth. The communion with Christ that it facilitates is a communion in the love of God for the world. We accept his forgiveness and offer it to one another. We commune with Christ crucified and risen for the world and renew our dedication to participate in his act of reconciling the world to God.

Postscript:

In God's self-impartation, the Church and the Kingdom of God meet each other and continue to interpenetrate one another until the time when God's dwelling place is with humanity and God is all in all (1 Cor. 15.28; Rev. 21.3). Then the Church and the reign of God will represent two sides of one reality. Until then, we groan in the Spirit for the liberty to come as we show forth signs of that liberty in our life and witness. The rains of the Spirit help to refresh our souls as we groan, work, and pray to grasp that reality that already grasps us more deeply than words can express.

PART SEVEN

REFLECTIONS, ASSESSMENTS, AND RESPONSES

12

'THE LEANING TOWER OF PENTECOSTAL ECCLESIOLOGY': REFLECTIONS ON THE DOCTRINE OF THE CHURCH ON THE WAY

VELI-MATTI KÄRKKÄINEN*

First Words

I have been to too many conferences and symposia in which responses, rather than being responses to other presentations, have been self-contained constructive proposals with little or no relation to the task given originally to the speaker. Hence, as soon as I was invited to serve as one of the respondents to the presentations at this conference, I decided to do just that, namely *to respond*.

I was also helped by the circumstances. For the past six weeks I have been travelling with my wife in various parts of Europe and have received the conference presentations by email sporadically. Literally, I have been reading and reflecting on them on the way. Travelling from one country to another, I have been reminded of the journey-like nature of all theology, including the theology of the Church. As long as theology is *in via*, it has the potential for development, self-correction, and learning.

Moreover, as I visited the Leaning Tower of Pisa in Italy, it appeared to me that that monument may provide me with an appropriate metaphor: similarly to that leaning tower, Pentecostal theology has been leaning in certain directions from the beginning. What

* Veli-Matti Kärkkäinen (Dr Theol, University of Helsinki, Finland) is Professor of Systematic Theology at Fuller Theological Seminary in Pasadena, CA, USA and Docent of Ecumenics at the University of Helsinki in Finland.

makes the tower of Pisa an interesting photography target is that it seems to be leaning no matter from which angle you are looking at it! Now it is time to find out what these directions have been and why it is that a *leaning position*—rather than a fixed one—may be to the advantage of this incipient doctrine of the Church. In other words, in light of the presentations given in this conference, I seek to discern the directions in which Pentecostal ecclesiology has been and is currently leaning.

Peter Althouse succinctly describes the current status of Pentecostal ecclesiology; his evaluation serves as the springboard for further developments as well: 'Although Pentecostalism is now over a century old, its theology of the church is sorely underdeveloped. In practice, Pentecostal churches eclectically borrow from other theological traditions and apply their practices in pragmatic and technical ways, but with little understanding of their philosophical and theological implications' (p. 225). That said, it is also true that tentatively and nonthematically, Pentecostal ecclesiology contains a lot of promise as its core values are being rediscovered, developed, and fine-tuned.

In my response, I will first offer some remarks on directions and developments taken by the conference contributors when it comes to various aspects of the Fivefold-Gospel-driven ecclesiology. In the second part, I will seek to give some advise as to what kinds of tasks lie ahead of us as we continue constructing an authentic ecclesiology, whether based on the Full Gospel scheme or not.

Looking at the Leaning Tower from Five Angles

With Chris Thomas I was at a World Council of Church's consultation on mission in Santiago de Chile in 2003. In one of the many personal conversations, Chris turned to me and said, 'Veli-Matti, we should do something more about constructing a Fivefold-Gospel-based Pentecostal doctrine of the church.' As soon as I heard this, I knew such a task is important and relevant for Pentecostal theologians. I also knew that Chris and others had already labored in that field. Since that conversation, the thought has never left me, and in my teaching of systematic theology at Fuller Theological Seminary, the University of Helsinki, and elsewhere, I have routinely mentioned that Pentecostal ecclesiology could be developed along these lines—but that that work has only been initiated and that I do not know what its results will be!

However, against my initial high hopes concerning the potential of the Fivefold Gospel as the basis for an ecclesiology, a number of doubts and questions have arisen in my mind. Ken Archer helpfully lists the typical challenges faced by any effort to build ecclesiology on the foundations of the Full Gospel scheme: '[I]t does not address all the theological loci. Or that the Fivefold gospel can no longer function in the same way as it did in the early classical period of Pentecostalism. Furthermore, some argue that we must speak of Pentecostalisms not Pentecostalism and such a work would be too narrow and only be representative of a narrow USA version of Pentecostalism' (p. 32). Furthermore, with reference to my own writings, Archer rightly notes that 'interestingly, even though he affirms the Fivefold gospel as important for informing and shaping ecclesiology, he never explains how it does so' (p. 26). 'Similarly,' Archer writes, 'Frank Macchia never identifies or explains the fivefold marks of the Church beyond reasserting the Fivefold gospel. How does the Fivefold gospel shape ecclesiology beyond offering a Pentecostal commentary upon the marks of the Church mentioned by the Nicene-Constantinopolitan Creed?' (p. 28).

At this point of investigation, I think it is premature to pass a final judgment with regard to whether an effort to build an ecclesiology on the basis of the Fivefold Gospel is feasible or not. That assessment can only be made once we have more materials in place. What helps us in this discerning process is to highlight some of the directions—leanings, if you will—along which Pentecostal theologians in this conference have developed main themes of the Full Gospel. Let me make four brief observations to that effect:

First, I am encouraged by the way Jesus' role as Redeemer and Sanctifier has been developed in these presentations. Rather than delving into the typical debates about justification or sanctification, typical in much of Evangelical and Protestant theologies, these writers aim at an inclusive, holistic, and socially-politically relevant account of salvation. In this regard, I find Archer's preference for 'Pentecostal *Soteriological* Ecclesiology'—instead of the typical *charismatic* ecclesiology—quite intriguing and promising. Those two ecclesiologies are complementary and belong to the texture of Pentecostal spirituality. I look forward to hearing more about that in the future. Matthias Wenk's search for 'a theology of holiness [that] would help either overcome or foster such individualistic inclinations within Pentecostalism' (p. 104) highlights the biblical link between holiness and community, including the principle of inclusiveness, as well as holiness and ethics at the personal and communal levels. According to him, 'From its very beginning Pentecostalism was known for its inclusive power, its potency in overcoming ethnic, gender, and social barriers between people' (p. 105). Darío López's subtitle, 'The God of Life and the Community of Life,' is indicative of the desire of several contributors to expand and make more inclusive Pentecostal pneumatology and ecclesiology, especially the vision for the Pentecostal understanding of the Church as liberationist, in search of justice, equality, and credible public witness. The figure of J. Moltmann looms large behind several presentations—even where his name is not mentioned. These inclusive soteriological visions as the context for ecclesiology offer a shining example of the right direction in which Pentecostal ecclesiology could be leaning—and at times is leaning—as long as it is not taken over by the opposite forces. Wynand de Kock does a valuable service to Pentecostal theology by highlighting the significance of two competing hermeneutics in the Pentecostal understanding of redemption. One is communal, turned towards inclusivity, openness to the world, and life-affirming; the other one is individualistic, exclusivistic, escapist, and blind to social implications such as racism and sexism.

Second, the two essays on Jesus' role as Spirit-Baptizer by Daniela Augustine and Simon Chan were the biggest surprises in terms of what I anticipated. Rather than focusing on typical Pentecostal themes related to Spirit-baptism and the 'initial evidence', these essays focus on constructing a pneumatological ecclesiology in the context of ecumenical discussion, particularly drawing from Orthodox writers. That approach has huge ecumenical implications. Those developments resemble in many ways Macchia's groundbreaking work on expanding and making more comprehensive the notion of Spirit-baptism in his landmark work *Baptized in the Spirit*. In many ways, these two essays could have joined the lead article of Archer in providing a wider perspective and context for reflections on Pentecostal ecclesiology.

Third, Kimberly Alexander's idea of 'The Healing Home Model' reminds me of Luther's idea of the Church as the hospital for the incurably sick. Luther's theology was based on the idea of the Christian as the 'Christ' to the neighbor because of the presence of Christ in the Spirit through faith (*in ipsa fide Christus adest*). This idea has an affinity with the Eastern soteriological concept of participation and union, a theme mentioned by Archer (p. 16), among others. Furthermore, Alexander's linking of healing to the Eucharist (pp. 198-99) is a theme well worth further exploration; it is an ancient belief of Christians that whatever other forms of healing there might be, the Table of the Lord is healing medicine not only to the 'soul' but also to the body. Importantly also, both Alexander and Opoku Onyinah question the ruling modernist epistemological model, which has helped much of mainline Christian spirituality miss the notion of healing, exorcism, and other miraculous works of salvation. For Onyinah the African cultures' openness to healing and 'spiritual dimensions' serves as a critique of Western reductionism, whereas for Alexander's American context, postmodernity is the reminder of the limits of the Enlightenment-based ideology. A proper theology of healing also calls for a robust theological anthropology, a theme yet to be developed by Pentecostals. Listening to the voices from the Global South helps Western Pentecostals seek a theological account of the human being and God's salvific vision, which in a nonthematic way was present in early Pentecostalism but which has subsequently been in danger of being forgotten.

Fourth, new directions are also being sought in the two essays focused on Jesus' role as the Soon-coming King. In what I find probably theologically the most pregnant statement of the relationship between the Triune God, eschatology, and the Church, Macchia writes (p. 249):

Eschatology thus qualifies the life and ministry of the Church precisely because the Church is constituted by the Spirit. The Church does not administer Spirit baptism, Spirit baptism administers the Church. Moreover, the Church is not founded by Christ and the apostles and then granted the Holy Spirit as an added bonus or supplemental gift. The Church is rather constituted by the outpouring and presence of the Spirit.

In other words, the Church is not first established by Christ and then—in an analogy of the Christmas Tree—decorated by the tinsel of the Spirit to make it more appealing. Rather, the pneumatological moment is as important as the Christological one. The Father uses the two hands—Christ and the Spirit—in all aspects of his work in the world, including the Church. This triune movement into which the Church is graciously called and included is eschatological: the Father is showing himself to be faithful to his creation as he redeems eternal promises made in Christ in the power of the Spirit. Hence, eschatology is about the kingdom of God, the righteous rule of the Triune God. Pentecostal theology has been leaning towards this orientation since its inception as it envisioned salvation in terms of the Full Gospel. However, it lost this inclusive and comprehensive vision as it aligned itself with conservative Protestantism.

Materially, the same trinitarian eschatological approach is present in the opening sentence of Althouse's essay. He incorporates into his reflections the important role of *ascension* of Christ, a theme too often missed by Pentecostals (p. 224): 'The gift of the Spirit promised in the ascension of Christ and fulfilled in the Spirit's descent, inaugurated the Church as the people of God under the eschatological reign of the Lord Jesus Christ (Acts 2.2-4).' Indeed, ascension rather than resurrection is the 'climax of the history of Jesus' (Althouse, p. 229). It is the ascended Christ who is the agent of the Pentecostal pouring out of the Spirit as the harbinger of the end times. No other contemporary theologian has developed the theme of ascension as powerfully as Karl Barth, whose insights are offered in the last part of his *Church Dogmatics* (IV/1). Macchia, Althouse, and other Pentecostal theologians who are familiar with Barth could draw valuable lessons from his masterful exposition.

Having looked briefly at the ways conference presentations are developing key themes of the Fivefold Gospel ecclesiology, let me acknowledge and challenge Archer's proposal, based on the earlier work of Thomas that seeks to integrate the fivefold ministry gifts of Christ (Eph. 4.11-13) and sacraments:

> Jesus is the Savior. The Church as the Redeemed Community and the ecclesiastical sacramental ordinance is Water Baptism. To this I would add apostles and the *apostolic* function of the community.

Jesus is the Sanctifier. The Church as a Holy Community and Footwashing is the ecclesiastical sign. To this I would add teachers and the *teaching* function of the community.

Jesus is Spirit Baptizer. The Church as a Charismatic Community and the ecclesiastical sign is Glossolalia. To this I would add the prophets and the *charismatic* function of the community.

Jesus is the Healer. The Church as a Healing Community with the ecclesiastical sign of praying for the sick with the laying on of hands and anointing with oil. To this I would add pastors and the *pastoral* function.

Jesus is Coming King. The Church as a Missionary Community with the Lord's Supper serving as the ecclesiastical sign. To this I would add the evangelists and the *evangelistic* function of the community.

My question to Thomas includes: (1) I need help in discerning the logic of the linking of Jesus' various roles with specific sacramental signs; or else, this link seems to me somewhat artificial and haphazard. With regard to Archer's expansion of Thomas's scheme, I will add a few more questions: (2) The way sacraments and gifts are mixed in this scheme calls for clarification. For example, what is the basis for linking footwashing with the teaching gift? (3) How is *glossolalia* to be understood as the 'missionary sign'? Aren't all the gifts 'missionary' signs, say, healing and words of wisdom? (4) The list of 'offices' or gifts of ministry listed in Ephesians 4 hardly is a comprehensive list, any more than any of the lists of the gifts. Even if it were, the logic of linking these offices with specific dimensions of ecclesiology calls for more explanation. Just to take one example: Isn't the apostolic task of the Church much more comprehensive than that related to salvation and water baptism?

Tasks for the Development of Pentecostal Ecclesiology

Robust Trinitarian Theology

The first urgent task for Pentecostal ecclesiological work, already started in several essays, is a robust trinitarian vision for the Church. This plea was made passionately by Chan. Similarly, de Kock (p. 52) reminded us of the ancient idea, prevalent especially in Eastern theology, of the Church as the image of the Trinity and the implications of the perichoretic indwelling of persons into an inclusive view of redemption. Above, I mentioned the important contributions to this theme by Macchia and Althouse.

Now, why is a robust trinitarian theology so essential to the task of constructing an ecclesiology? In my understanding, trinitarian theology offers resources for several interrelated tasks. Let me just outline three of those:

1.   The Whole History of Jesus: A Trinitarian Spirit-Christology helps rediscover the whole history of Jesus as the background and power for the coming to being and continued existence of the Church. What ancient creeds miss in their otherwise healthy trinitarian orientation is the lack of focus on the earthly life of Jesus. As Moltmann pointedly remarks, in the creeds, between the clauses 'conceived of the virgin Mary' and 'suffered under Pontius Pilate' there is only a comma! The teachings, healings, exorcisms, invitation to sinners and outcasts, baptism with the Holy Spirit, and inauguration of the kingdom are left out. Pentecostal Spirit-Christology, with its accent on Jesus as Healer and Baptizer with the Spirit, could be a God-sent corrective. The full force of that rediscovery just needs to be added to ecclesiology.

2.   Spirit-Christology: Against misunderstandings prevalent among poorly informed observers of Pentecostalism, the Pentecostal movement does not represent pneumatocentrism. Its distinctive feature is a thoroughgoing Spirit-Christology. I am using the term Spirit-Christology in a nontechnical sense, meaning that I do not mean by it any specific type of Spirit-Christology as those are available in contemporary theology. I simply mean the integral, robust mutual conditioning of the work of the Son and Spirit throughout the Gospels and its development in much of patristic theology, both Eastern and Western. In everything that the Son does, the Spirit is present and an agent and vice versa—and this in a healthy trinitarian context.

3.   The Role of the Father: Trinitarian theology may also help Pentecostal theology and ecclesiology rediscover the importance of the first article of the creed, that on the Father and the Father's work in creation and in the world. There is some truth to

the claim of the Anglican charismatic Tom Smail, noted by Chan, who speaks of *The Forgotten Father* in much of Pentecostal theology. Chan's suggestion of turning to Orthodox trinitarian understanding in which the monarchy of the Father is at the center is worth exploring; most Pentecostals so far have been turned on by social trinitarianism. Be that as it may, trinitarian theology fosters a robust creation theology. Creation theology, in part, strengthens holistic theology and ecclesiology. The following statement by Althouse sounds very promising to me (p. 224): 'Creation itself is the focus of hope for its eschatological renewal in that the Spirit depicted as a "violent wind [that] came from heaven and filled the whole house", alludes to the creation narrative of Genesis when the Spirit of God (wind) broods over the waters (Gen. 1.2).'

Communion Ecclesiology

If there is any theme in contemporary ecumenical ecclesiological discussion about which there is virtual unanimity, it is the importance of *koinonia*, communion. Under the guidance of the Orthodox John Zizioulas, current theology has rediscovered the biblical and patristic notion of the Church as *koinonia*. In Pentecostal parlance, this is called the Church as the *fellowship*. Now, the English term 'fellowship' is of course shallow and almost meaningless. But as a translation from the biblical term *koinonia* it is, as *Lumen Gentium* # 9 says, a powerful claim according to which God did not intend to save persons as individuals but rather as a bonded people. The beginning chapters of the Book of Acts, dear to Pentecostals, provide us with a powerful resource. In the long-standing international dialogue between Roman Catholics and Pentecostals, a landmark document was produced, titled *Perspectives on Communion*. It makes great reading for both Pentecostals and others.

Trinity and communion belong together. The eternal love relationship between Father, Son, and Spirit represents the primary mode of communion. As Zizioulas says, the Christian God does not exist first as 'one' but as three, persons-in-relation. The Church is the image of God. A trinitarian communion theology is the best medicine for the rampant individualism of the cultures of the Global North.

Theology of Charisms and the Charismatic Structure of the Church

In the conference presentations, surprisingly, there is a conspicuous lack of discussion on charisms as an integral part of the life and mission of the Church as well as development of the theme of the charismatic structure of the Church. Macchia begins that discussion with reference to Hans Küng's highly important insights in his landmark work *The Church*. Much more is needed in this area in order for a robust theology of charisms to emerge.

A fruitful way—again in keeping with a trinitarian Spirit-Christology—is the link between not only charisms and Pentecost but also charisms and the *ascension* of Christ, a theme opened up by Althouse. According to Ephesians 4, it is the ascended Christ who gives gifts to the Church, gifts having to do with Church offices. Ernst Käsemann, the former-generation NT scholar, famously claimed that these gifts—call them also charisms—are nothing less than participation in the power and continuing ministry of the ascended Christ in the Church. Hence, the gifts, offices, charisms are both Christological and pneumatic in nature.

Basic Questions of the Ecclesiality of the Church

Behind the question of the ecclesiality of the Church is simply the question of what makes the Church, church, i.e. the conditions of the Church. Free Churches, among which Pentecostalism is usually counted, have a vastly different interpretation from both the Roman Catholic and Orthodox Churches; and there is a different orientation even between Free Churches and Mainline Protestants. The questions of sacraments and episcopacy loom large in those debates.

Part of this discussion is the question of the marks of the Church, a theme mentioned briefly by Daniel Castelo and Augustine. Archer (p. 28) refers to Macchia's idea of the basic features of the Fivefold Gospel as the 'ecclesiological marks'.

A number of potentially fruitful themes emerge out of the investigation into the marks of the Church. Let me just mention two: (1) It could be claimed that apostolicity is a defining feature of Pentecostal spirituality and ecclesiology. It is not for nothing that from the beginning Pentecostals have often identified themselves as *apostolic* churches. Apostolicity for Pentecostals means continuity with the apostolic church of the Book of Acts. (2) It may be the case that what other traditions, particularly Roman Catholics, call 'catholicity,' in Pentecostal parlance is called the Full Gospel, i.e. a Gospel that is 'whole,' not lacking anything, as the Greek term literally says.

I find Castelo's 'turn' to imagination as a way of doing ecclesiology a most intriguing and promising move. What other 'method' would fit in so smoothly with the continuing, Spirit-led reflection on the nature and mission of the Christian community for the movement born of the Spirit!

13

WHY THE CHURCH NEEDS A FULL GOSPEL: A REVIEW AND REACTION TO PENTECOSTAL ECCLESIOLOGY*

ROBERT POPE**

In his erudite and comprehensive account of Pentecostal theology, Keith Warrington warns that 'to understand Pentecostalism, it is a significant advantage to be a Pentecostal'.[1] There is probably more than a modicum of truth in that statement, in much the same way as it could be said, for example, that rocket scientists hold a considerable advantage over the rest of us when it comes to discussing and understanding rocket science. As Dr Warrington points out, Pentecostals might well emphasize a common experience (i.e. Spirit baptism) and the practicalities of a lived faith over and above the details of a theological system, yet most would affirm that they belong squarely within the fold of historical, Trinitarian Christianity securely grounded in the life, death, resurrection (and ascension) of Jesus Christ and the story of the proclamation of the gospel by the

* In writing this 'response', I am aware of Veli-Matti Kärkkäinen's criticism of those commissioned to 'respond' but who instead present 'self-contained constructive proposals'. The reader may judge whether or not what follows is a 'constructive proposal'. It was nevertheless written in *response* to the papers as prepared for and delivered at the Conference on Pentecostal Ecclesiology held at Bangor University, 28-29 July 2010.

** Robert Pope (PhD, University of Wales), formerly Reader in Theology and Head of the School of Theology and Religious Studies at Bangor University, is Reader in Theology at the University of Wales Trinity St David, Lampeter in South Wales, UK.

[1] Keith Warrington, *Pentecostal Theology: A Theology of Encounter* (London: T & T Clark, 2008), p. viii.

disciples and apostles in the ancient world. Furthermore, they would claim this to be public truth with an obvious mission to the world rather than some kind of esoteric mystery which can be revealed only to the initiated. It is not unreasonable to suggest, then, that while engaging in the task of explaining Pentecostal theology might well be evidence of a desire for self-understanding rather than for a Pentecostal apologetic to the wider church (and world), its forms and content should not be totally beyond those who belong to other Christian communities.

Pentecostal theology, while pursued by Pentecostals for Pentecostals, must also be a public theology challenging the world and the rest of the Church with its insight, emphasis, and understanding. It is of course right and proper that Christian communities seek to understand belief and practice and to express that understanding in a coherent if not also systematic manner, but theological construction for consumption by their own constituency, important as such an exercise might be, is only part of the task for Pentecostals. All theology should be ecumenical, not in the sense that the theological enterprise can only be done alongside representatives from all branches of the Christian Church, and where contributions balance each other in order that nothing distinctive is identified and no-one is in any way offended, but in the sense that it offers insights into the meaning and value of the gospel to the whole household of God. It seems, then, that the presence and participation of a non-Pentecostal in a colloquium on Pentecostal ecclesiology can be justified after all! The value of the exercise has as much to do with the disposition and sympathy of the participants as it does with their denominational affiliation or their ecclesiastical or devotional preferences.[2]

Having said that, I must admit that listening to the papers was an experience similar to eavesdropping on someone else's conversation. During the conference, on the whole, Pentecostals were speaking to each other, making claims for what it is that Pentecostals believe and, with perhaps greater alacrity, propounding with confi-

---

[2] At this point it is worth noting my appreciation of the fellowship as well as the intellectual stimulation which I experienced at the Conference. I am aware that I do not refer in this piece to all participants by name, but that in no way should suggest that I do not hold all of the papers to have offered significant contributions to the debate.

dence what Pentecostals do.[3] The fact that this led on occasion to disagreement between the participants is evidence of the diversity that lies at the heart of this global movement. Indeed, the colloquium confirmed, and even affirmed, diversity arising from context—both social and theological. Speakers and participants hailed from North America, Latin America, Africa, Asia, and Europe, and appeal was made to the Eastern Orthodox and Roman Catholic as well as Reformed traditions, not to mention the invocation of what is sometimes the more nebulous concept of 'orthodox Christianity' itself. This has amply demonstrated that while there is much agreement between Pentecostals, the theological understanding and the Christian practice which follows will make for a 'messy' church (or messy churches). This seems to be a principle affirmed in these papers as an inevitable result of the Spirit's guidance, even if the term itself has not been used. Maybe this in itself is a gift that can be offered to ecumenical theology, especially given the prominence of 'messiness' in some forms of emerging church and of 'fresh expressions', and this is so even if a messy ecclesiology in some senses is not an ecclesiology at all, and certainly poses problems when it comes to the discussion of church order, to which ecclesiologies must inevitably lead. Nevertheless, while God is a God of order and not chaos (1 Cor. 14.33), he is not to be domesticated into our own ideas and our own sense of ecclesiastical orderliness. The Spirit blows where he will (Jn 3.8) and cannot be bound by earthly and human structures and forms. So a Pentecostal ecclesiology will affirm that while the Spirit comforts and encourages the Church, he also challenges, stimulates, provokes, and transforms it. Thus while order is of the *esse* of the Church, the shape of that order is a matter of the *bene esse* of the Church; order is a theological datum, but the form it takes is contingent. Ecclesiology emanates from theology (rather than from sociological, empirical or pragmatic considerations). So where should we begin?

---

[3] Take, for example, S.A. Ellington's assertion that 'the essential emphasis of Pentecostalism is not a teaching which must be believed or a proof which can be deduced and defended against all challenges, but a God who must be reckoned with in direct encounter'. S.A. Ellington, 'Pentecostalism and the Authority of Scripture', in *Journal of Pentecostal Theology* 9 (1996), pp. 16-38 [17], quoted in Warrington, *Pentecostal Theology*, p. 20.

The Gospel and the Church

More than anything else, the papers presented at the conference and published here confirm the importance of the 'fivefold', or 'full' gospel. This is as good a starting point as any. In fact, without a *full* gospel, there could not be a church. It is not so much that Jesus as redeemer, sanctifier, Spirit-baptizer, healer, and coming king constituted the framework for the conference's discussion. In as much as this was the designated format of the conference it was inevitable that it would be prominent in what was said. Instead, this format has allowed the affirmation of Christ's salvific work as the very essence of the Christian good news. In this way the essentially transformational power of the gospel becomes the bedrock from which we formulate the understanding of the Church, thus confirming that the several papers which claim ecclesiology to be an outworking of soteriology are making an apposite and important point.

However, the Church is no mere institution, nor is it the natural or even the practical consequence of the existence of individual Christian believers, transformed by Christ through the Spirit. Of course, in Christian experience the Church succeeds other theological considerations; those who experience the reality of Christ's saving work in their lives will, secondarily, become aware of and become members of the Church. Yet it is important also to recognize that the Church also precedes the experience of salvation. Those who become members of the Church in time join something which as both an empirical or temporal institution and as a spiritual reality *precedes* our experience of it. The Church is in this sense not constituted by its members, it is not the sum total of the saints through time and space, but it is in fact the creature of God's holy word (*creatura verbi divini*) constituted by the Spirit. It is as God's gracious utterance towards humankind and through humankind to the created order (as, in the Church, they become the bearers of divine good news) that the Church can be understood as the community of the full gospel of Christ as redeemer, sanctifier, spirit-baptizer, healer, and coming king. And it can be understood as such even when it is not necessarily experienced as such. As Wynand de Kock observes, the Church 'is at once redeemed, un-redeemed, and a redeeming force'—a point to which I will return.

This tension between the theological *reality* which the Church represents and the empirical *actuality* which we experience lies behind the discussion in many of these papers. But it is important to acknowledge that this is a positive rather than a negative and restricted tension. It is not so much that what can be experienced in the present has to be qualified by its limitations, its weaknesses, its failings, its lack of fullness. Instead, the inevitable tension in which the Church exists suggests that the fullness that God intends for his creation, in terms of redemption, healing, sanctification, and empowerment, can be a reality now, in the present, even if only in part and grasped 'as in a mirror dimly' (1 Cor. 13.12). Peter Althouse puts it this way: 'The Church as the body of the crucified and risen Christ is the eschatological community, who by the promise of the Spirit given at Pentecost lives in the tension of the already and the not yet of the eschaton'. The 'not yet' corresponds to the promise that what is known in part shall be known fully ('face to face' to continue with Paul's description to the Corinthians). As such it is part of God's liberating and redeeming action. Even when known partially, its effect is not to restrict human beings but to release and to empower them to lives of worship, witness, and service so that the light of God's Kingdom may break into the world in judgement and transformation of all the life-denying 'powers and principalities' which currently hold sway in personal and social life. That is why the tension of the 'already' and 'not yet' is not a disappointing discovery, but is in fact the essence of *good* news.

Grace, Faith, and the Church

There were many meaningful phrases uttered during the conference and I would like to draw attention to those which both highlight this sense of the Church's prior existence as the product of God's prevenient grace, and those which emphasize that the Church's empirical existence—even when all evidence might suggest the contrary—as the sacramental means of grace to a sinful, powerless, and sick humanity and to a fallen world.

Daniela Augustine's passionate appraisal of the Church as *empowered* community revolves, appropriately enough, around the 'public statement' of God at Pentecost where, by Spirit baptism, the disciples of Jesus are identified as the sons and daughters of God and charged with bringing the good news of justice, healing, reconciliation, and restoration to the world. Her thesis reminds us of three things. First, that the Church is the product of God's action not of ours; second, that this is a *public* action—the Church is not called to hide away in secret but to be in itself the proclamation of God's word to the world; third, that this word is a word of *good* news, which brings reconciliation and restoration and declares the advent of God's kingdom of love. This is not to deny that the Church's witness in the world is dependent on its members or that Christians have lived—and continue to live—in contexts in which, for safety's sake, it is necessary to keep their faith hidden from the prying eyes of neighbours and the officers of the state. Furthermore, it cannot be denied that the Church, and those who belong to it, have on occasion obscured rather than manifested the good news. As Frank Macchia points out: 'There is no question but that the Church falls short of the reality for which prophets and sages had yearned. The relationship between the Church and eschatology implies recognition of the weakness or fallen-ness of the Church'. But none of this changes the starting point for the doctrine of the Church or the theological reality that ecclesiology seeks to uphold. The Church is the Church because of God and not because of human beings.

This leads us to a phrase used by Kenneth Archer, where he referred to the Church as an 'ontological witness in the world'. This statement reminds us that it is not so much that the 'local church is to carry on the mission of Christ' but that, as the body of Christ, it is *de facto* that mission. Only as the embodiment, or even the incarnation, of that mission can it be the community of the redeemed, the sanctified, the empowered, the healers and the healed, and the eschatologically prepared. Without its institution and constitution by God, which is prior to all earthly manifestations and all human ideas about the structural form which it should take, the Church is no more than a gathering of individuals of common mind whose significance is hardly greater than any other human gathering, such as a sporting or cultural event. But because it is instituted and constituted by God, the Church is the redeeming, reconciling, evangelical (in the sense of good news) presence of God. As such the Church is the body of Christ, it is the sacramental presence of God's transformative Word and Spirit in the world, it is characterized by the marks of the fivefold gospel and 'the gates of hell shall not prevail against it' (Mt. 16.18). Human fallibility must be faced and dealt with—as we shall see—but it does not change the essential theological nature and truth about the Church because the theological reality of the Church is grasped by faith and not by sight.

For Jan Milič Lochman (erstwhile Professor of Systematic Theology in the University of Basel), this is expressed in the Apostles' Creed by the absence of a preposition. The Apostles' Creed, he says, does not declare 'I believe *in* the church' as it declares that 'I believe *in*' God, Father, Son and Holy Spirit but instead states 'I believe … the church'. The reason for this, he asserts, is that the Church is the result of belief in the Triune God.[4] Lochman acquired this point from Calvin, though the latter admitted that he did 'not wish to dispute over words', partly because he recognized that other ancient sources—the Nicene Creed included—do not omit the preposition.[5] While this suggests that this particular grammatical argument ought not be overdone, the substantive point remains valid. The Church is not an article of belief for the Christian. Instead, it is a reality made effective by the presence of God in Christ in the power of the Holy Spirit. It exists because of the Triune God, his prevenient grace and his soteriological and sustaining activity in history. And it is grasped, experienced and lived in the world by faith.

In this way, the Church, as the Christocentric ecclesial community, empowered by the Spirit, is a sacramental sign of God's grace. These papers affirm something of the distinctiveness of Pentecostal practice in the way in which laying on of hands and glossolalia (both of which are widely practised by Pentecostals as well as by Christians of other denominations) and foot washing (which is perhaps not quite so widespread) constitute sacramental actions (though I realize that the word 'sacrament' is considered problematic in some quarters). But in some ways these acts possess sacramental significance because they are *ecclesial* acts and as the product of God's creative Word, and thus as the 'ontological witness to the world', the Church is God's means of proclaiming his grace and embodying it in the world. As Wynand de Kock observes: 'the re-

---

[4] Jan Milič Lochman, *The Faith We Confess: An Ecumenical Dogmatics* (trans. David Lewis; Edinburgh: T & T Clark, 1984), pp. 197-98.

[5] John Calvin, *Institutes of the Christian Religion* (trans. F.L. Battles; ed. J.T. McNeill; London: SCM, 1960), II, I.2, p. 1013.

deemed community is also a sacrament, since the Spirit enables the Church to transmit the grace of God, in Christ, through the world. The Church signals to the world that there is life, in and beyond this life and that intimacy with God is possible, in and beyond our broken relationships'. God still makes his grace available through the Church, as the body of Christ, as the gathered community of saints, even though the Church on earth is not perfect, has not been perfected and awaits perfection. God still makes his grace available through the Church, even though the Church on earth is made up of finite, fallible and feeble human beings. If it were not, how could it be a vehicle of *grace*?

Thus the Church is the body of Christ in that it is called, sent, and empowered by Christ through the Spirit to continue his ministry in the world. As a result, it has a paradoxical (or, in Peter Althouse's words, ambiguous) existence. The Church is simultaneously the community which celebrates, witnesses to, and proclaims the mighty acts of God in Christ, achieved, accomplished, and completed in his life, death, resurrection (and ascension), *and* at the same time it is the community which lives in the expectation of fulfilled promise, when God will be 'all in all' (1 Cor. 15.28). As such the Church is an eschatological community where the eschatological realities and truths are vouchsafed by its institution and constitution by God's Holy Spirit. Indeed, it is, historically, the Spirit's outpouring on the day of Pentecost which marks the Church as eschatological community—a fact that resonates deeply with Pentecostals as seen in these papers. In this regard, some assistance can be gained from the American theologian Gabriel Fackre, who has recently suggested that it is the 'signs of the Spirit', as gleaned from the account of Pentecost recorded in Acts 2, which enable the actualization and the manifestation of the Church in history. But while the Church's existence as eschatological community is safeguarded by the Spirit's presence, this is manifest in a number of ways, named in Acts 2. He puts it in this way:

> Not only does the church witness to the world through the signs of the Spirit what will be at the End, but it also *participates* now, albeit brokenly, in the kingdom that is to come. Those who trust the *kerygma* [the proclamation of the gospel] truly celebrate that gospel in the *leitourgia* [the work of the people in worship, prayer and praise], and live out that faith in the love poured forth in *di-*

akonia [the enactment of the gospel through the meeting of need] and *koinonia* [the living out of the gospel by the gathered community], are citizens of the Realm to be.[6]

The Paradox of the Church

From all this, we can draw a number of conclusions about the Church and about the Pentecostal contribution to ecclesiology. First of all, the Church is the salt of the earth (Mt. 5.13), the bride of Christ (Eph. 5.23-32); it is God's own people (1 Pet. 2.9) and it is the body of Christ (1 Cor. 12.27). At the same time, with the rest of creation, it too groans 'in travail' waiting in hope 'that the creation itself will be set free from its bondage to decay and will obtain the freedom of the glory of the children of God' (Rom. 8.21). It is the community where the Kingdom of God is graciously and proleptically present, but which looks to its future consummation when it will be known in its fullness.

This paradox, or ambiguity, was clear in the papers outlining the Church as the redeemed community, the holy community, the empowered community, and the healing community. Wynand de Kock's humbling testimony and insightful paper confirmed to us that the Church is the redeemed community, that needs redemption and yet somehow then remains the redeeming force of God in the world. This could, *mutatis mutandis* be applied to doctrines of sanctification, empowerment, and healing. In all these doctrinal realities we acknowledge that we live in some form of interim where they are powerfully available to God's people, but they are not available in their fullness. This leads me to make two further points.

First of all it seems reasonable to suggest that it is the eschatological lens which enables us to make sense of, and to live out, the other four claims of the fivefold gospel. I take my cue here from Frank Macchia, who wrote: 'As a living hope for the coming Kingdom of God, eschatology pervades all aspects of Christian life and thought. It provides all other doctrinal discussions with their dynamism, hope, and critical realism.'[7] I have no desire to offend any-

---

[6] Gabriel Fackre, *The Church: Signs of the Spirit and Signs of the Times: The Christian Story—A Pastoral Systematics V* (Grand Rapids, MI: Eerdmans, 2007), p. 11.

[7] I am aware that Simon Chan suggested that 'Spirit baptism' was 'the one [element of the fivefold gospel] through which we could make sense of all the

one, but this is where Christians must beware that eschatology is both badly misunderstood and undermined when it is hijacked by dispensational and millennialist debates—or at least when those debates descend into a dry exercise in arithmetic. Those things are at best secondary. Eschatology's primary aspect, and one that offers a liberative and liberated vision for our ecclesiological understanding and practice is that of Christ the King who has already walked on the earth, but who will come again 'to judge the quick and the dead' as the classical ecumenical creeds put it. One of the mysteries revealed by the incarnation is that it is only the supernatural, transcendent and miraculous God who can be of any help at all in the natural, the immanent, and the ordinary. And this means that even when there is no miracle, no holiness, no healing, and no transcendence, then the hope of the gospel for eschatological sanctification, restoration, healing, and wholeness remains because the promises of God transcend our everyday existence with its challenges, its disappointments and its problems. If it did not, then it would have no power whatsoever in the face of sickness, suffering, and injustice which all human beings, in varying degrees, have to face day by day. Only then can the Church, even in its weakness, stand against the powers and principalities of this world and declare the justice and righteousness of God. Darío López Rodríguez humbles us with his account of ecclesiology written from the context of work with the poor. He demonstrates that eschatology motivates and arouses the Church into pronouncing judgement on sin and evil not only in individuals but also—and probably primarily—in social, political, economic structures and institutions. '[T]he affirmation of Christian hope becomes a prophetic critique of the kingdoms of this world and why believers should be warned of their temporal, transitory and finite nature'. As such we can say that: 'The Church does more than merely point to a reality beyond itself. By virtue of its participation in the life of God, it is not only a sign and instrument, but also a genuine foretaste of God's kingdom, called to show forth visibly, in the midst of history, God's final purposes for human-

---

others'. It is true that this might make a clearer, and specifically *Pentecostal* contribution to the debate. But as it is admitted by a number of scholars in this collection that Spirit-baptism is an eschatiological event, there may also be some truth to my claim.

kind.'[8] In this way it challenges the *status quo* while simultaneously suggesting the way to transform it.

We gain little by trying to work out when and how the eschatological consummation of creation will occur (not to mention the 'tribulation' that might precede it). But looking in faith to Christ's coming and all that represents in terms of the completion of God's will for creation, we can live in the present in the living hope that God's will will be fulfilled, the creation will arrive at its consummation and the Kingdom will be established in its fullness. In that day, despite all the words that have been spoken and will be spoken, human mouths will fall silent and God will have the final word.

Second, the hope which the eschatological orientation of the good news offers to Christians, to Christian community, and to the world, is wrapped up in the fact that this final word has already been heard in the Word made flesh. In this way, as Daniela Augustine confirms, we can affirm realized eschatology, or an inaugurated eschatology, and as Peter Althouse argued (during the conference), we are orientated back to the Christ event and to the empowering outpouring of God's Spirit on the day of Pentecost in order to be orientated forward to the final consummation of all things. Of course, there is a danger here. To believe in a 'fully realized eschatology' runs the risk of believing that the present is all that there is, a nightmare scenario effectively outlined by Michael Frost and Alan Hirsch (and quoted by Peter Althouse), and one which is not restricted to North America:

> The nihilistic *eros* of the consumer society, which seems to have drawn much of American Christianity into its wake, creates a desire that can never be satisfied. Ads and shop windows offer us a perpetual stream of icons promising to fulfill our ambitions to have the life that they represent: a fully realized eschatology.[9]

The 'already' demanded by a culture of immediacy must be modified, challenged, even judged, by the 'not yet' of eschatological hope or else it becomes a prison in which human beings are condemned

---

[8] Graham Cray, *et al.*, *Mission-shaped Church: Church Planting and Fresh Expressions of Church in a Changing Context* (London: Church House Publishing, 2004), p. 95.

[9] Michael Frost and Alan Hirsch, *The Shaping of Things to Come: Innovation and Mission for the Twenty-first Century Church* (Peabody MA: Hendrickson, 2003), p.6. Quoted by Peter Althouse.

to a future in which the possibilities and potentialities of change as well as the promise of consummation are all denied, vision is lost, and the people perish (Prov. 29.18).

The Church as Community of the Full Gospel

The insistence that the Church is characterized by the 'already' present power of the consummated creation, when the *oikoumene* is fully redeemed, healed, and empowered, has to remain qualified by the confession that it continues to long for redemption, healing, and empowerment and indeed that it lives often in an unredeemed state, suffering from sickness and lacking in power. Kimberley Alexander helps us to see that this is primarily a positive state of affairs by speaking of 'sacramental signs' in the present and the promise of 'signs following', 'revealing to all the Creator Spirit, already at work in the earth, healing the pains of the past and moving towards the Day when all will be healed.'

The Church is sacramentally the reality of God's gracious *being for* humankind and the world. It is simultaneously the proclamation of the good news and the empowered community in the present and the foretaste of what is to come. And it is all this while also being preoccupied with and populated by human beings who are, as Luther reminded us, *simul Justus et Peccator*. There really is, then, salvation, sanctification, baptismal power, healing in the Body of Christ. And at the same time, there really is not. But because both the manifestation and the apparent withholding of these things are viewed eschatologically they remain real for now and a hope for the future.

Perhaps more than anything else, the pattern of the fivefold gospel as the framework for ecclesiological discussion reminds us that the Church is the *Church* only because Jesus redeems, sanctifies, empowers, heals, and instills in us the hope for his return. This leads to a high view of the Church as the most prominent agent of grace in the divine economy. But the gospel is only *good* news because we know that these things are beyond ourselves and constantly require the transforming power of the Trinitarian God, active in history through what Irenaeus called his 'two hands', the Son and the Spirit. While we might strive to make the high view of the Church visible in the world, we know that when we fall short of the ideal we remain the objects of God's mercy and loving kindness. It is vital that we make this aspect of the Church visible too. For only then will the Church be the testimony and witness to the fullness of the gospel of Jesus Christ.

14

CONCLUDING REFLECTIONS

WILLIAM K. KAY[*]

The chapters in this book were originally delivered at a conference at Bangor University, Wales, in the summer of 2010. Two years beforehand, in response to Chris Thomas' bold vision, he and I began to plan a conference on Pentecostal ecclesiology. From the start it was clear that, if we were to reflect the sheer scale of Pentecostalism, we needed to gather an international band of scholars. We wanted men and women from every part of the world to which the Pentecostal movement had spread during the 20th century. By inviting a balance of speakers, we were able to assemble men and women from the global West and the global East so that Asia (Simon Chan) might dialogue with Latin America (Darío López) or so that the North (Veli-Matti Kärkkäinen) might speak with the global South (Opoku Onyinah). We secured a financial subvention from Bangor University and this enabled our cast to be assembled. In order to ensure high quality contributions, we asked our speakers to submit their texts before we met and then, when we did meet, there was an opportunity for everyone to ask questions or challenge presumptions, a process that continued informally during the meals and which eventually slightly modified some of the contributions.

In the 1900s Pentecostals were derided and even caricatured for their absence of theology and their unthinking embrace of wild spiritual experience. But as the 20th century passed, Pentecostals began to build colleges and universities and their sons and daughters entered higher education and gained the full range of under-

---

[*] William K Kay (DD, University of Nottingham) is Professor of Theology at Glyndŵr University, North Wales, UK.

graduate and research degrees. As a result the papers given here are enriched by the benefits of prolonged study as well as by the continuing infusion of spiritual experience. We think that everybody who committed to this conference would be happy to attend a Pentecostal congregation, and some of them work as pastors and preachers when they are not lecturing on campuses. We believe that the contributions that you have read in the preceding chapters provide the framework for a truly universal understanding of Pentecostal ecclesiology, one that gives weight to Pentecostal distinctives stretching back in time to the early revivals which eventually gave birth to the entire Pentecostal movement.

Using the structure of the fivefold gospel which has been at the heart of Pentecostalism for more than 100 years, our speakers have constructed a vision of the Church that is both practical and ideal and it is for these reasons that we believe the chapters assembled here will have an ongoing significance.

My own brief reflections are designed to fill out the picture further by suggesting future additional lines of enquiry or reflection that could be build on the substantial achievements already made.

First, it is noticeable that we have not dealt with parachurch organisations at all. Much of the focus of our attention has been on congregations and of the outworking of the fivefold gospel in the life of congregations. But, as we know, a huge amount of Christian activity is devolved to parachurch organisations that have fluid structures, varied aims, and questionable oversight. Parachurch organisations rarely practice any sacraments or see themselves as promoting every aspect of the fivefold gospel. It is true that parachurches sometimes are built around a particular ministry gift like that of an evangelist with the result that the parachurch is an evangelistic organisation with that one task in mind. It functions simply to express the need for those outside the Church to become members of it. Other parachurch organisations, particularly those that have a missionary emphasis, may be related to one or multiple denominations and here they may express a variety of doctrinal positions. But in any case it is difficult to see exactly how the New Testament pattern and its theological concepts can be applied to parachurch organisations with any precision. Moreover, it is not easy to see how parachurches should be related to churches. Some parachurch organisations (e.g. the Full Gospel Businessmen's Fellowship) specifically exclude ordained ministry from office with the result that they are deliberately lay-led organisations. Others, like those that are evangelistic, will almost invariably be centred upon the ministry of a particular ordained person who may or may not retain denominational credentials.

We need a way of discussing the ecclesiological nature of parachurches. If, on the one hand, the Church is marked by its capacity to preach the Word and to enact sacraments, then we have to say that the parachurch is not Church. Yet, on the other hand, parachurches do pursue many of the functions that one would expect churches to fulfill. They occupy a theologically anomalous position allowing us to classify them either within the greater concept of the Church or, alternatively, allowing us to see them as undesirable pseudo-churches taking money and energy away from congregational life and weakening the influence of recognised ministers.

Second, there is a need for empirical theology as well as speculative and theoretical theology. It is from empirical theology that we learn exactly what members of the Church currently believe and not what it is that they historically have believed or should believe. It is by empirical theology that we discover which factors influence church life. Is there any practical difference between those churches which believe that speaking in tongues functions as the initial evidence of baptism in the Holy Spirit and those which do not? Do the Orthodox and Roman practices of confession lead to sanctification in the sense understood by Pentecostal churches? What are the lifestyle or attitudinal differences between Pentecostal churches in the Wesleyan stream and those in the 'finished work' stream? Do those with a strong eschatological expectation have different attitudes to the contemporary age from those whose eschatological expectations are more diffuse? Is the Church in Africa significantly different from the Church in Asia or Europe and, if it is, can we isolate cultural and contextual factors by empirical means? Can we discover an equation that would allow us to work along these lines: core beliefs + context = actual beliefs? Can we discover whether cultural practices influence theological praxis and, if we can, how should we relate all these empirically discovered beliefs to the wider range of theological beliefs drawn from 20 centuries of theological reflection? My own wish would be to find an honourable place for empirical theology alongside systematic and dogmatic theology so that each could interact with the other.

Third, although it is often said that very little has been written by Pentecostals on ecclesiology, I want to draw attention to the British Pentecostal, Donald Gee (1891-1966), who wrote about spiritual gifts and church life in the late 1920s and 1930s. His books remained in print for more than 20 years and he did attempt to show how spiritual gifts operating in congregations would influence congregational life.[1] Similarly, he attempted to show how spiritual gifts might be linked with the emergence of a Pentecostal conception of ministry based upon the fivefold gifting found in Ephesians 4. The evangelist would manifest gifts of healing, teachers would manifest words of wisdom, and so on. By exposition of Scripture he showed how congregational life ought to be theologically understood drawing from Pentecostal theology rather than from the traditions of those churches from which Pentecostals had originally come. He argued from a biblical basis rather than from historical exemplars or from expediency. Although he never framed his discussion within the larger span of systematic theology, he took the first step towards a Pentecostal ecclesiology that could be understood by pastors and disseminated by Bible studies. In this respect he gave to English-speaking congregations a pattern that had much merit and created space where the Spirit of God might work.

Fourth, it is reasonable to argue that theology of the kind ably exemplified in the preceding chapters is the internal driving force that presses out towards the concrete embodiment of the Church. Theology is the DNA that is the key for understanding the ecclesiastical phenotype. Theology is the master discipline enabling us to understand the origins and intricate internal balances within the life of contemporary congregations. In this important sense theology gives us a plan for the future as well as a way of understanding the past. By measuring congregations all over the world against the fivefold gospel, we can see how these congregations fall short of the

---

[1] Gee's first book, *Concerning Spiritual Gifts,* was published in 1928; *The Ministry Gifts of Christ* followed in 1930 and *Concerning Shepherds and Sheepfolds* in the same year. This trio of books gave British Pentecostalism, and eventually Pentecostalism in many parts of the world (because they were all widely translated), an understanding of itself that remained largely intact until the healing evangelists and the faith movement of the 1940s and 1950s offered a competing interpretation.

ideals for which they ought to strive. In this sense the fivefold gospel provides a paradigm and a diagnostic tool, by which we can assess church programs and create new initiatives. For every congregation, the pastor or bishop or local superintendent may ask, 'to what extent does this congregation manifest the full range of activities implied by the fivefold gospel?' and in the light of the answers that are given may begin to plan remedial action.

Fifth, in speaking of the theology of the Church we need also recall ecumenical dialogue both with Roman Catholic and with Orthodox communities. It is here that I have to do what many Pentecostals do when they speak of those things that concern them deeply. I must give personal testimony. I was brought up in the Russian Orthodox Church and baptised into it. My mother was Russian though, because she married an Englishman, she very quickly adapted to British life. But in our home we had icons on the walls and at regular intervals we attended the great feasts of the Church. We celebrated Easter at the correct time according to the ancient calendar and we learnt to say in Russian after a lengthy midnight mass, 'Christ is risen'. And yet I want to say that the Orthodox Church for all the beauty of its liturgy needs a greater humility than is often found among its strongest defenders. I lived within the Orthodox Church and yet I did not find Christ. This is something to do with the Old Church Slavonic in which the liturgy was sung. When I became a Protestant (which rejoiced in a language I understood), it soon became apparent to me that the Orthodox Church lacked a proper mechanism by which to offer social critique, and I saw this in the doctrine of the Russian Orthodox Church which stated that 'the will of the Czar is the will of God', a doctrine that appeared to the taken directly from the pages of the Old Testament and which had nothing to do with the way the earliest Christians understood their relation to political authority (Acts 4.19).[2] While not wishing in any way to exculpate the murderous activities of the Bolsheviks, I note the way Russian revolutionaries treated the Orthodox Church. I understood that there was a deep hatred among

---

[2] 'The Russian Church has often been criticized for its submissiveness to secular authority ... its total subordination to the temporal power came comparatively late ... virtually making the priests into salaried servants of the state', in Max Hayward (1979), *The Russian Empire: a Portrait in Photographs* (London: Jonathan Cape, 1979), p. 17.

peasants against aspects of the Church's mindless support for a political regime in desperate need of reform. When I saw the Orthodox Church close up, I understood its weaknesses and its fissiparous tendencies.

And then in the other direction and in the Roman Catholic Church I see the outrageous scandals that have been associated with its unwillingness to face up to paedophile priests and, when I talk to my liberal Catholic friends, I understand the need for a new Catholic Reformation. The time must surely come when married priests are allowed. It is never been clear to me why, if the primacy of St Peter is foundational, subsequent Roman Catholic priests should be required to be celibate when St Peter himself was married.

These are matters for prolonged discussion. There are many places where this discussion may be held but one of the most fruitful is surely to be found within the borders of the Academy, especially in academic conferences and in personal contact between scholars belonging to different traditions. The conference on which this particular book was based drew from a truly international spectrum of Pentecostal positions. Without threat and across the meal table or at the podium a full and frank exchange of views can occur. I had not realised that Karl Barth and Hans Küng would dine together in what might be a mini-ecumenical dialogue. Somewhere in Küng's memoirs, *My Struggle For Freedom*, where he recalls his fellowship with Barth, he reports that Catholics and Protestants will be reconciled at the Last Day … but only in the afternoon!

In its churches ad through its pastors Pentecostalism stands across the world as a testimony to the work of the Holy Spirit in the 20th century. In both directions, towards Orthodoxy and Roman Catholicism, Pentecostalism brings a message of spiritual renewal to ecumenical discussion, but it does so while recognising that both these great arms of the Christian tradition are themselves in need of reform. It will not be sufficient for Pentecostalism to adapt itself so as to accommodate its beliefs and practices to unreformed Orthodoxy or to unreformed Catholicism. Rather Pentecostalism, while it needs a perpetual cleansing and renewal within its own life, must join hands with the best and the most gracious of those elements in the other great traditions of the Church in all its historical totality.

Index of Biblical (and Other Ancient) References

Index of Names

Other Books from CPT Press

R. Hollis Gause, *Living in the Spirit: The Way of Salvation* (2009). ISBN 9780981965109

Kenneth J. Archer, *A Pentecostal Hermeneutic: Spirit, Scripture and Community* (2009). ISBN 9780981965116

Larry McQueen, *Joel and the Spirit: The Cry of a Prophetic Hermeneutic* (2009). ISBN 9780981965123

Lee Roy Martin, *Introduction to Biblical Hebrew* (2009). ISBN 9780981965154

Lee Roy Martin, *Answer Key to Introduction to Biblical Hebrew* (2009). ISBN 9780981965161

Lee Roy Martin, *Workbook for Introduction to Biblical Hebrew* (2010). ISBN 9780981965185

Martin William Mittelstadt, *Reading Luke–Acts in the Pentecostal Tradition* (2010). ISBN 9780981965178

Roger Stronstad, *The Prophethood of All Believers* (2010). ISBN 9780981965130

Kristen Dayle Welch, *'Women with the Good News': The Rhetorical Heritage of Pentecostal Holiness Women Preachers* (2010). ISBN 9780981965192

Steven Jack Land, *Pentecostal Spirituality: A Passion for the Kingdom* (2010). ISBN 9780981965147

Made in the USA
Middletown, DE
28 December 2018